CASEBOOK

GENERAL EDITOR: A. E. Dyson

Jonson

Every Man in his Humour
and
The Alchemist

A CASEBOOK

EDITED BY

R. V. HOLDSWORTH

Selection, editorial matter and Introduction
© R. V. Holdsworth 1978

First published 1978 by
THE MACMILLAN PRESS LTD
London and Basingstoke
Associated companies in Delhi Dublin
Hong Kong Johannesburg Lagos Melbourne
New York Singapore and Tokyo

Printed in Hong Kong by
L. Rex Offset Printing Co., Ltd.

British Library Cataloguing in Publication Data

Jonson 'Every man in his humour' and
  'The alchemist'. – (Casebook series).
  1. Jonson, Ben. Every man in his humour.
  2. Jonson, Ben. Alchemist, The
  I. Holdsworth, Roger Victor   II.   Series
  822′.3   PR2613

  ISBN 0–333–19205–2
  ISBN 0–333–19206–0   Pbk

CONTENTS

ACKNOWLEDGEMENTS

The editor is grateful to Miss Sara Pearl and Mr. T. P. Dolan for their assistance and advice, and to the Una Ellis-Fermor Memorial Trust for a grant towards the work.

The editor and publishers wish to thank the following who have kindly given permission for the use of copyright material: Anonymous reviews from *The Times*, 'Comic Cockneys: *Every Man in His Humour* at Stratford' (7 August 1937), 'A Boisterous Modern Farce' (2 April 1935), reproduced from *The Times* by permission. J. B. Bamborough, extract from *Ben Jonson* (1970), by permission of the editor and Hutchinson Publishing Group Limited. J. A. Barish, extracts from *Ben Jonson and the Language of Prose Comedy*, pp. 98–104, 130–41, by Jonas A. Barish, Cambridge, Mass.: Harvard University Press, copyright © 1960 by the President and Fellows of Harvard College, reprinted by permission; and from 'Feasting and Judging in Jonsonian Comedy' from *Renaissance Drama*, new ser., v (1972), by permission of the author and Northwestern University Press. H. Holland Carter, extract from Introduction to *Every Man in his Humor* (1921), by permission of Yale University Press Limited. I. Donaldson, essay 'Language, Noise, and Nonsense: *The Alchemist*' from *Seventeenth-Century Imagery*, ed. Earl Miner, © 1971 by The Regents of the University of California, reprinted by permission of University of California Press. A. Richard Dutton, essay 'The Significance of Jonson's Revision of *Every Man in his Humour*' from *Modern Language Review*, LXIX (1974), reprinted by permission of the author and the editors. T. S. Eliot, extracts from 'Ben Jonson' from *Selected Essays* (1920), by permission of Faber & Faber Limited. William Empson, article '*The Alchemist*' from *The Hudson Review*, XXII, No 4 (Winter 1969–70), copyright © 1970 by *The Hudson Review*, Inc., and reprinted by permission. P. Fleming, review of *The Alchemist* from the *Spectator* (24 January 1947), reprinted by permission. B. Gascoigne, review 'All that Glisters' from the *Spectator* (7 December 1962), reprinted by permission. C. H. Herford and P. and E. Simpson, extracts from *Complete Critical Edition of Ben Jonson* (11 volumes), published by Oxford University Press, reprinted by permission of the publisher. G. B. Jackson, extracts from Introduction to *Every Man in his Humour* (1969), by permission of Yale University Press Limited. A. B. Kernan, extracts from *The Cankered Muse: Satire of the English Renaissance* (1959), by permission of Yale University Press Limited. L. C. Knights, extracts from *Drama and Society in the Age of Jonson* (1937), by permission

of the author and Chatto & Windus Limited. J. W. Lever, extract from
Introduction to *Every Man in his Humour* (1971), by permission of the
editor and The University of Nebraska Press. H. Levin, extracts from
Introduction to *Ben Jonson: Selected Works* (1938), published by The
Nonesuch Press, reprinted by permission of The Bodley Head. F. H.
Mares, extract from Introduction to *The Alchemist* (1967), by permis-
sion of the editor and Methuen Educational Limited. E. B. Partridge,
extracts from *The Broken Compass: A Study of the Major Comedies of Ben
Jonson* (1958), by permission of the author and Chatto & Windus
Limited. J. B. Steane, extracts from Introduction to *The Alchemist*
(1967), by permission of the author and Cambridge University Press.
F. L. Townsend, extract from *Apologie for Bartholmew Fayre: The Art of
Jonson's Comedies*, by permission of the Modern Language Association of
America. K. Tynan, extract from *He That Plays The King* (1950), by
permission of the author. Irving Wardle, article 'Comic Intrigue' from
The Times (10 February 1970), reproduced from *The Times* by
permission. The publishers have made every effort to trace the
copyright-holders, but if they have inadvertently overlooked any, they
will be pleased to make the necessary arrangement at the first
opportunity.

NOTE ON TEXTS AND ABBREVIATIONS

All references to and quotations from the works of Jonson have been
standardised in accordance with the text of C. H. Herford and P. and E.
Simpson, *Ben Jonson*, 11 volumes (Oxford, 1925–52), except that i/j and
u/v spelling forms have been altered to conform with modern practice.
This edition is referred to throughout as Herford and Simpson. Where
confusion is possible, textual references to the quarto (1601) and folio
(1616) versions of *Every Man in his Humour* are distinguished by the
letters Q and F. In Parts Two and Three all the titles printed within
quotation marks have been supplied by the Editor. All other editorial
additions are enclosed between square brackets.

GENERAL EDITOR'S PREFACE

The Casebook series, launched in 1968, has become a well-regarded library of critical studies. The central concern of the series remains the 'single-author' volume, but suggestions from the academic community have led to an extension of the original plan, to include occasional volumes on such general themes as literary 'schools' and genres.

Each volume in the central category deals either with one well-known and influential work by an individual author, or with closely related works by one writer. The main section consists of critical readings, mostly modern, collected from books and journals. A selection of reviews and comments by the author's contemporaries is also included, and sometimes comment from the author himself. The Editor's introduction charts the reputation of the work or works from the first appearance to the present time.

Volumes in the 'general themes' category are variable in structure but follow the basic purpose of the series in presenting an integrated selection of readings, with an Introduction which explores the theme and discusses the literary and critical issues involved.

A single volume can represent no more than a small selection of critical opinions. Some critics are excluded for reasons of space, and it is hoped that readers will pursue the suggestions for further reading in the Select Bibliography. Other contributions are severed from their original context, to which some readers may wish to turn. Indeed, if they take a hint from the critics represented here, they certainly will.

A. E. DYSON

To J. B. Bamborough

INTRODUCTION

Every Man in his Humour is a striking example of the extraordinary self-consciousness with which Jonson, in later years, shaped and portrayed his artistic career. It was not his first play. When it was performed in September 1598 at the Curtain playhouse by the Lord Chamberlain's Men (the company for which Shakespeare wrote and acted), its author, aged twenty-six, had already written *The Case is Altered*, a comedy of romantic entanglements, and several plays for Henslowe's companies which had caused him to be cited as one of 'our best for Tragedie'. He had also collaborated, with Thomas Nashe, on *The Isle of Dogs*, a notorious political satire 'contanynge very seditious and sclandrous matter' which had earned him a spell in prison in 1597. But Jonson ignored all these earlier pieces when he compiled his folio *Works* of 1616. He placed *Every Man in his Humour*, in a carefully revised form, at the front of the volume, and added a preface dedicating the play to his old schoolmaster, William Camden, which introduced it as '*of the fruits*' of his dramatic labours '*the first*'. Taxed with this falsehood, Jonson might have replied that this description represented a 'likenesse of Truth'[1] more true, because more illuminating, than the actual facts. *Every Man in* was the first example of the kind of drama he wanted to write, and be known by; the play in which he found his voice and style. More than this, it marked, as its author became well aware, a watershed in the development of English drama. Earlier comedies – for example Henry Porter's *The Two Angry Women of Abingdon* – had brought onto the stage recognisable Elizabethan bourgeois types, but *Every Man in* was the first to give such dramatisations of contemporary ·manners firm moral direction and force; and earlier comedies – for example George Chapman's *An Humorous Day's Mirth*, and Jonson's own *The Case is Altered* – had made play with 'humours', featuring characters stamped by a habitual foible or quirk of disposition; but *Every Man in* was the first to make personality, rather than narrative complications, the primary interest; the first, in the words of Jonson's Oxford editors, to make 'the exhibition of Humours the sole function of plot', and thus throw 'into the background, once for all, the comedy of mere intrigue'.[2] Jonson shows the same retrospective awareness of *Every Man in* as his real point of departure in the Induction to his last completed play, *The Magnetic Lady* (1632). Here 'the *Author*, beginning his studies of this kind, with *every man in his Humour* . . . and since, continuing in all his *Playes*, especially those of the *Comick* thred', presents himself as *the* poet of the humours, whose subject has always been 'the manners of men, that went along with the times'. My works, Jonson wanted to imply, are a unified corpus, which implement as a whole a deliberate programme of ethical and aesthetic reform. When Thomas Dekker sneered at Jonson as 'that *selfe-creating Horace*'[3] he was inadvertently making an astute point about Jonson's careful moulding of a literary identity.

Jonson's regard for *Every Man in* is also evident in the Prologue he prefixed to the folio text, where with splendid assertiveness (or, from another point of view, monomaniac arrogance) he holds up the play as a perfect fusion of classical form with contemporary subject-matter. It observes the classical prescriptions for comedy, yet offers 'an Image of the times' (that is, an interpretation and a judgement, as well as a description) by means of 'deedes, and language, such as men doe use' ('men' as distinct from the 'monsters' of popular sensational drama). The result is exemplary: 'one such . . . as other plays should be'. But the most striking evidence of Jonson's regard for the play is his painstaking revision of the version first seen in 1598. This version, published in quarto in 1601, is set in Florence and has Italian characters. In the folio, the setting is transferred to London, and the characters given English names, as follows:

Q	F
Lorenzo Senior	Knowell
Prospero	Wellbred
Thorello	Kitely
Stephano	Stephen
Doctor Clement	Justice Clement
Bobadilla	Bobadill
Musco	Brainworm
Cob	Cob
Giuliano	Downright
Lorenzo Junior	Edward Knowell
Biancha	Dame Kitely
Hesperida	Bridget
Peto	Formal
Matheo	Matthew
Piso	Cash
Tib	Tib

In addition, Jonson tightened up the play's finale, omitting an unnecessary entrance by Giuliano (Q, v i 60), abridging Musco's long-winded recapitulation of his day's activities, and eliminating Lorenzo Junior's eloquent but in context awkwardly static defence of poetry. Clement's busy judgement-giving is simplified, and also lightened:

Matheo and Bobadilla are not made to parade humiliatingly as emblems of literary and military fraudulence and folly, but merely excluded from the socially re-unifying wedding supper.

When Jonson made the revision is uncertain: he took care to cover his tracks, introducing no new topical references into the play which would suggest a date later than that of the original performance. It may have been towards the end of 1604, in time for a production at court on 2 February 1605, and in support one can point to the vogue for citizen comedy around this date and to Jonson's own developing interest in the genre evidenced by *Eastward Ho!* (1604). On the other hand, it may have been as late as 1612–13, when he would have been editing the material to be included in the *Works*, and some scholars have preferred this date on the grounds that the revised *Every Man in* often displays a prose style as subtle, varied and vigorous as that of Jonson's greatest prose comedies, *Epicoene, or The Silent Woman* (1609) and *Bartholomew Fair* (1614). As to the reasons for the revision, Jonson himself supplies a partial explanation in a typical piece of oblique and ironic self-reference in *Bartholomew Fair*. Here we find the amateur dramatist John Littlewit, who has transferred the story of Hero and Leander to an up-to-date London setting so as 'to reduce it to a more familiar straine for our people' and make it less 'learned, and poeticall' and more '*moderne* for the times': 'for the *Hellespont* I imagine our *Thames* here, and then *Leander*, I make a Diers sonne, about *Puddle-wharfe*: and *Hero* a wench o' the *Banke-side*' (v iii 116–24). It is a policy Leatherhead the puppet-master fully approves: 'Your home-borne projects prove ever the best, they are so easie, and familiar, they put too much learning i' their things now o' dayes' (v i 14–16). *Every Man in*, too, is made more 'familiar' and less 'learned, and poeticall'. The Rialto becomes the Exchange, and Clement's house is moved from 'yonder by Saint *Anthonies*' to 'here, in *Colman*-street'. The abstract, rhetorical style of Old Knowell and Kitely is toned down in favour of a more concrete, colloquial idiom and Clement's Latin quotations disappear. At the same time, Jonson the moral teacher would expect us to recognise a further motive for the revision. As J. W. Lever notes, 'the Florence of the quarto version was a purely conventional backcloth for English characters and manners';[4] by removing this convention, and making explicit what had remained implicit in the original, Jonson was seeking to implicate his English audience more directly in the 'Image of the times' the play presents.

Several excellent studies of the revision have appeared in this century, and the reader is urged to consult those of H. H. Carter, Herford and Simpson, and J. W. Lever (in their editions of the play), which are not included in the present volume. In the two that are, Jonas A. Barish analyses the more assured command of dramatic prose which enables Jonson to substantiate his characters and sharpen his satire; and

A. Richard Dutton argues that the new setting, though inadequately focused, is a function of Jonson's 'firmer ethical grasp' of his material. Two features of the revision have not been noted. One is the more overt emphasis on the typically Jonsonian theme of linguistic integrity, a character's attitude to language as the measure of his moral and intellectual health. In both quarto and folio, this idea is embodied most vividly in Bobadill, one of the great Jonsonian masters of the use of jargon to mystify and impress, and a normative touchstone is established in the Knowells, father and son, who stand up for linguistic straightforwardness and restraint. Young Knowell, for example, rebukes the extravagance of Wellbred's declarations that he will unite him with Bridget: 'Nay, doe not sweare. . . . Hold, hold, be temperate' (IV v 25–9); and Old Knowell chides Brainworm, in his disguise as Fitzsword, for verbal posturing:

> Nay, nay, I like not those affected othes;
> Speake plainely man. . . .
>   Ile prove thee, if thy deedes
> Will carry a proportion to thy words.   (II v 127–32)

Several new touches in the folio extend this theme more explicitly to other characters. In the quarto, Stephen's idiotic aspirations to fashion and gentility are signalled thus:

and a man have not skill in hawking and hunting now a daies, ile not give a rush for him; hee is for no gentlemans company.

                                        (I i 37–40)

In the folio, knowledge of the words is all he requires:

an' a man have not skill in the hawking, and hunting-languages now a dayes, I'll not give a rush for him. They are more studied then the *Greeke*, or the *Latine*. He is for no gallants companie without 'hem.

                                        (I i 40–4)

Similarly, Brainworm, who stands at the opposite end of the play's intellectual spectrum, is assessed as a deceiver in the folio in terms of his ability as a manipulator of words. Young Knowell calls him 'a weaver of language' (III v 27–8), and Old Knowell marvels 'Is it possible . . . that thou should'st disguise thy language so, as I should not know thee?' (V iii 81–2). Even the revision, however, cannot be said to be *about* language in the way that is true of, say, *The Alchemist*, and indeed in the play's own terms the theme remains – despite its occurrence also in the poetic malpractices of Matthew – imperfectly realised. Stephen's 'hawking, and hunting-languages' are never heard of again, and the Knowells' normative function is compromised by their readiness to approve or indulge in verbal trickery when it suits them (thus, Old

Knowell excuses his opening of the letter addressed to his son by means of a quibble: 'Yet, I am EDWARD KNO'WELL too . . .': another folio addition). Also, the moral implications of Brainworm's skill in linguistic fraud, which associates him with the similarly accomplished Bobadill (a parallel underlined by their being both in different ways fake soldiers) are evaded rather than faced in the play's conclusion. Brainworm is fêted for his 'wit', while Bobadill is dismissed as a sham: a contrast which tends to equate goodness with success.

The other aspect of the revision which has not received its due concerns two cases of apparent inconsistency, where touches of Italian local colour in the quarto have been allowed to survive into the English version. At IV viii 16–39 the pathologically suspicious Kitely, like his quarto counterpart, is induced by Prospero – Wellbred into the panic-stricken belief that his wife has put poison on his clothes. An eighteenth-century commentator rightly associated this idea with 'the dark and fatal revenges of Italian jealousy', but went on to censure its presence in the folio as something Jonson 'forgot to change':

Nothing could be more in character than this surmise, supposing the persons, as was the case at first, to have been native of Italy. But had Jonson recollected, it is probable he would have varied the thought, to adapt it more consistently to the genius and manners of the speaker.[5]

This is to underestimate the meticulous (some critics would add, deadening) craftsmanship Jonson exercised on his plays, down to the smallest and seemingly most random detail. The effect of crazy incongruity produced by this lurid 'Italian' notion's being entertained by a London businessman is clearly deliberate. Kitely's mental world seems all the more ludicrously wrapped in fantasy, all the more intransigently out of touch with the humdrum realities of the worlds of family and business which he actually inhabits. So also with another apparent oversight, the repetition of Bobadill's wistful memories of Venetian swordplay (Q,IV iv 11; F, IV ix 12). In the quarto, Venice is appropriate simply because it is the neighbouring state. In the new setting of the folio it acquires a sheen of romantic glamour, making it a fit location for the escapist dreams of a down-at-heel English 'captain' who has just had the hard truth of 'your base wood' imprinted on him in London. 'Mistakes' such as these are a good example of what Swinburne meant when he declared 'There is nothing accidental in the work of Ben Jonson.'[6]

The presentation of humour-dominated personalities in *Every Man in*, and more especially in the harsher 'comical satires' which followed it – *Every Man out of his Humour* (1599), *Cynthia's Revels* (1600), and *Poetaster* (1601) – rapidly earned Jonson a reputation as a snarling satirist, vindictive, ill-tempered, cynical, and haughtily condescending. Ac-

cording to Dekker in *Satiromastix, or The Untrussing of the Humorous Poet*
(1601), Jonson's aim was 'to flirt Inke in everie mans face', particularly
that of his fellow Londoner:

thou cryest ptrooh at worshipfull Cittizens, and cal'st them Flat-caps, Cuckolds,
and banckrupts, and modest and virtuous wives punckes cockatrices.[7]

His muse was directed by his own defects of character, not by any moral
sense: '*Thy pride and scorne made her turne Saterist, / And not her love to
virtue* (as thou Preachest)'.[8] Another commentator, one 'W. I.'
(probably John Weever) in *The Whipping of the Satire* (1601), accused
him both of cashing in on the 'newfangled neoterisme' of humours ('you
made sale of your Humours to the Theater, and there plaid Pee boh
with the people in your humour, then out of your humour'), and of
adopting an intolerably knowing attitude towards his public:

Monsieur Humorist, you . . . talke of mens humours and dispositions, as though
you had beene a Constellation-setter seven yeres in the firmament, or had cast
account of every mans nativitie with the starres.[9]

An arrogant sense of superiority is what motivates him (W. I. suggests
that Jonson wants 'to taxe all the world, like Augustus Cesar'), and as a
result his work is less 'morall medicine' than 'mortall poyson'.

It is not difficult to answer such charges. To begin with, in making the
exposure of folly his primary aim, Jonson was fulfilling a time-honoured
function of the comic poet. Sidney had stated it clearly in his *Apology for
Poetry* when he declared that 'comedy is an imitation of the common
errors of our life', represented 'in the most ridiculous and scornful sort
that may be, so as it is impossible that any beholder can be content to be
such a one'.[10] Moreover, in his cultivation of humours Jonson was not
being original; he was taking over a psychological explanation of moral
defects which by 1598 was well established. Nashe had used it six years
earlier in *Pierce Penniless*:

the Divell . . . is onely a pestilent humour in a man, of pleasure, profit, or
policie, that violently carries him away to vanitie, villanie, or monstrous
hypocrisie[11]

and Thomas Wright was soon to give it definitive treatment in his
treatise *The Passions of the Mind in General* (1604), to which Jonson
contributed a commendatory poem. According to Wright, 'he that
loveth, hateth, or by any other passion is vehemently possessed, judgeth
all things that occurre in favor of that passion, to be good and agreeable
with reason', and this is a perfect description of the mental processes of
Jonson's humour characters, all of whom, to borrow Bacon's phrase, are
guilty of 'submitting the shows of things to the desires of the mind'.[12]
Indeed, one may go further and point out that, far from being

'newfangled' in his humour comedy, Jonson had simply spotted that the fashionable term 'humour' really described a quality or constituent of comedy which all comedies contain. Henri Bergson's definition of this quality in *On Laughter* makes the connection clear:

> At the root of the comic there is a sort of rigidity which compels its victims to keep strictly to one path, to follow it straight along, to shut their ears and refuse to listen. . . . A stubborn spirit ends by adjusting things to its own way of thinking, instead of accommodating its thoughts to the things.[13]

One might argue that humour theory did at least enable Jonson to depict characters tyrannised by a particular foible or vice, and that this allowed him to exhibit types of folly with a distinctive clarity and force; but this too had been a feature of comedy from Aristophanes onwards. 'When did satiric comedy ever cease', a recent editor of *Every Man in* has observed, 'to isolate the follies of mankind, for ridicule and castigation? Jonson attempted the illusion of novelty by giving them a topical name and a topical dress.'[14]

There is, however, a further reason why Jonson found humour theory congenial. As many critics note, it provided a convention through which he could express his own, pessimistic view of human nature as something essentially closed and remote, immune to instruction or reproof. A humour, as Congreve observes, 'cannot be wholly changed', and in *Every Man in* one finds this idea constantly applied to the characters. 'It will never out o' the flesh that's bred i' the bone', Downright grumbles concerning Wellbred's rakishness, 'counsell to him, is as good, as a shoulder of mutton to a sicke horse' (II i 71–4). Knowell Senior echoes these sentiments when he laments the loose living of his son:

> it is gone into the bone alreadie.
> . . . This die goes deeper then the coate,
> Or shirt, or skin. It staines, unto the liver,
> And heart, in some. (II v 28–31)

Stephen is, and is held up as being, a classic example of human immutability, 'eene past hope / Of all reclaime' (I i 62–3), 'stupiditie it selfe' (III v 6–7). Bridget can only wonder at the 'strength' of the 'extreme conceits' (IV viii 31) which keep her brother Kitely insulated within his fantasy world.

This notion of human beings' deep resistance to change crucially affects both the action and the endings of Jonson's comedies. Because the characters occupy fixed positions, the action often proceeds in an atmosphere of sharp verbal and physical conflict, of brawls and blows, giving an effect well described by Aldous Huxley:

> [Jonson's] characters are not human, but rather marionettes of wood and metal

that collide and belabour one another, like the ferocious puppets of the Punch and Judy show, without feeling the painfulness of the proceeding.[15]

And because they cannot learn or develop by themselves, change has to be imposed on them, often violently, from without. Even *Every Man in*, regarded by most critics as Jonson's most genial play, contains the narrowly averted sword-fight in Kitely's house, the hectic quarrel outside Cob's, three on-stage beatings, Clement's terrorising of Cob and Brainworm and the public burning of Matthew's poems. The impositions of change sometimes make Jonson's endings seem improbable or arbitrary or inappropriately harsh. Arthur Sale boldly asserts of *Every Man in* that 'the characters are *in* their Humour and then *out*, and there is nothing more to be said',[16] yet the exclusion of Stephen, Matthew and Bobadill from the festive supper – comedy's symbol of a newly integrated and harmonious society – strikes a discordantly punitive and negative note. It is not just that these three are not shown to have reformed: none of the other characters much cares whether they have or not. It is enough that they have been humiliated into silence. With Kitely the problem is different, and perhaps more serious, since it raises the question of probability. J. W. Lever thinks that he is 'jerked back into sanity by Clement's commonsense advice', and this is what Jonson means us to believe; but many critics, for example William Oxberry, have remained utterly unconvinced: 'The *constitutional* failing of such a man as *Kitely*, could never be cured in the abrupt manner here represented'.[17] 'To bee a foole borne, is a disease incurable', as Volpone remarks (*Volpone*, ii ii 159).

Discussion of the moral perspective of Jonson's comedies has naturally tended to focus on the above-mentioned features, and until recently the standard conclusion has been that his regular aim was to write 'an excellent *comoedy* of affliction' (to borrow Clerimont's phrase in *Epicoene*[18]), in order to dramatise the view of human nature which he sets out in *Discoveries*:

Passions are spirituall Rebels, and raise sedition against the understanding. . . . *Natures* that are hardned to *evill*, you shall sooner breake, then make straight; they are like poles that are crooked, and dry: there is no attempting them.

(ll. 30–8)

If the use of inherently unreformable characters in order to demonstrate the need for moral reform looks like poor tactics, then this, according to the standard view, is because Jonson's method is primarily descriptive, not prescriptive: he wants to show how bad (vain, avaricious, anti-social etc.) people can be, not how good they could and should become. In fact this view, as the essay by Gabriele Bernhard Jackson reprinted in this collection makes clear, is very incomplete. It leaves out of account

Jonson's fascinated interest in the sheer *fact* of eccentricity, an interest which tends to overturn the ostensible castigatory and didactic structure of his plays. Do we really feel, as Dutton and Barish suggest, that Knowell and Kitely are 'embodiments of a diseased condition' which 'attacks the fabric of natural social harmony', that Cob's mind is 'streaked by . . . coarse skepticism' and 'credulousness', or that Bobadill 'becomes contemptible in direct proportion to the skill and effort he expends on his impostures'? Edward Knowell may exclaim 'O, manners! that this age should bring forth such creatures! that Nature should bee at leisure to make 'hem!' (iv vii 146–8), and no doubt in the play's didactic scheme he and Wellbred are meant to represent 'the balanced personalities against whom the unbalanced are measured';[19] but the impression created by the ridicule and the attempts at normative contrast is of the less imaginative members of a society ganging up on the more colourfully unorthodox individuals within it in order to browbeat them into a dull and featureless conformity. *Every Man in* succeeds, Miss Jackson argues, 'not by enforcing a concept of balance but by impressing upon us the overwhelming force of imbalance'; and far from despising such a figure as Bobadill, we are made to feel that 'the road of normality from which he has diverged is lost to view, and well lost, behind the picturesque landscape of the territory in which he has arrived.' Overtly proclaiming the need to subscribe to a commonly defined, objective idea of reality, the play covertly demonstrates the attractions of subjective experience. Viewed thus, Bobadill's 'egoism' becomes his tenaciously preserved sense of himself, and his 'wantonnesse of language' the idiom in which this sense is embodied and expressed. In a suggestive remark, Thomas Wright compares a passion or humour to 'greene spectacles, which make all thinges resemble the colour of greene'.[20] What sense can I make of someone's impertinently telling me that I ought to prefer things in their 'real' colours? *My* world – and surely yours too? – is green. What other colour is there?

The eccentrics of *Every Man in* do not protest their uniqueness with the vociferous, heroic defiance one encounters in Jonson's later comedies. There is no one quite of the stature of Puntarvolo in *Every Man out*, described in 'The Names of the Actors' as one consciously 'consecrated to singularity' and 'resolving (in despight of publike derision) to sticke to his owne particular fashion, phrase, and gesture'; or of Humphrey Wasp in *Bartholomew Fair*, who announces 'I have no reason, nor I will heare of no reason, nor I will looke for no reason, and he is an Asse, that either knowes any, or lookes for't from me' (iv iv 42–4); or, perhaps most magnificently of all, Fitzdottrel in *The Devil is an Ass*, who, when all is lost, declares,

> I will not think; nor act;
> Nor yet recover; do not talke to me!
> I'll runne out o' my witts, rather then heare;
> I will be what I am, *Fabian Fitz-Dottrel*,
> Though all the world say nay to't.   (IV vii 90–4)

But it is possible to experience a similar sense of awe when confronting the impregnable doltishness of Stephen and Matthew, or the superb mental resilience of Bobadill. (In the quarto Jonson had Bobadill explain, 'I am armd in soule agaynst the worst of fortune' – v v 370–1; in the folio he deleted this probably because he realised it was self-evident.) Kitely reveals yet greater strengths. Consider his masterly reply when Wellbred tells him that the suggestion about poison was only a joke:

> Am I not sicke? how am I, then, not poyson'd?
> Am I not poyson'd? how am I, then, so sicke?
>   (IV viii 38–9)

Wellbred may well wonder 'what a strange, and idle imagination is this?'; empirical argument wilts before such psychological self-sufficiency. A further point arises from these lines. In their beautiful pseudo-logical circularity, suggesting a state of mind which is secluded and self-contained, they illustrate very clearly what is perhaps the essential reason for Jonson's ambivalent attitude towards his humour characters: namely, the similarity between the typical mental stance of the characters and Jonson's idea of the poet. It is not just that 'The lunatic, the lover, and the poet / Are of imagination all compact', as Shakespeare, or rather Theseus, observes in *A Midsummer Night's Dream*. The self-involved, solipsistic condition of a character like Kitely may be compared with Jonson's more individual presentation of the poet as isolated hero, 'high, and aloofe', his own law-maker, 'Who (like a circle bounded in it selfe) / Contaynes as much, as man in fulnesse may'.[21] T. S. Eliot's remark that Jonson 'created his own world' points to a further correspondence. Kitely and Bobadill also create their own worlds, and in *The Alchemist* (by which time Jonson had no doubt become fully conscious of the analogy) this is literally true of Sir Epicure Mammon, who duplicates the procedures of the author in whose play he is appearing by announcing himself 'In *novo orbe*', filling his brave new world with images fabricated by his imagination, advocating the transmutation of 'Nature' by means of 'art' so as to restore a golden age (I iv 25–9), and firmly ignoring those who, like Surly, sceptically question the value of his vision. In the later *Bartholomew Fair*, to take one other example, this author – character mirroring occasions some wry self-mockery. Here one finds not only the dramatist Littlewit imitating

Jonson by applying classical subject-matter to modern life, but, in the Induction, the stage-keeper of the Hope theatre convicting Jonson of the very self-involvement which typifies his own characters: 'these Master-*Poets*, they will ha' their owne absurd courses; they will be inform'd of nothing!' (ll. 26–7). James Joyce said that Jonson was one of the few authors whose works he had read all through. Perhaps he recognised that they offer not only an image of the times but an ironic and self-dramatising portrait of the artist.

All this is not to deny that *Every Man in* is an early play, in which Jonson was feeling his way towards the kind of form his comic vision required. The plot, in particular, betrays a certain tentativeness. Like many Elizabethan comedies, the main action of *Every Man in* imitates a standard plot of the Greek and Roman New Comedy of Menander, Plautus and Terence: that of the tyrannical, killjoy father (the *senex*) who attempts to inhibit the amatory career of his son, and who is eventually defeated when the hero, assisted by a wily household slave (the *servus*), succeeds in marrying the girl of his choice. In New Comedy, and in Shakespeare, this plot embodies a social and individual meaning well described by Northrop Frye:

> As the hero gets closer to the heroine and opposition is overcome, all the right-thinking people come over to his side. Thus a new social unit is formed on the stage, and the moment that this social unit crystallizes is the moment of the comic resolution. In the last scene, when the dramatist usually tries to get all his characters on the stage at once, the audience witnesses the birth of a renewed sense of social integration. In comedy as in life the regular expression of this is a festival, whether a marriage, a dance, or a feast. . . . The essential comic resolution, therefore, is an individual release which is also a social reconciliation. The normal individual is freed from the bonds of a humorous society, and a normal society is freed from the bonds imposed on it by humorous individuals.[22]

In *Every Man in*, the opening scenes orientate the play towards this meaning (notice, for example, the reference to the redemptive power of love at I ii 129), and the last act attempts to realise it. But what happens in between makes the attempt a failure. Jonson's real aim, it soon becomes clear, is not to narrate and celebrate the purging and reintegration of a society, but to display and relish the variety, absurdity and zaniness of human nature – and this largely by means of characters (Cob, Bobadill, Stephen, Matthew) who do not contribute materially to either of the play's plot-lines at all. The result is that Edward's fortunes become of incidental interest, and his off-stage courtship and marrying of Bridget appears as though hurried in as an afterthought to fulfil the requirements of the intrigue launched in Act I. Gifford suggests that Bridget is 'won . . . with little wooing' because this was 'then the case'. The reason is, rather, that Jonson's delighted contemplation of eccentric behaviour has got the better of his nominal commitment to the New Comedy formula.

This antagonism between the structure of *Every Man in* and Jonson's imaginative inclination becomes all the clearer if one examines the comments of two critics who interpret the play in what may be called Shakespearean terms. For Dutton the actions of Old Knowell are 'socially divisive and morally degenerate', and 'perhaps the central theme of the play' is 'suspicious rather cynical old age . . . out of tune with regenerative nature and society, represented here by the playful vitality of the young men'. For J. A. Bryant, describing the play's overall structure, the action

parallels the predictable course of a disease, moving from symptoms to aggravation to crisis to cure. That is to say, the structure of the play, like the main characters in it, participates in the analogy which the title suggests. We can say that Acts I and II present the accumulation of symptoms, Act III the aggravation, Act IV the crisis, and Act V the cure, sought by those who are potentially capable of normality and thrust upon those who are incorrigible fools.[23]

Both readings seem to me very forced. Regarding Dutton's, not only do the separate centres of interest created by Cob and Bobadill and company distract attention from the 'central', thematic conflict he describes, the conflict itself hardly conforms to the terms of his description. It is true that Jonson, trying to preserve the New Comedy formula, imputes to Knowell some of the divisive traits of the *senex*: Brainworm calls him a cunning old man, 'a foxe in yeeres' (II v 136), and Wellbred in his letter accuses him of stinginess (I ii 75–7); but these comments have nothing to do with the originally eccentric character Jonson actually creates. The real Old Knowell is an amiable figure, fussy and garrulous and somewhat opinionated, but often commonsensical and certainly not tyrannical or degenerate.[24] The case of Kitely, age's other representative, is similar. It is the bizarreness of his behaviour, and the obsessive state of mind it implies, which commands Jonson's interest, and ours. His social divisiveness and degeneracy remain theoretical considerations, because the play does not communicate a notion of 'society', in the sense of a group of people defined and linked by mutual rights, affections, and responsibilities, with comparable force. The treatment of both characters reflects Jonson's failure, or rather unconscious refusal, to subordinate his interest in oddity to the age – youth conflict, with its attendant themes of social and domestic order, which his New Comedy plot supplied. As to Bryant's disease analogy, which seems plausible applied to a summary of the plot, the problems are, firstly, the disruptive vitality and attractiveness of the officially 'diseased' characters, as noted above; secondly, the fact

that, read or seen, the play itself does not convey the sense of purposeful
movement which Bryant's interpretation demands. The reader's or
spectator's experience is more likely to be that described by Wallace A.
Bacon:

at the outset of the play we think we are intended to fix our attention on the visit
of young Knowell to Wellbred, with complications arising from the elder
Knowell's pursuit. This turns out to be essentially a false clue, for as the play
moves along, our attention finds itself unable with any comfort closely to relate
scenes, and we finally settle for the individual scenes as being good fun in
themselves.[25]

This fragmentariness is always a potential weakness in a Jonson play.
Because his principal aim is to exhibit the characters in their typical
mental attitudes, the danger is that scene will follow scene in a loose,
directionless way until the parade of grotesques (and the play) is
complete. In later plays Jonson overcame this by sharply restricting his
locations (Volpone's bedchamber, Lovewit's house, the fair at Smithfield) and concentrating his characters' attention on a single target (a
legacy, the elixir, a licence); but in *Every Man in* with its twenty changes
of scene and diversity of purposes there is no such 'Center attractive'[26]
or unifying symbol to hold the play together. A story is launched,
directing us forward, offering a connecting thread and prompting us to
ask 'what happens next?', but the displays of humours foster an
impression that this question is of no consequence; that the play's
meaning is somehow outside its story. Hence, whatever Jonson's
intention, the play does not in retrospect naturally organise itself into
the coherently significant pattern Bryant describes. What one remembers is an assortment of tricks, confrontations, and set speeches
(Knowell on filial education, Cob on herrings, Bobadill on national
defence) which demonstrate in a rich and vivid way how incorrigibly
freakish human beings can be.

However, the remarkable success of *Every Man in* on the stage is good
evidence that this structural uncertainty is not (despite William
Archer's irate denunciation) gravely damaging. The quarto title-page
says performances were given 'Sundry times', and this suggestion of
early popularity is supported by John Aubrey in *Brief Lives* who states
that after an inauspicious beginning Jonson 'undertooke again to write
a Playe, and did hitt it admirably well, viz. *Every Man . . .* which was his
first good one'. According to a later tradition, begun by Nicholas Rowe
in 1709, it was Shakespeare who made the first performance possible.
Rowe records that

[Shakespeare's] Acquaintance with *Ben Johnson* began with a remarkable piece
of Humanity and good Nature; Mr. *Johnson*, who was at that Time altogether
unknown to the World, had offer'd one of his Plays to the Players, in order to

have it Acted; and the Persons into whose Hands it was put, after having turn'd it carelessly and superciliously over, were just upon returning it to him with an ill-natured Answer, that it would be of no service to their Company, when *Shakespear* luckily cast his Eye upon it, and found something so well in it as to engage him first to read it through, and afterwards to recommend Mr. *Johnson* and his Writings to the Publick. After this they were profess'd Friends; tho' I don't know whether the other ever made him an equal return of Gentleness and Sincerity.[27]

Shakespeare idolatry stands behind this last sentence, a form of worship which in the eighteenth century mythologised Jonson as an envious, splenetic and rule-bound pedant who set off by contrast the natural native genius of the Gentle Will – but the main fact of Rowe's account may well be true, and if so the play in question is almost certainly *Every Man in*. Independent evidence of Shakespeare's involvement in the first production is provided by Jonson himself, in the cast list which he appended to the folio text, where 'WILL. SHAKESPEARE.' appears as one of the 'principall Comoedians' who acted in the 1598 performance. Which part did Shakespeare play? The assumption has usually been Knowell Senior, since his name appears in the corresponding place (first) in the list of dramatis personae at the front of the folio, and Shakespeare's knowledge of character is indicated by Polonius in *Hamlet*, for whom, it has been plausibly argued, Knowell Senior was a partial model.[28] The 1937 production capitalised on this assumption by making up the actor playing Knowell to look like Shakespeare. It seems more likely to me, however, that Shakespeare took the part of Kitely. Several scholars have noticed detailed reminiscences of this character in Shakespeare's plays, notably *The Merry Wives of Windsor* and *Othello* (of which Kitely's quarto name, Thorello, is a near anagram), and to these I can add the following echo:

> My brother *Prospero* (I know not how)
> Of late is much declin'd from what he was,
> And greatly alterd in his disposition.   (Q, I iv 32–4)

I have of late – but wherefore I know not – lost all my mirth, foregone all custom of exercises; and indeed it goes so heavily with my disposition . . . .
                                                       (*Hamlet*, II ii 295–7)

Chance recollection of this sort, a matter of unremarkable turns of phrase, is just what one would expect if Shakespeare had memorised the part two or three years before.[29]

The play's later stage history is equally noteworthy. David Garrick's production at Drury Lane in 1751 was one of the great successes of the eighteenth-century theatre, remaining in more or less continuous repertory until 1798 and supplying Garrick, who played Kitely, with one of his most famous roles. Garrick made many alterations, chiefly because, as he explained, 'The Language & Characters of Ben Jonson (and particularly of the Comedy in question) are much more difficult than those of any other writer',[30] but he stayed faithful to Jonson's conception. Apart from Kitely, the production's great triumph was Henry Woodward's Bobadill, played with 'calm composure', 'Reserve and Gravity',[31] very differently from the blustering *miles gloriosus* figure some modern critics suppose him to be; though this interpretation did not prevent Woodward, in III i, from demonstrating the inferiority of Stephen's sword by treading on it. This production was the first, of any play, to introduce the convention of historic costuming. Garrick's dress as Kitely (rather too upper-class looking) can be seen in the portrait by Sir Joshua Reynolds. Two other famous actors were soon to play Kitely: Kean in 1816 and Macready in 1838. Hazlitt's review of the former production is especially valuable, particularly for its endorsement of what many readers must feel, that Bobadill's defeat is 'the only affecting circumstance in the play' and compared with him Wellbred and Edward seem 'insipid'. Macready's Kitely, according to Robert Browning, was 'superb from his flat cap down to his shining shoes'.[32] On 20 September 1845 a company of literary amateurs (several were writers for *Punch*) performed the play at Miss Kelly's Theatre, Soho, with Charles Dickens as Bobadill. According to John Forster, who also took a role, their success 'out-ran the wildest expectation', Dickens presenting in Bobadill – perhaps less perceptively than Woodward – 'a richly coloured picture of bombastical extravagance and comic exaltation'.[33] Between 1845 and 1848 further performances were given in London, Manchester and Liverpool. This century has seen several fine professional productions, but none for the past forty years. This is a pity, since reviewers have often confessed themselves agreeably surprised that a play which is not easy to follow in the study should work so well on the stage.

Every Man in resembles *The Alchemist* in a number of ways. Brainworm, like Face, is a tricky domestic servant who is also a comic overreacher. Eventually he tries one ploy too many and is forced to admit 'I have made a faire mash on't' (IV xi 76), just as Face, an 'oreweaning raskall', finds he has too many schemes to cope with when Lovewit returns. In both plays also, the dupes of the tricksters are prey to delusive hopes and impressions the insubstantiality of which is imaged in similar ways. Smoke, puffed from the pipes of Bobadill and his cronies, becomes a kind of visible symbol of delusiveness in *Every Man in*, III v, and it suggests the same idea in *The Alchemist*, in which the reader must imagine clouds of smoke from Subtle's laboratory periodically drifting across the stage;[34] also, when Brainworm speaks of Knowell as 'travelling with the expectation of wonders . . . at length [to] be deliver'd of aire' (IV vi 54–5), he is describing very exactly the

experience not only of Volpone and Mosca's victims in *Volpone*, for whom 'all turnes aire' (I iv 159), but also of Subtle, Dol and Face's in *The Alchemist*, who discover that '*it* [the philosopher's stone], *and they, and all in* fume *are gone*' (Argument, l. 12). Finally, both plays are resolved by a very wayward arbitrator who sets great store by wit and jest, and who (as in Roman comedy) lets off the wily servant for his skill as a provider of mirth. These parallels suggest that a comparison of the two plays might be profitable. What is it that makes *The Alchemist* the richer and more brilliant of the two, and indeed, as Ian Donaldson puts it in the last sentence of the critical studies in this volume, 'one of the great comedies of the world'?

Perhaps the most obvious feature is the play's structure. *Every Man in*, for all Brainworm's busy doings, retains the air of a static exhibition of diverse comic types. *The Alchemist* offers an even greater variety of eccentrics, each involved in a separate 'plot' (seven in all), but ties them firmly together by making each a part of the central business venture of Subtle, Face and Dol. Moreover, despite its greater wealth of comic material, the play conveys a sense of purposeful, and constantly accelerating, movement. Dryden pointed out in his famous 'examen' of *Epicoene* that 'the business . . . rises in every act. The second is greater than the first; the third than the second; and so forward to the fifth.'[35] Precisely the same is true of *The Alchemist*. There is, most obviously, a carefully phased build-up of characters: five appear in Act I, seven in II, eight in III, nine in IV, and twelve – or, including the neighbours, officers and parson, twenty-one – in V. There is also an accumulation of ever more complex intrigues, so that one has the sense of watching a juggler add more and more objects to those already in the air, and anticipating with ever greater suspense the inevitable loss of control. And there is, finally, as in *Sejanus* and *Volpone*, a sense of rising tension conveyed by the rogues' alliance itself, as Face and Subtle, reunited into a precarious partnership by Dol in the opening scene, gradually revert to a state of rivalry and begin to work against each other to secure the upper hand. The result is a crescendoing concentration and pace which is quite absent from *Every Man in*. Here one finds no equivalent to the climactic catastrophe which topples tricked and trickster alike, while Brainworm, denied any motive stronger than a taste for practical jokes, remains a peripheral and bewildering figure.

Another aspect of Jonson's greater maturity in *The Alchemist* is his more complex use of the contemporary London setting. Not only is the life of Jacobean London, its sights and sounds, customs, trades, and streets, densely particularised; the fictional location (a house in Blackfriars) is also where the first production actually took place (the Blackfriars 'private house'), and the imagined time (the autumn of 1610) is contemporaneous with the date of that production, and thus

Jonson is conducting a kind of running joke aimed at his audience, whose houses would have been standing empty while they were watching the play (as indeed would Jonson's own, which was just round the corner). This gives a special edge to the stock notion of a play as *speculum vitae*, a mirror of life; though today, of course, we have to make a historical leap to retrieve the full irony of Jonson's device. Another feature of the setting requires no such adjustment. This is Jonson's brilliant use of the actual physical confines of the stage to suggest a room, in which, as Face says, the rogues are 'entrench'd . . . against a world' (iii iii 34–5). Some remarks by a modern playwright, Harold Pinter, who is recurrently fascinated by this situation, indicate its powerfulness as a stage device:

Two people in a room – I am dealing a great deal of the time with this image of two people in a room. The curtain goes up on the stage, and I see it as a very potent question: What is going to happen to these two people in the room? Is someone going to open the door and come in?[36]

In *The Alchemist*, Dol's peering through the window, the constant knockings on the door, keep us tensely aware of the unseen world outside the room, a potential source of profit but also of threat. At any moment the shelter might become a prison, and when Lovewit returns and Face at once announces 'We are undone, and taken' (iv vii 114) it suddenly does.

One further aspect of the play's formal organisation invites comparison with *Every Man in*: its uninhibited reworking of the New Comedy formula. Here we may look again at Northrop Frye's definition of the typical Roman and Shakespearean comic structure:

The normal action is the effort of a young man to get possession of a young woman who is kept from him by various social barriers. . . . [This structure] normally begins with an anticomic society, a social organization blocking and opposed to the comic drive, which the action of the comedy evades or overcomes.[37]

The Alchemist incorporates New Comedy elements – for example, the motif of the empty house taken over by a servant and his accomplice appears in Plautus's *Mostellaria* – but it ironically inverts this formula. Had Jonson followed it straightforwardly, Surly would be the play's hero and agent of release, and the rogues the representatives of the anticomic society. Surly would overcome the rogues, and the play would end with his marriage to Dame Pliant and general reconciliation. The play Jonson wrote is very different. Surly is the focus of the anticomic mood, and the rogues represent the essential comic virtues of vitality and joy. In the dénouement Surly goes off baffled and single, Face is undefeated, and Lovewit, whose name associates him with the rogues, wins the girl and the wealth. As in *Every Man in*, Jonson ends *The*

Alchemist traditionally with a marriage, but he does not attempt to assert that the traditional concomitants of this ending, individual self-discovery and a heightened sense of social unity, are also present. Lovewit's marriage seems a purely superficial change. Everything stays basically just as it was.

This is a very bold and unsettling structure, and it has prompted, not surprisingly, some disapproval and a good many different critical readings. The conclusion, in particular, has been frequently attacked. In 1695 John Dennis found the play 'to be more dexterously perplexed, than to be happily disentangled'; in 1783 Thomas Davies was more specific:

the catastrophe [i.e. dénouement] is surely a bad one; a gentleman of fortune joining with his knavish servant, to cheat a parcel of bubbles of their money and goods, is equally mean and immoral.

And in our own century a French critic has branded the conclusion 'le gros défaut, le seul peut-être de la pièce', adding, 'on ne peut ni l'expliquer ni l'excuser'.[38] Other commentators have attempted, nevertheless, an explanation. Of these, the least successful is Collier's, who argues that the play ends morally because Face makes 'an Apology before he leaves the *Stage*'. Collier misses, rather absurdly, a heavy layer of irony. Face's plea to the audience for pardon is backed up by a bribe, which is no less than an offer of a share in the spoils: 'this pelfe, . . . if you doe quit me, rests / To feast you often' (v v 163–4). Other critics argue, hardly more plausibly, that the conclusion does not mean what it seems to mean. J. V. Holleran (see Select Bibliography) suggests that Lovewit's triumph is really a hollow one, since he must now constantly suspect Face and must pay for the cleaning of his house; to which one might reply, no less, or more, relevantly, that he can give Face the sack if he wants to and has now enough money to buy several new houses. Edward B. Partridge (see below, Part Three, section 2) argues that the conclusion should be seen as sternly punitive: 'all endure the most comic of all punishments: they remain themselves – a deadly retribution if one is a fool like Mammon or a rascal like Face'. If Jonson intended this, he has certainly not conveyed it with sufficient explicitness. As the play stands, Face's being allowed to remain himself seems more like a reward. A more attractive account is that of Alvin B. Kernan:

If alchemy is ever possible, the play seems to be saying, then its true powers are the wit and the quickness of such clever characters as Face and Subtle, who always manage to turn a dollar somehow . . . when Lovewit materializes at the beginning of Act v, far from being a *deus ex machina* he is simply the embodiment, in a more respectable form, of that mental agility and histrionic skill, that wit, which we have been watching throughout the play with such fascination as it appears in Face and Subtle, turning the rough opportunities of life into pure gold. Lovewit's marriage with the rich widow and his seizure of all the loot stored in his cellar is the perfect ending of the play, the triumph of true alchemy, the wit which achieves riches and happiness by making the most of such chances as the world throws its way.[39]

Perhaps the main aim of Jonson's ending, however, is to leave the audience in a state of difficulty which no interpretation can entirely allay. A basic law of Elizabethan comedy, followed, at least in letter, in all Jonson's other plays, was that 'the conclusion showes, the confusion of Vice, and the cherishing of Virtue'.[40] In place of such an ending, Jonson leaves us wondering who are the wicked and who are the virtuous in his play. Are we, for example, to believe Lovewit's glib explanation to the dupes at v v 29–37 concerning his knowledge of the affair, or has Face put him more fully in the picture than he admits? And in his final speech, is his argument setting an 'ungratefull' attitude against 'some small straine / Of his owne candor' a piece of facile, self-extenuating casuistry, or a reasonable view that rigid moral standards are sometimes inappropriate? Before we can ponder such questions, Face steps forward with a plea for acquittal which questions our right to make any judgements at all. When he addresses the audience as 'my country' and looks forward to the reception of 'new ghests', his ostensible meaning is respectively 'fellow countrymen' and 'new spectators'; but the first phrase could mean 'rogues just like me' and the second 'new guests in Lovewit's house, i.e. dupes'. Acquit me, in other words, on the grounds that none of you is any different from the characters in this play. In ending the play at this point, Face and Jonson spring their last and most devastating trap. We applaud, because the play is over; but it appears that we are applauding the argument that Face has just advanced. Or perhaps we would be inclined to do so anyway? If we are in retrospect 'ashamed to have laughed', as Dryden says, it is surely because we have been suddenly involved with uncomfortable closeness in the play's processes of moral comment and discovery.

What moral discoveries does the play make? Views vary greatly. For Edmund Wilson the answer is none at all: *The Alchemist* is a spirited but themeless romp, 'one of the funniest [plays] in English', but no more than 'a picaresque farce, fundamentally not different from the Marx brothers'.[41] Other critics find the play deeply and austerely moral. For Corbyn Morris, writing in 1744, Jonson is sternly, even sadistically, bent on demonstrating that his characters are in the last degree mean, sordid, and despicable, and for William Gifford in the next century Jonson is attacking social pests, whom he exhibits in 'an odious and disgusting light' in order to 'extirpate [them] . . . from the commerce of real life'. A similar view is held by many modern critics. L. C. Knights, for example, believes that *The Alchemist* is 'built on the double theme of lust and greed, and the whole play is constructed so as to isolate and magnify the central theme'; Edward B. Partridge that it is the work of 'a moral idealist and dogmatic Christian' who as well as condemning the sins of avarice and hypocrisy in general is exposing alchemy as 'fraudulent', 'impious', and 'obscene'; and Alan C. Dessen that it is an up-dated Morality play which dramatises 'the campaign of the Vices against humanity'.[42] Other critics, for example Bamborough, Empson, and Steane, while also convinced of Jonson's moral and intellectual seriousness, find a strong measure of gaiety and wit in the play which tempers and complicates our response to its characters, particularly the rogues.

Of these three approaches the last seems to me the most rewarding, and that of the moralistic critics potentially the most restricting. (Nowadays many would regard Wilson's comparison with the Marx brothers as an illuminating piece of praise.) To dismiss the rogues as simply wicked or sordid misses a lot in the play which gains them sympathy. They are vastly outnumbered, 'the few . . . against a world' (III iii 34–5); they take a detached, self-criticising pride in their skill as swindlers: 'O, but to ha' gull'd him, / Had beene a maistry' says Subtle about Surly (III iii 7–8), as though gulling were an academic pursuit in which there are recognised standards of excellence; and their breezy jollity puts them on the side of life against those who would cramp and depress it, and this is the side which comedy always backs (thus, in the first scene, Dol's chief objection to their neighbours is that they 'scarse have smil'd twise, sin' the king came in'). Similarly, to take Surly as the play's moral spokesman, 'the single voice of truth and sanity in the midst of a world of lies and self-deceptions',[43] is to take him too readily at his own estimation and to ignore the implications of his name. In some respects Surly is the comic equivalent of the embittered railer of Jacobean tragedy, such as Middleton's Vindice; in others he looks forward to Justice Adam Overdo, the self-appointed seeker-out of 'enormity' in *Bartholomew Fair*, whose moral absolutism has eventually to yield to the painful lesson that he is 'but *Adam*, Flesh, and blood'. The play accords him, as Steane observes, no authority. His status is undermined by compromising parallels: like Dapper he is a gamester; like Ananias he hates philosophy (cf. II iii 264, 310 and III i 10); like Mammon he is adept in the language of compliment when it suits him (his praise, in Spanish, of Dame Pliant at IV iv 63–4 closely echoes Mammon's of Dol at IV i 141–3); and like Face, but less successfully, he tries his hand at disguise. In II i, in which Mammon and Surly, alone on the stage, offer a revealing physical contrast ('the fat knight, and the leane gentleman'), Surly's refusal to indulge his friend's expansive dreams makes him appear less commonsensical than a mean-spirited spoilsport, and in his attempts to deflate them he early forfeits our support by being brutally coarse (ll. 42–5). 'You are too foule', Mammon tells him, and the comment seems just. The gulls, too, are presented ambiguously, so that condemnation of their greed and folly is checked by other responses. They arrive, for the most part, with modest ambitions, and are swept up into fantasy, finding they have entered a magic place in which, as Subtle tells Ananias, 'You may be any thing' (III ii 53). In reality they are the deserving victims of their own conceited illusions, but the versions of reality which the play offers – Drugger's worms, Face's description of Subtle's poverty, Surly's sneering – give these illusions a poignant attractiveness and force. The gulls are, moreover, as M. C. Bradbrook notes, 'enriched with potent gifts of imagination and hope';[44] so much so, that in the case of Dapper it is almost with relief, with a grateful sense of something saved, that we see him leave the stage with his dreams intact to await his birthright ('three or four hundred chests of treasure, / And some twelve thousande acres of *Faerie* land'). Blindfolded, pinched, locked in the privy and utterly forgotten for half the play, he at last achieves his meeting with the Queen of Fairy and 'cannot speake, for joy'. It is a beautiful and touching moment, which the blatancy of his folly fails to impair. And even the play's most unpleasantly predatory characters, the Anabaptists, are partly redeemed by their inability to recognise their own absurdity; as Empson remarks, 'one does not much hate them, because they are so funny'.

These ambivalences reflect a tension at the heart of the play. On the one hand it condemns the encroachment of money on morality, and portrays man's limitless capacity to be idiotic and self-deceived. On the other it celebrates the optimism and energy of man's unconquerable mind, his limitless power to alchemise the world into the forms which his imagination conceives. We may see this conflict, if we wish, as one between opposing 'world pictures' – medieval and Renaissance, or Christian and humanist; but it is possible to associate it also with an opposition of attitudes in Jonson's own personality. Viewed thus, *The Alchemist* might be said to dramatise the collision between Jonson the pessimistic *censor morum* of *Discoveries* and the dramatic prefaces, whose 'whole Discourse', as he lay paralysed in old age at his house in Blackfriars, 'Was how Mankinde grew daily worse and worse', and Jonson the delighter in contrivance, who once himself dressed up as an astrologer, 'in a Longe Gowne & a whyte beard at the light of a Dimm burning candle', in order to play a joke on a lady; between Jonson the literary theorist, to whom imagination seemed less important than the need for judgement, craftsmanship, and rational control, and Jonson the inventive artist, who once 'consumed a whole night in lying looking to his great toe, about which he hath seen tartars & turks Romans and

Carthaginions feight in his imagination'; a collision perhaps summed up in his friend Drummond's memorandum that 'He can set Horoscopes, but trusts not in them.'[45]

The play's richest embodiment of this conflict is Sir Epicure Mammon. This character is at once luxurious monster and childlike dreamer whose visions fill the mind with wonder; at once Tiberius (who offered a prize to anyone who could invent for him a new sin) and Don Quixote. Partridge solemnly dissects the meaning of his name and Bamborough calls him the play's 'real villain', but other critics, for example Marianna Da Vinci Nichols, find him heroic:

Sir Epicure's heady language evokes a response in us far different from moral disapproval. . . . He is capable of touching our secret dreams because we suspect he is innocent as well as ridiculous, generous rather than merely greedy. . . . He is unreal; yet we don't want him to waken from his dream world for he echoes anti-social wishes of our own. Better still, he assures us they are harmless. Sir Epicure's cry 'O my voluptuous mind!' can be beginning and ending, for his exuberance illustrates the unfathomable power of language to create.[46]

Mammon speaks in the soaring cadences and high astounding terms of Marlowe's Tamburlaine and Faustus (a style denounced as flying 'from all humanity', 'vitious . . . gaping, swelling, and irregular' by Jonson in Discoveries), and like them he lives perpetually in the future. Faustus worships a succubus as Helen of Troy and Mammon hails the commonest of prostitutes ('all things in Common') as a Hapsburg princess. Although The Alchemist is a comedy, the effect of these transplantations is far from ludicrous. As with Marlowe's tragic individualists, Mammon's fantastic ambitions and opulent verse disarm criticism, so that to disapprove seems small-minded, and his solipsism and unworldliness reveal him at once as pathetically vulnerable and marked down for disaster. Face's summary of his career in Act v has the ring of an epitaph:

> he would ha' built
> The citie new; and made a ditch about it
> Of silver, should have runne with creame from Hogsden. . . .
>   (v v 76–8)

Dessen thinks these lines 'a bitter reductio of Sir Epicure's original hopes and pretensions . . . the final pronouncement in Jonson's exposé of Sir Epicure Mammon'.[47] It is also possible to read them as a moving tribute, an admiring and nostalgic survey which offers us a last wistful glimpse of dazzling possibilities as the dream fades out. Jonson probably did not intend an overt echo of Marlowe here (it was Faustus, we remember, who wished to surround Germany with walls of brass), but the double response, the conflicting sense of grandeur and folly, is typically Marlovian.

Mammon's seductive verbal adventures point to another aspect of this play's greatness: its rich and brilliant language. Jonson had an acute ear for different styles of speech, and *The Alchemist* is the result of a sharp aural as well as visual scrutiny of his fellow Londoners. Eighteenth-century critics often accuse him of exaggeration, but in fact the current jargons of alchemy, tobacco-dealing, and quarrelling were quite technical and bizarre enough for his purpose, and are faithfully reproduced.[48] The Anabaptists, too, speak the authentic language of their sect. Compare this passage from a contemporary religious treatise, which distinguishes different types of the puritan fanatic precisely as Jonson distinguishes Tribulation from Ananias:

The Puritan or Separatist . . . are according to their own definition, refined protestants, but to others, Gospellers out of their wits; men drunken with their owne wine, but with difference, some more soberly besotted, other more frantickely intoxicated. . . . These men I say are sacrilegers: for first they have defiled our holy sacraries, with their Bedlam Rhetoricke . . . tearming them *Temples of Baal, sties of Antichrist, cages of uncleane birds, &c.* Nay, some have commenced to such a degree of holy frenzie, that they have abhorred the very tongue wherein superstition hath talked, as the language of the beast, (then happily true, when themselves do speake it.) . . . tell mee what manner of propositions these be: *Tythes, Prelacies, Churches, demeanes, & dignities are all Antichristian, the markes of the beast, the garments of the whoore, the sties of the devill.*[49]

It is not surprising that to some of his contemporaries Jonson should have seemed merely a superficial recorder, 'a meere spunge', as he wryly described himself in *Poetaster*, 'nothing but humours, and observation; he goes up and downe sucking from every societie, and when he comes home, squeazes himself drie againe' (IV iii 104–7). But the linguistic design of *The Alchemist* transcends mere verisimilitude. Partridge draws attention to the play's intricate webs of imagery, and Mares to the way Jonson differentiates and defines his characters by means of their habits of speech. Kernan notices how Jonson's language evokes a densely cluttered and chaotic universe packed with random objects – 'pepper, sope, / Hops, or tabacco, oat-meale, woad, or cheeses' – through which his characters move in a state of permanent mental seclusion.[50] Ian Donaldson, in a fine essay, discusses the play's insistent concern with linguistic distortion and collapse. If one is inclined anywhere to quarrel with Donaldson's argument, it may be over a failure to allow that *The Alchemist* may embody a rather more ambiguous view of verbal disorderliness than Jonson sets out in *Discoveries*. Here Jonson's position is unequivocal: 'Wheresoever, man-ners, and fashions are corrupted, Language is. It imitates the publicke riot . . . wantonnesse of language [is the sign] of a sick mind' (ll. 954–8).

In the play the rogues' exuberant sporting with words – Face conjugating the superiority of things Spanish (iv v 8 ff.), Subtle anticipating how Surly will be 'sok'd, and strok'd, and tub'd, and rub'd', etc. (iv iii 97 ff.) – generates an infectious sense of delight, intellectual and aesthetic, which runs counter to the moral thesis. This is the case even, and especially, with the alchemical jargon. Harold Pinter, in such pieces as *Trouble in the Works* and *The Caretaker*, is often claimed as the first English playwright to extract poetry and verbal magic from the vocabularies of plumbing and home-decorating. Jonson does something very similar in *The Alchemist*.

The *Alchemist* has had the most brilliant stage history of all Jonson's plays, outshining even *Volpone*. Its early success is indicated in a letter by a scandalised university don, Henry Jackson, who saw the play in Oxford in September 1610 at a time when the plague had closed the London theatres:

> Over these past days the King's Men have been here. Their acting received very great applause in a full theatre. But they appeared wicked (deservedly so) to holy and learned men, because, not content with attacking alchemists, they most foully violated the sacred scriptures themselves. Naturally they twitted the Anabaptists; and as a result beneath their costumes wickedness lurked. (Our religious men, shame to say, flocked there most eagerly.) Never have our theatres thundered with greater applause than when that rascal in disguise entered, he who, in order to expose the holiness of the Anabaptists as spurious, for the spectators to laugh at, wickedly and outrageously defiled the scriptures.[51]

Possibly it was similar puritan sympathies which some years later motivated those who, according to Robert Herrick, 'hist / At thy uneqal'd Play, the *Alchymist*' ('Upon Mr. Ben Jonson'). There were frequent revivals before and after the Restoration, and Pepys noted in his diary 'a most incomparable play' after seeing a performance on 22 June 1661. The eighteenth century was the peak of the play's success on the stage. Between 1709 and 1776 it was in almost continuous production, becoming particularly popular after 1721, when the bursting of the South Sea Bubble lent it a special topical appeal. This was also the period of the extraordinary popularity of the part of Drugger, about whom, R. G. Noyes remarks, 'more was written up to Garrick's death than about any other comic character except Falstaff'.[52] William ('Pinky') Pinkethman brought the part into prominence between 1709 and 1731, and the farcical talents of Theophilus Cibber, who replaced him, increased its success. Cibber's accidental breaking of a urinal during one performance became standard to the role. On 21 March 1743 David Garrick's production opened to instant acclaim, with Garrick as Jonson's tobacconist. In this version the text was cut by almost a thousand lines, reducing the playing time to two hours and three minutes, and Drugger's popularity was reflected in a revision whereby he, and not Kastril, became the chief beater-away of Surly in IV vii. The degree of Garrick's success in the role can be gauged from such contemporary interludes as *Drugger's Jubilee* (1770) and *Abel Drugger's Return from the Fête Champêtre at Marybone Gardens* (1774), the naming of a London tobacco-shop 'The Abel Drugger', and two plays by Francis Gentleman, *The Tobacconist* (1770), a rewriting of *The Alchemist* in which Drugger becomes the hero, and *The Pantheonites* (1773), which, in the manner of modern film sequels, features Dan Drugger, the great-grandson of Jonson's Abel. Garrick produced the play once or twice every year until 1776, three years before his death, and intermittent performances continued until 1787. After this, unless we count Edmund Kean's revival of *The Tobacconist* in 1815, *The Alchemist* disappeared completely from the stage until 1899, when William Poel's Elizabethan Stage Society performed the play at the Apothecaries' Hall, Blackfriars, on the site of its first theatre. From this time onwards productions have been frequent, though not always as successful as the production of 1947, when Drugger was played by Alec Guinness. In 1962 Tyrone Guthrie employed a modernised text in the interests of intelligibility, a disastrous strategy in a play where obscurantism is itself a central concern. In the 1970 Chichester Festival production, directed by Peter Dews, the 'plethora of funny hats, funny voices, custard pies and chamber pots suggested a belief that the only way to deal with Jonson's rich, intricate verbal invention was to bury it under farcical hubbub'.[53] Jonson, not the most temperate of persons, would have had strong words to say to both these directors. Slapstick he explicitly repudiates in the Prologue to *Volpone*, where we are told that a sign of 'his playes worth' is that 'no egges are broken; / Nor quaking custards with fierce teeth affrighted'. As for the modernising of his text, Jonson held 'that to be the most unlucky *Scene* in a *Play*, which needs an Interpreter; especially, when the *Auditory* are awake' (Induction to *The Magnetic Lady*, ll. 145–7). Since he would have included readers, along with spectators, in this last remark, we may be sure that he would have had words to say to the contributors in this Casebook as well.

NOTES

1. *Discoveries*, l. 774 (Herford and Simpson, vol. VIII, p. 587).

2. Herford and Simpson, vol. I, p. 343.

3. *Satiromastix*, ed. F. Bowers, *The Dramatic Works of Thomas Dekker*, 4 vols (Cambridge, 1953–61) v ii 138.

4. J. W. Lever, Introduction to *Every Man in his Humour* (London, 1972) p. xxi.

5. Peter Whalley (ed.), *The Works of Ben Jonson*, 7 vols (London, 1756) vol. I, pp. xi–xii.

6. A. C. Swinburne, *A Study of Ben Jonson* (London, 1889) p. 9.

7. *Satiromastix*, IV ii 77, IV iii 194–6; cf. Kitely, who fears that he will be mocked 'all over, / From my flat cap, unto my shining shoes' (III i 109–10; added, however, in the folio).

8. *Satiromastix*, v ii 216–17.

9. Herford and Simpson, vol. IX, p. 332.

10. Katherine Duncan-Jones and J. Van Dorsten (eds), *Miscellaneous Prose of Sir Philip Sidney* (Oxford, 1973) pp. 95–6. Cf. Jonson's own definition of comedy in *Every Man out of his Humour*, III vi 207–9: 'a thing throughout pleasant, and ridiculous, and accommodated to the correction of manners'.

11. R. B. McKerrow (ed.), *The Works of Thomas Nashe*, 5 vols (London, 1904–10) vol. I, p. 220.

12. Thomas Wright, *The Passions of the Mind in General* (London, 1604) p. 49; Francis Bacon, *The Advancement of Learning* (London, 1605) II iv 2.

13. Trans. C. Brereton and F. Rothwell (London, 1935) p. 185.

14. Arthur Sale (ed.), *Every Man in his Humour*, 2nd edition (London, 1949) p. xviii.

15. Aldous Huxley, 'Ben Jonson' in *On the Margin* (London, 1923) pp. 200–1.

16. Sale (ed.), *Every Man in*, p. xvii.

17. William Oxberry (ed.), *The New English Drama*, 18 vols (London, 1818–23) vol. XVI, p. ii.

18. *Epicoene*, II vi 35–6. Clerimont is describing the baiting of Morose, in which he is assisting.

19. Judd Arnold, *A Grace Peculiar: Ben Jonson's Cavalier Heroes* (Philadelphia, 1972) p. 16. Discussing Kitely, Arnold seems to me to indulge in some fantasising of his own when he states that 'Kitely's puritanical loathing is, of course, a mask for almost lustful desires.'

20. Wright, *Passions of the Mind*, p. 49.

21. 'Apologetical Dialogue' appended to *Poetaster*, l. 238; 'An Ode to Himself' (*Underwood*, XXIII) l. 36; *Cynthia's Revels*, v viii 19–20. With Bobadill's remark quoted above cf. 'An Ode to Himself', ll. 16–17: 'Minds that are great and free, / Should not on fortune pause.'

22. Northrop Frye, 'The Argument of Comedy' in L. Lerner (ed.), *Shakespeare's Comedies: An Anthology of Modern Criticism* (Harmondsworth, 1967) pp. 316–17.

23. J. A. Bryant, 'Jonson's Revision of *Every Man in his Humor*', *Studies in Philology*, LIX (1962) 649–50.

24. Cf. the comment of William Oxberry in *The New English Drama*, vol. XVI, p. iii: '*Old Knowell* is sensible and tedious. He moralizes in good set terms, and utters some wholesome truisms, which are apt to task the patience of the audience very severely.'

25. Wallace A. Bacon, 'The Magnetic Field: The Structure of Jonson's Comedies', *Huntington Library Quarterly*, XIX (1955–6) 137. In his valuable discussion of Shakespearean dramatic structure Emrys Jones points out that 'Plays are made of scenes before they are made of words . . . the scene is the primary dramatic unit, the unit in terms of which [the dramatist] will work out his play' (*Scenic Form in Shakespeare* (Oxford, 1971) p. 3). It is perhaps the

obviousness of this method of composition in Jonson which constitutes one aspect of his inferiority, as a dramatist, to Shakespeare.

26. Jonson's own term for this structural device in *The Magnetic Lady*, Induction, l. 108. See the articles by Thomas Greene and Ray L. Heffner Jr listed in the Select Bibliography. Judd Arnold, in *A Grace Peculiar*, p. 9, argues that Brainworm is the 'Center attractive' of *Every Man in*.

27. Nicholas Rowe (ed.), *The Works of Mr. William Shakespeare*, 6 vols (London, 1709) vol. I, pp. xii–xiii.

28. Claire McGlinchee, ' "Still Harping": Ben Jonson's *Every Man in his Humour* as a Source of Polonius' Precepts Speech', *Shakespeare Quarterly*, VI (1955) 362–4.

29. See also S. Sewell, 'The Relation between *The Merry Wives of Windsor* and Jonson's *Every Man in his Humour*', *Shakespeare Association Bulletin*, XVI (1941) 175–89; P. Mueschke and J. Fleisher, 'Jonsonian Elements in the Comic Underplot of *Twelfth Night*', *PMLA*, XLVIII (1933) 722–40; Jones, *Scenic Form in Shakespeare*, pp. 149–51; Lever, Introduction to *Every Man in*, pp. xxiv–xxvi; George C. Taylor, essay listed in the Select Bibliography.

30. D. M. Little and G. M. Kahrl (eds), *The Letters of David Garrick* (London, 1963) vol. I, p. 304. Garrick's view still, regrettably, prevails; cf. Ivor Brown's review of the 1937 production, where the director is praised for 'extracting what will tell with a contemporary audience from a good deal of topical matter inevitably dead' (*The Observer*, 8 Aug 1937, p. 11).

31. See Herford and Simpson, vol. IX, p. 179, and the anonymous *London Chronicle* article below, Part Two, section 1.

32. Herford and Simpson, vol. IX, p. 181.

33. John Forster, *The Life of Charles Dickens*, 3 vols (London, 1872–4) vol. II, pp. 182–6. At least one member of the audience was less enthusiastic: 'Lord Melbourne said before the curtain rose that it was a dull play, "with no μῦθος [story] in it," that was his expression. Between the acts he exclaimed in a stentorian voice, heard across the pit, "I knew this play would be dull, but that it would be so damnably dull as this I did not suppose' (L. Strachey and R. Fulford (eds), *The Greville Memoirs*, vol. V (London, 1936) p. 236).

34. Cf. also *Bartholomew Fair*, III vi 32–3: 'the smoake of tabacco, to keepe us in mist and error'.

35. *Of Dramatic Poesy, An Essay*, in W. P. Ker (ed.), *Essays of John Dryden* (New York, 1961) vol. I, p. 88.

36. Quoted in Martin Esslin, *The Theatre of the Absurd*, revised edition (Harmondsworth, 1968) pp. 265–6.

37. Northrop Frye, *A Natural Perspective* (New York, 1965) pp. 72–3.

38. John Dennis, letter to Congreve (June 1695) in J. C. Hodges (ed.), *William Congreve: Letters and Documents* (London, 1964) p. 174; Thomas Davies, *Dramatic Miscellanies*, 3 vols (London, 1783–4) vol. II, p. 107; Maurice Castelain, *Ben Jonson: L'Homme et L'Œuvre* (Paris, 1907) p. 351.

39. Alvin B. Kernan (ed.), *The Alchemist* (New Haven, Conn., and London, 1974) p. 13.

40. George Whetstone, Dedication to *Promos and Cassandra* (London, 1578).

41. Edmund Wilson, 'Morose Ben Jonson' (see Select.Bibliography).

42. Alan C. Dessen, '*The Alchemist*: Jonson's "Estates" Play', *Renaissance*

Drama, VIII (1965) 38. For an entertaining review, and dismissal, of over-solemn readings of the play, see Richard Levin's essay listed in the Select Bibliography.

43. Dessen, in *Renaissance Drama*, VIII, 46–7.

44. M. C. Bradbrook, *The Growth and Structure of Elizabethan Comedy*, 2nd edition (Harmondsworth, 1963) p. 156.

45. See Herford and Simpson, vol. I, pp. 113, 141.

46. Marianna Da Vinci Nichols, 'Truewit and Sir Epicure Mammon: Jonson's Creative Accidents', *Ariel*, VII, no. 4 (1976) 15–19.

47. Dessen, in *Renaissance Drama*, VIII, 42.

48. Similarly, much of the play's action could easily have formed a fairly routine day in the life of a Jacobean alchemist and astrologer. Readers who doubt this should compare Simon Forman's diary published in A. L. Rowse's *Simon Forman: Sex and Society in Shakespeare's Age* (London, 1974) pp. 279–99. The Dapper plot is based on fact; see Herford and Simpson below, Part Three, section 1.

49. Roger Gostwyke, *The Anatomy of Ananias: or, God's Censure against Sacrilege* (Cambridge, 1616) pp. 64–8.

50. Jonson's vision here may be compared with Milton's of Chaos in *Paradise Lost*, Bk II, 890–967, with its whirl of 'embryon atoms' and 'universal hubbub wild / Of stunning sounds and voices all confused'; and both with the mechanico-materialistic universe posited by the new science and empirical philosophy of Bacon, Locke and Newton, with its separation of matter and mind.

51. Herford and Simpson, vol. IX, p. 224 (trans. from the Latin by T. P. Dolan).

52. R. G. Noyes, *Ben Jonson on the English Stage 1660–1776* (Cambridge, Mass., 1935) p. 103.

53. Ronald Bryden, in the *Observer*, 26 July 1970, p. 24.

PART ONE

Comment on Jonsonian Comedy 1668–1938

John Dryden (1668)

The greatest man of the last age (*Ben. Johnson*) was willing to give place
to [the Ancients] in all things: He was not onely a professed Imitator of
Horace, but a learned Plagiary of all the others; you track him every
where in their Snow: If *Horace, Lucan, Petronius Arbiter, Seneca*, and
Juvenal, had their own from him, there are few serious thoughts which
are new in him; you will pardon me therefore if I presume he lov'd their
fashion when he wore their cloaths. . . .

'Tis evident that the more the persons are, the greater will be the
variety of the Plot. If then the parts are manag'd so regularly that the
beauty of the whole be kept intire, and that the variety become not a
perplex'd and confus'd mass of accidents, you will find it infinitely
pleasing to be led in a labyrinth of design, where you see some of your
way before you, yet discern not the end till you arrive at it. And that all
this is practicable, I can produce for examples many of our English
Playes: as the Maids Tragedy, the Alchymist, the Silent Woman. . . .

I think [Jonson] the most learned and judicious Writer which any
Theater ever had. He was a most severe Judge of himself as well as
others. One cannot say he wanted wit, but rather that he was frugal of it.
In his works you find little to retrench or alter. Wit and Language, and
Humour also in some measure we had before him; but something of Art
was wanting to the *Drama* till he came. He manag'd his strength to more
advantage then any who preceded him. You seldome find him making
Love in any of his Scenes, or endeavouring to move the Passions; his
genius was too sullen and saturnine to do it gracefully, especially when
he knew he came after those who had performed both to such an height.
Humour was his proper Sphere, and in that he delighted most to
represent Mechanick[1] people. . . . He borrow'd boldly from [the
Ancients]. . . . But he has done his Robberies so openly, that one may
see he fears not to be taxed by any Law. He invades Authors like a
Monarch, and what would be theft in other Poets, is onely victory in
him. . . . If I would compare him with *Shakespeare*, I must acknowledge
him the more correct Poet, but *Shakespeare* the greater wit. *Shakespeare*
was the *Homer*, or Father of our Dramatick Poets; *Johnson* was the *Virgil*,
the pattern of elaborate writing; I admire him, but I love *Shakespeare*.

. . . by humour[2] is meant some extravagant habit, passion, or
affection; particular . . . to some one person: by the oddness of which,
he is immediately distinguish'd from the rest of men; which being lively
and naturally represented, most frequently begets that malicious

pleasure in the Audience which is testified by laughter: as all things which are deviations from common customes are ever the aptest to produce it: though by the way this laughter is onely accidental, as the person represented is Fantastick or Bizarre; but pleasure is essential to it, as the imitation of what is natural. The description of these humours, drawn from the knowledge and observation of particular persons, was the peculiar genius and talent of *Ben. Johnson*.

SOURCE: extract from *Of Dramatick Poesie, An Essay* (1668).

NOTES

1. [Low-life.]
2. [I.e. the method of character presentation. In the preceding paragraph 'humour' has the common meaning.]

William Congreve (1695)

The Character of *Cob* in *Every Man in his Humour*, and most of the under Characters in *Bartholomew Fair*, discover only a Singularity of Manners, appropriated to the several Educations and Professions of the Persons represented. They are not Humours but Habits contracted by Custom. Under this Head may be ranged all Country Clowns, Sailers, Tradesmen, Jockeys, Gamesters and such like, who make use of *Cants* or peculiar *Dialects* in their several Arts and Vocations. One may almost give a Receipt[1] for the Composition of such a Character: For the Poet has nothing to do, but to collect a few proper Phrases and terms of Art, and to make the Person apply them by ridiculous Metaphors in his Conversation, with Characters of different Natures. Some late Characters of this kind have been very successful; but in my mind they may be Painted without much Art or Labour; since they require little more, than a good Memory and Superficial Observation. But true *Humour* cannot be shewn, without a Dissection of Nature, and a Narrow Search, to discover the first Seeds, from whence it has its Root and growth. . . .

I take [Humour] to be, *A singular and unavoidable manner of doing, or saying any thing, Peculiar and Natural to one Man only; by which his Speech and Actions are distinguish'd from those of other Men*.

Our *Humour* has relation to us, and to what proceeds from us, as the Accidents have to a Substance; it is a Colour, Taste, and Smell, Diffused through all; thô our Actions are never so many, and different in Form, they are all Splinters of the same Wood, and have Naturally one Complexion; which thô it may be disguised by Art, yet cannot be wholly changed: We may Paint it with other Colours, but we cannot change the Grain. So the Natural sound of an Instrument will be distinguish'd, thô the Notes expressed by it, are never so various, and the Divisions never so many. Dissimulation, may by Degrees, become more easy to our practice; but it can never absolutely Transubstantiate us into what we would seem: It will always be in some proportion a Violence upon Nature.

A Man may change his Opinion, but I believe he will find it a Difficulty, to part with his *Humour*, and there is nothing more provoking, than the being made sensible of that difficulty. Sometimes, one shall meet with those, who perhaps, Innocently enough, but at the same time impertinently, will ask the Question; *Why are you not Merry? Why are you not Gay, Pleasant, and Cheerful?* then instead of answering, could I ask such one; *Why are you not handsome? Why have you not Black Eyes, and a better Complexion?* Nature abhors to be forced.

SOURCE: extracts from letter to John Dennis, 10 July 1695.

NOTE

1. [Formula, recipe.]

Corbyn Morris (1744)

Ben Johnson has *Humour* in his *Characters*, drawn with the most masterly Skill and Judgment; In Accuracy, Depth, Propriety, and Truth, he has no *Superior* or *Equal* amongst *Ancients* or *Moderns*; But the *Characters* he exhibits are of a *satirical*, and *deceitful*, or of a *peevish*, or *despicable* Species; as *Volpone, Subtle, Morose*, and *Abel Drugger*; In all of which there is something very justly to be *hated* or *despised*; And you feel the same Sentiments of *Dislike* for every other *Character* of *Johnson*'s; so that after you have been gratify'd with their *Detection* and *Punishment*, you are quite tired and disgusted with their Company: – Whereas *Shakespear*, besides the peculiar *Gaiety* in the *Humour* of *Falstaff*, has guarded him from disgusting you with his *forward Advances*, by giving him *Rank* and *Quality*; from being *despicable* by his real good *Sense* and excellent *Abilities*; from being *odious* by his *harmless Plots* and *Designs*; and from being *tiresome* by his inimitable *Wit*, and his new and incessant *Sallies* of highest *Fancy* and *Frolick*. . . .

Johnson in his COMIC Scenes has expos'd and ridicul'd *Folly* and *Vice*; *Shakespear* has usher'd in *Joy, Frolic* and *Happiness*. – The *Alchymist*,

Volpone and *Silent Woman* of *Johnson*, are most exquisite *Satires*. The *comic*
Entertainments of *Shakespear* are the highest Compositions of *Raillery*,
Wit and *Humour*. *Johnson* conveys some Lesson in every Character.
Shakespear some new Species of Foible and Oddity. The one pointed his
Satire with masterly Skill; the other was inimitable in touching the
Strings of Delight. With *Johnson* you are confin'd and instructed, with
Shakespear unbent and dissolv'd in Joy. *Johnson* excellently concerts his
Plots, and all his Characters unite in the one Design. *Shakespear* is
superior to such Aid or Restraint; His Characters continually sallying
from one independent Scene to another, and charming you in each with
fresh Wit and Humour.

It may be further remark'd, that *Johnson* by pursuing the most useful
Intention of *Comedy*, is in Justice oblig'd to *hunt down* and *demolish* his
own Characters. Upon this Plan he must necessarily expose them to
your *Hatred*, and of course can never bring out an amiable Person. His
Subtle, and *Face* are detested at last, and become mean and despicable.
Sir *Epicure Mammon* is properly trick'd, and goes off ridiculous and
detestable. The *Puritan Elders* suffer for their Lust of Money, and are quite
nauseous and abominable; And his *Morose* meets with a severe
Punishment, after having sufficiently tir'd you with his Peevishness. –
But *Shakespear*, with happier Insight, always supports his Characters in
your *Favour*. His Justice *Shallow* withdraws before he is tedious; The
French Doctor, and *Welch* Parson, go off in full Vigour and Spirit;
Ancient *Pistoll* indeed is scurvily treated; however, he keeps up his
Spirits, and continues to threaten so well, that you are still desirous of his
Company; and it is impossible to be tir'd or dull with the gay unfading
Evergreen *Falstaff*.

But in remarking upon the Characters of *Johnson*, it would be unjust
to pass *Abel Drugger* without notice; This is a little, mean, sneaking,
sordid Citizen, hearkening to a Couple of Sharpers, who promise to
make him rich; they can scarcely prevail upon him to resign the least
Tittle[1] he possesses, though he is assur'd, it is in order to get more; and
your Diversion arises, from seeing him *wrung* between *Greediness* to *get*
Money, and *Reluctance* to *part* with any for that Purpose. His Covetousness continually prompts him to follow the Conjurer, and puts him at
the same Time upon endeavouring to stop his Fees. All the while he is
excellently managed, and spirited on by *Face*. However, this Character
upon the whole is *mean* and *despicable*, without any of that free spirituous
jocund Humour abounding in *Shakespear*. But having been strangely
exhibited upon the Theatre, a few Years ago, with odd Grimaces and
extravagant Gestures, it has been raised into more Attention than it
justly deserved; [2] It is however to be acknowledg'd, that *Abel* has no
Hatred, Malice or Immorality, nor any assuming Arrogance, Pertness
or Peevishness; And his eager Desire of getting and saving Money, by

Methods he thinks lawful, are excusable in a Person of his Business; He is therefore not odious or detestable, but harmless and inoffensive in private Life; and from thence, correspondent with the Rule already laid down, he is the most capable of any of *Johnson*'s Characters, of being a Favourite on the Theatre.[3]

It appears, that in Imagination, Invention, Jollity and gay Humour, *Johnson* had little Power; But *Shakespear* unlimited Dominion. The first was cautious and strict, not daring to sally beyond the Bounds of Regularity. The other bold and impetuous, rejoicing like a Giant to run his Course, through all the Mountains and Wilds of Nature and Fancy.

It requires an almost painful Attention to mark the Propriety and Accuracy of *Johnson*, and your Satisfaction arises from Reflection and Comparison; But the Fire and Invention of *Shakespear* in an Instant are shot into your Soul, and enlighten and chear the most indolent Mind with their own Spirit and Lustre. – Upon the whole, *Johnson*'s Compositions are like finished Cabinets, where every Part is wrought up with the most excellent Skill and Exactness; – *Shakespear*'s like magnificent Castles, not perfectly finished or regular, but adorn'd with such bold and magnificent Designs, as at once delight and astonish you with their Beauty and Grandeur.

SOURCE: extracts from *An Essay towards Fixing the True Standards of Wit, Humour, Raillery, Satire, and Ridicule* (1744).

NOTES

1. [Smallest thing.]

2. [Referring to the farcical interpretation of Drugger by Theophilus Cibber, who took the part from 1731 to 1746. Thomas Davies comments: 'Mr. Garrick freed the stage from the false spirit, ridiculous squinting, and vile grimace, which, in Theophilus Cibber, had captivated the public for several years, by introducing a more natural manner of displaying the absurdities of a foolish tobacconist' – *Dramatic Miscellanies*, 3 vols (London, 1783–4) vol. II, p. 107.]

3. [Morris has remarked: 'The *Business* of COMEDY is to exhibit the whimsical *unmischievous Oddities*, *Frolics*, and *Foibles* or *Persons* in *real Life*; And also to *expose* and *ridicule* their *real Follies*, *Meanness*, and *Vices*. The *former*, it appears, is more pleasurable to the Audience, but the *latter* has the Merit of being more instructive' – *Essay*, p. 32.]

46   THOMAS DAVIES

Thomas Davies (1783)

Of all our old playwrights, Jonson was the most apt to allude to local
customs and temporary follies. . . . It was a constant complaint of the
old actors, who lived in Queen Anne's time, that if Jonson's plays were
intermitted for a few years, they could not know how to personate his
characters, they were so difficult, and their manners so distant, from
those of all other authors. To preserve them required a kind of stage
learning which was traditionally hoarded up. . . .

To understand Jonson's comedies perfectly, we should have before us
a satirical history of the age in which he lived. I question whether the
diligence of Mr. Steevens and Mr. Malone[1] could dig up a very
complete explanation of this author's allusions. Mr. Colman, after all
the pains and skill he could bestow on this comedy,[2] found that it was
labour lost; there was no reviving the dead.

SOURCE: extracts from *Dramatic Miscellanies*, vol. II (1783).

NOTES

1. [George Steevens and Edmond Malone, editors of Shakespeare and
scholars of the drama.]
2. [*Epicoene*, adapted by George Colman in 1776.]

William Gifford (1816)

In the plots of his comedies, which were constructed from his own
materials, he is deserving of undisputed praise. Without violence,
without, indeed, any visible effort, the various events of the story are so
linked together, that they have the appearance of accidental introduction; yet they all contribute to the main design, and support that
just harmony which alone constitutes a perfect fable. Such, in fact, is the
rigid accuracy of his plans, that it requires a constant and almost painful
attention[1] to trace out their various bearings and dependencies.
Nothing is left to chance; before he sat down to write, he had evidently
arranged every circumstance in his mind; preparations are made for
incidents which do not immediately occur, and hints are dropped which
can only be comprehended, at the unravelling of the piece. The play
does not end with Jonson, because the fifth act is come to a conclusion;
nor are the most important events precipitated, and the most violent
revolutions of character suddenly effected, because the progress of the

story has involved the poet in difficulties from which he cannot otherwise extricate himself. This praise, whatever be its worth, is enhanced by the rigid attention paid to the unities; to say nothing of those of place and character, that of time is so well observed in most of his comedies, that the representation occupies scarcely an hour more on the stage than the action would require in real life.

With such extraordinary requisites for the stage, joined to a strain of poetry always manly, frequently lofty, and sometimes almost sublime, it may, at first, appear strange that his dramas are not more in vogue; but a little attention to his peculiar modes and habits of thinking will, perhaps, enable us in some measure to account for it. The grace and urbanity which mark his lighter pieces he laid aside whenever he approached the stage, and put on the censor with the sock. This system (whether wise or unwise) naturally led to circumstances which affect his popularity as a writer; he was obliged, as one of his critics justly observes, 'to hunt down his own characters',[2] and, to continue the metaphor, he was frequently carried too far in the chase.

But there are other causes which render his comedies less amusing than the masterly skill employed upon them would seem to warrant our expecting. Jonson was the painter of humours not of passions. It was not his object (supposing it to have been in his power) to assume a leading passion, and so mix and qualify it with others incidental to our common nature, as to produce a being instantly recognized as one of our kind. Generally speaking, his characters have but one predominating quality: his merit (whatever it be) consists in the felicity with which he combines a certain number of such personages, distinct from one another, into a well ordered and regular plot, dexterously preserving the unities of time and place, and exhibiting all the probabilities which the most rigid admirer of the ancient models could possibly demand. Passions indeed, like humours, may be unamiable; but they can scarcely be uninteresting. There is a natural loftiness and swelling in ambition, love, hatred, &c. which fills the mind, and, when tempered with the gentler feelings, interests while it agitates. Humours are far less tractable. If they fortunately happen to contain in themselves the seeds of ridicule; then indeed, like the solemn vanity of Bobadill and the fantastic gravity of Puntarvolo, they become the source of infinite amusement; but this must not always be looked for: nor should we degrade Jonson by considering him in the light of a dramatic writer, bound, like the miserable hirelings of the modern stage, to produce a certain *quantum* of laughter. Many humours and modes of common life are neither amusing in themselves, nor capable of being made so by any extraneous ingenuity whatever: the vapourers in *Bartholomew Fair*, and the jeerers in the *Staple of News* are instances in point. – But further, Jonson would have defeated his own purpose, if he had attempted to elicit entertainment from them: he wished to exhibit them in an odious and disgusting light, and thus to extirpate what he considered as pests, from the commerce of real life. It was in the character of the poet to bring forward such nuisances as interrupted the peace, or disturbed the happiness of private society; and he is therefore careful to warn the audience, in his occasional addresses, that it is less his aim to *make their cheeks red* with laughter[3] than to feast their understanding, and minister to their rational improvement.

SOURCE: extract from Introduction to *The Works of Ben Jonson* (1816).

NOTES

1. [See Corbyn Morris's final paragraph above.]
2. [Corbyn Morris; see above.]
3. [See Prologue to *Volpone*, l. 35.]

William Hazlitt (1819)

The superiority of Shakspeare's natural genius for comedy cannot be better shewn than by a comparison between his comic characters and those of Ben Jonson. The matter is the same: but how different is the manner! The one gives fair-play to nature and his own genius, while the other trusts almost entirely to imitation and custom. Shakspeare takes his groundwork in individual character and the manners of his age, and raises from them a fantastical and delightful superstructure of his own: the other takes the same groundwork in matter-of-fact, but hardly ever rises above it; and the more he strives, is but the more enveloped 'in the crust of formality' and the crude circumstantials of his subject. His genius (not to profane an old and still venerable name, but merely to make myself understood) resembles the grub more than the butterfly, plods and grovels on, wants wings to wanton in the idle summer's air, and catch the golden light of poetry. Ben Jonson is a great borrower from the works of others, and a plagiarist even from nature; so little freedom is there in his imitations of her, and he appears to receive her bounty like an alms. His works read like translations, from a certain cramp manner, and want of adaptation. Shakspeare, even when he takes whole passages from books, does it with a spirit, felicity, and mastery over his subject, that instantly makes them his own; and shews more independence of mind and original thinking in what he plunders without scruple, than Ben Jonson often did in his most studied passages, forced from the sweat and labour of his brain. His style is as dry, as literal, and meagre, as Shakspeare's is exuberant, liberal, and unrestrained. The one labours hard, lashes himself up, and produces little pleasure with all his fidelity and tenaciousness of purpose: the other, without putting himself to any trouble, or thinking about his success, performs wonders. . . . I do not deny Jonson's power or his merit; far from it: but it is to me of a repulsive and unamiable kind. He was a great man in himself, but one cannot readily sympathize with him. His works, as the characteristic productions of an individual mind, or as records of the manners of a particular age, cannot be valued too highly; but they have little charm for the mere general reader. Schlegel observes, that whereas Shakspeare gives the springs of human nature, which are always the same, or sufficiently so to be interesting and intelligible; Jonson chiefly gives the *humours* of men, as connected with certain arbitrary or conventional modes of dress, action, and expression, which are intelligible only while they last, and not very interesting at any time.[1] Shakspeare's characters are men; Ben Jonson's are more like machines, governed by mere routine, or by the convenience of the poet, whose property they are. In reading the one, we are let into the minds of his characters, we see the play of their thoughts, how their humours flow and work: the author takes a range over nature, and has an eye to every object or occasion that presents itself to set off and heighten the ludicrous character he is describing. His humour (so to speak) bubbles, sparkles, and finds its way in all directions, like a natural spring. In Ben Jonson it is, as it were, confined in a leaden cistern, where it stagnates and corrupts; or directed only through certain artificial pipes and conduits, to answer a given purpose. The comedy of this author is far from being 'lively, audible, and full of vent': it is for the most part obtuse, obscure, forced, and tedious. He wears out a jest to the last shred and coarsest grain. His imagination fastens instinctively on some one mark or sign by which he designates the individual, and never lets it go, for fear of not meeting with any other means to express himself by. A cant phrase, an odd gesture, an old-fashioned regimental uniform, a wooden leg, a tobacco-box, or a hacked sword, are the standing topics by which he embodies his characters to the imagination. They are cut and dried comedy; the letter, not the spirit of wit and humour. Each of his characters has a particular cue, a professional badge which he wears and is known by, and by nothing else. . . . There is almost a total want of variety, fancy, relief, and of those delightful transitions which abound, for instance, in Shakspeare's tragi-comedy. In Ben Jonson, we find ourselves generally in low company, and we see no hope of getting out of it. He is like a person who fastens upon a disagreeable subject, and cannot be persuaded to leave it. His comedy, in a word, has not what

Shakspeare somewhere calls 'bless'd conditions'. It is cross-grained, mean, and mechanical. It is handicraft wit. Squalid poverty, sheer ignorance, bare-faced impudence, or idiot imbecility, are his dramatic common-places – things that provoke pity or disgust, instead of laughter. His portraits are caricatures by dint of their very likeness, being extravagant tautologies of themselves; as his plots are improbable by an excess of consistency; for he goes thorough-stitch with whatever he takes in hand, makes one contrivance answer all purposes, and every obstacle give way to a predetermined theory. . . . He would no more be baffled in the working out a plot, than some people will be baffled in an argument. 'If to be wise were to be obstinate', our author might have laid signal claim to this title. Old Ben was of a scholastic turn, and had dealt a little in the occult sciences and controversial divinity. He was a man of strong crabbed sense, retentive memory, acute observation, great fidelity of description and keeping in character, a power of working out an idea so as to make it painfully true and oppressive, and with great honesty and manliness of feeling, as well as directness of understanding: but with all this, he wanted, to my thinking, that genial spirit of enjoyment and finer fancy, which constitute the essence of poetry and of wit. The sense of reality exercised a despotic sway over his mind, and equally weighed down and clogged his perception of the beautiful or the ridiculous. He had a keen sense of what was true and false, but not of the difference between the agreeable and disagreeable; or if he had, it was by his understanding rather than his imagination, by rule and method, not by sympathy, or intuitive perception of 'the gayest, happiest attitude of things'. There was nothing spontaneous, no impulse or ease about his genius: it was all forced, up-hill work, making a toil of a pleasure. And hence his overweening admiration of his own works, from the effort they had cost him, and the apprehension that they were not proportionably admired by others, who knew nothing of the pangs and throes of his Muse in child-bearing. In his satirical descriptions he seldom stops short of the lowest and most offensive point of meanness; and in his serious poetry he seems to repose with complacency only on the pedantic and far-fetched, the *ultima Thule* of his knowledge. He has a conscience of letting nothing escape the reader that he knows. *Aliquando sufflaminandus erat*,[2] is as true of him as it was of Shakspeare, but in a quite different sense. He is doggedly bent upon fatiguing you with a favourite idea; whereas, Shakspeare overpowers and distracts attention by the throng and indiscriminate variety of his.

SOURCE: extracts from *Lectures on the English Comic Writers* (1819).

NOTES

1. [A. W. Schlegel, *A Course of Lectures on Dramatic Art and Literature*, trans. J. Black, 2 vols (London, 1815) vol. II, p. 287.]

2. ['Sometimes he needed checking.' In *Discoveries*, l. 659, Jonson applies this quotation, minus the mitigating *aliquando*, to Shakespeare.]

Samuel Taylor Coleridge (*c.* 1820)

. . . Ben's *personæ* are too often not characters, but derangements; – the hopeless patients of a mad-doctor rather, – exhibitions of folly betraying itself in spite of existing reason and prudence. He not poetically, but painfully exaggerates every trait; that is, not by the drollery of the circumstance, but by the excess of the originating feeling. . . .

The defect in Morose, as in other of Jonson's *dramatis personæ*, lies in this; – that the accident is not a prominence growing out of, and nourished by, the character which still circulates in it, but that the character, such as it is, rises out of, or, rather, consists in, the accident. Shakspeare's comic personages have exquisitely characteristic features; however awry, disproportionate, and laughable they may be, still, like Bardolph's nose, they are features. But Jonson's are either a man with a huge wen, having a circulation of its own, and which we might conceive amputated, and the patient thereby losing all his character; or they are mere wens themselves instead of men, – wens personified, or with eyes, nose, and mouth cut out, mandrake-fashion. . . .

Ben Jonson is original; he is, indeed, the only one of the great dramatists of that day who was not either directly produced, or very greatly modified, by Shakspeare. In truth, he differs from our great master in every thing – in form and in substance – and betrays no tokens of his proximity. He is not original in the same way as Shakspeare is original; but after a fashion of his own, Ben Jonson is most truly original.

The characters in his plays are, in the strictest sense of the term, abstractions. Some very prominent feature is taken from the whole man, and that single feature or humour is made the basis upon which the entire character is built up. Ben Jonson's *dramatis personæ* are almost as fixed as the masks of the ancient actors; you know from the first scene – sometimes from the list of names – exactly what every one of them is to be. He was a very accurately observing man; but he cared only to observe what was external or open to, and likely to impress, the senses. He individualizes, not so much, if at all, by the exhibition of moral or intellectual differences, as by the varieties and contrasts of manners,

modes of speech and tricks of temper; as in such characters as
Puntarvolo, Bobadill, &c.

I believe there is not one whim or affectation in common life noted in
any memoir of that age which may not be found drawn and framed in
some corner or other of Ben Jonson's dramas; and they have this merit,
in common with Hogarth's prints, that not a single circumstance is
introduced in them which does not play upon, and help to bring out, the
dominant humour or humours of the piece. Indeed I ought very
particularly to call your attention to the extraordinary skill shown by
Ben Jonson in contriving situations for the display of his characters.[1] In
fact, his care and anxiety in this matter led him to do what scarcely any
of the dramatists of that age did – that is, invent his plots. It is not a first
perusal that suffices for the full perception of the elaborate artifice of the
plots of *The Alchemist* and *The Silent Woman*; – that of the former is
absolute perfection for a necessary entanglement, and an unexpected,
yet natural, evolution.

Ben Jonson exhibits a sterling English diction, and he has with great
skill contrived varieties of construction; but his style is rarely sweet or
harmonious, in consequence of his labour at point and strength being so
evident. In all his works, in verse or prose, there is an extraordinary
opulence of thought; but it is the produce of an amassing power in the
author, and not of a growth from within. Indeed a large proportion of
Ben Jonson's thoughts may be traced to classic or obscure modern
writers, by those who are learned and curious enough to follow the steps
of this robust, surly, and observing dramatist.

SOURCE: extracts from *Literary Remains* (1836).

NOTE

1. 'In Jonson's comic inventions,' says Schlegel, 'a spirit of observation is
manifested more than fancy' [A. W. Schlegel, *A Course of Lectures on Dramatic Art
and Literature*, trans. J. Black, 2 vols (London, 1815) vol. II, p. 286; slightly
misquoted].

T. S. Eliot (1920)

In contrast, not with Shakespeare, but with Marlowe, Webster, Donne,
Beaumont, and Fletcher, [Jonson] has been paid out with reputation
instead of enjoyment. He is no less a poet than these men, but his poetry
is of the surface. Poetry of the surface cannot be understood without
study; for to deal with the surface of life, as Jonson dealt with it, is to deal

so deliberately that we too must be deliberate, in order to understand. Shakespeare, and smaller men also, are in the end more difficult, but they offer something at the start to encourage the student or to satisfy those who want nothing more; they are suggestive, evocative, a phrase, a voice; they offer poetry in detail as well as in design. So does Dante offer something, a phrase everywhere (*tu se' ombra ed ombra vedi*) even to readers who have no Italian; and Dante and Shakespeare have poetry of design as well as of detail. But the polished veneer of Jonson reflects only the lazy reader's fatuity; unconscious does not respond to unconscious; no swarms of inarticulate feelings are aroused. The immediate appeal of Jonson is to the mind; his emotional tone is not in the single verse, but in the design of the whole. But not many people are capable of discovering for themselves the beauty which is only found after labour; and Jonson's industrious readers have been those whose interest was historical and curious, and those who have thought that in discovering the historical and curious interest they had discovered the artistic value as well. When we say that Jonson requires study, we do not mean study of his classical scholarship or of seventeenth-century manners. We mean intelligent saturation in his work as a whole; we mean that in order to enjoy him at all, we must get to the centre of his work and his temperament, and that we must see him unbiased by time, as a contemporary. And to see him as a contemporary does not so much require the power of putting ourselves into seventeenth-century London as it requires the power of setting Jonson in our London. . . .

Jonson's drama is only incidentally satire, because it is only incidentally a criticism upon the actual world. It is not satire in the way in which the work of Swift or the work of Molière may be called satire: that is, it does not find its source in any precise emotional attitude or precise intellectual criticism of the actual world. It is satire perhaps as the work of Rabelais is satire; certainly not more so. . . .

Largely on the evidence of the two Humour plays, it is sometimes assumed that Jonson is occupied with types; typical exaggerations, or exaggerations of type. The Humour definition, the expressed intention of Jonson, may be satisfactory for these two plays. *Every Man in his Humour* is the first mature work of Jonson, and the student of Jonson must study it; but it is not the play in which Jonson found his genius: it is the last of his plays to read first. If one reads *Volpone*, and after that re-reads the *Jew of Malta*; then returns to Jonson and reads *Bartholomew Fair*, *The Alchemist*, *Epicoene* and *The Devil is an Ass*, and finally *Catiline*, it is possible to arrive at a fair opinion of the poet and the dramatist.

The Humour, even at the beginning, is not a type, as in Marston's satire, but a simplified and somewhat distorted individual with a typical mania. In the later work, the Humour definition quite fails to account for the total effect produced. The characters of Shakespeare are such as might exist in different circumstances than those in which Shakespeare sets them. The latter appear to be those which extract from the characters the most intense and interesting realization; but that realization has not exhausted their possibilities. Volpone's life, on the other hand, is bounded by the scene in which it is played; in fact, the life is the life of the scene and is derivatively the life of Volpone; the life of the character is inseparable from the life of the drama. This is not dependence upon a background, or upon a substratum of fact. The emotional effect is single and simple. Whereas in Shakespeare the effect is due to the way in which the characters *act upon* one another, in Jonson it is given by the way in which the characters *fit in* with each other. The artistic result of *Volpone* is not due to any effect that Volpone, Mosca, Corvino, Corbaccio, Voltore have upon each other, but simply to their combination into a whole. And these figures are not personifications of passions; separately, they have not even that reality, they are constituents. It is a similar indication of Jonson's method that you can hardly pick out a line of Jonson's and say confidently that it is great poetry; but there are many extended passages to which you cannot deny that honour.

> I will have all my beds, blowne up; not stuft;
> Downe is too hard. And then, mine oval roome,
> Fill'd with such pictures, as TIBERIUS tooke
> From ELEPHANTIS: and dull ARETINE
> But coldly imitated. Then, my glasses,
> Cut in more subtill angles, to disperse,
> And multiply the figures, as I walke. . . .

Jonson employs immense dramatic constructive skill: it is not so much skill in plot as skill in doing without a plot. He never manipulates as complicated a plot as that of *The Merchant of Venice*; he has in his best plays nothing like the intrigue of Restoration comedy. In *Bartholomew Fair* it is hardly a plot at all; the marvel of the play is the bewildering rapid chaotic action of the fair; it is the fair itself, not anything that happens in the fair. In *Volpone*, or *The Alchemist*, or *The Silent Woman*, the plot is enough to keep the players in motion; it is rather an 'action' than a plot. The plot does not hold the play together; what holds the play together is a unity of inspiration that radiates into plot and personages alike.

We have attempted to make more precise the sense in which it was said that Jonson's work is 'of the surface'; carefully avoiding the word 'superficial'. For there is work contemporary with Jonson's which is superficial in a pejorative sense in which the word cannot be applied to Jonson – the work of Beaumont and Fletcher. If we look at the work of Jonson's great contemporaries, Shakespeare, and also Donne and

Webster and Tourneur (and sometimes Middleton), they have a depth, a third dimension, as Mr. Gregory Smith[1] rightly calls it, which Jonson's work has not. Their words have often a network of tentacular roots reaching down to the deepest terrors and desires. Jonson's most certainly have not; but in Beaumont and Fletcher we may think that at times we find it. Looking closer, we discover that the blossoms of Beaumont and Fletcher's imagination draw no sustenance from the soil, but are cut and slightly withered flowers stuck into sand.

> Wilt thou, hereafter, when they talk of me,
> As thou shalt hear nothing but infamy,
> Remember some of these things? . . .
> I pray thee, do; for thou shalt never see me so again.

> Hair woven in many a curious warp,
> Able in endless error to enfold
> The wandering soul. . . .

Detached from its context, this looks like the verse of the greater poets; just as lines of Jonson, detached from their context, look like inflated or empty fustian. But the evocative quality of the verse of Beaumont and Fletcher depends upon a clever appeal to emotions and associations which they have not themselves grasped; it is hollow. It is superficial with a vacuum behind it; the superficies of Jonson is solid. It is what it is; it does not pretend to be another thing. But it is so very conscious and deliberate that we must look with eyes alert to the whole before we apprehend the significance of any part. We cannot call a man's work superficial when it is the creation of a world; a man cannot be accused of dealing superficially with the world which he himself has created; the superficies *is* the world. Jonson's characters conform to the logic of the emotions of their world. They are not fancy, because they have a logic of their own; and this logic illuminates the actual world, because it gives us a new point of view from which to inspect it.

. . . We turn to Mr. Gregory Smith's objection – that Jonson's characters lack the third dimension, have no life out of the theatrical existence in which they appear – and demand an inquest. The objection implies that the characters are purely the work of intellect, or the result of superficial observation of a world which is faded or mildewed. It implies that the characters are lifeless. But if we dig beneath the theory, beneath the observation, beneath the deliberate drawing and the theatrical and dramatic elaboration, there is discovered a kind of power, animating Volpone, Busy, Fitzdottrel, the literary ladies of *Epicoene*, even Bobadill, which comes from below the intellect, and for which no theory of humours will account. . . . We may say with Mr. Gregory Smith that Falstaff or a score of Shakespeare's characters have

a 'third dimension' that Jonson's have not. This will mean, not that
Shakespeare's spring from the feelings or imagination and Jonson's
from the intellect or invention; they have equally an emotional source;
but that Shakespeare's represent a more complex tissue of feelings and
desires, as well as a more supple, a more susceptible temperament.
Falstaff is not only the roast Manningtree ox with the pudding in his
belly; he also 'grows old', and, finally, his nose is as sharp as a pen. He
was perhaps the *satisfaction* of more, and of more complicated feelings;
and perhaps he was, as the great tragic characters must have been, the
offspring of deeper, less apprehensible feelings: deeper, but not
necessarily stronger or more intense, than those of Jonson. It is obvious
that the spring of the difference is not the difference between feeling and
thought, or superior insight, superior perception, on the part of
Shakespeare, but his susceptibility to a greater range of emotion, and
emotion deeper and more obscure. But his characters are no more
'alive' than are the characters of Jonson.

The world they live in is a larger one. But small worlds – the worlds
which artists create – do not differ only in magnitude; if they are
complete worlds, drawn to scale in every part, they differ in kind also.
And Jonson's world has this scale. His type of personality found its relief
in something falling under the category of burlesque or farce – though
when you are dealing with a *unique* world, like his, these terms fail to
appease the desire for definition. It is not, at all events, the farce of
Molière: the latter is more analytic, more an intellectual redistribution.
It is not defined by the word 'satire'. Jonson poses as a satirist. But satire
like Jonson's is great in the end not by hitting off its object, but by
creating it; the satire is merely the means which leads to the æsthetic
result, the impulse which projects a new world into a new orbit. In *Every
Man in his Humour* there is a neat, a very neat, comedy of humours. In
discovering and proclaiming in this play the new genre Jonson was
simply recognizing, unconsciously, the route which opened out in the
proper direction for his instincts. His characters are and remain, like
Marlowe's, simplified characters; but the simplification does not consist
in the dominance of a particular humour or monomania. That is a very
superficial account of it. The simplification consists largely in reduction
of detail, in the seizing of aspects relevant to the relief of an emotional
impluse which remains the same for that character, in making the
character conform to a particular setting. This stripping is essential to
the art, to which is also essential a flat distortion in the drawing; it is an
art of caricature, of great caricature, like Marlowe's. It is a great
caricature, which is beautiful; and a great humour, which is serious.
The 'world' of Jonson is sufficiently large; it is a world of poetic
imagination; it is sombre. He did not get the third dimension, but he
was not trying to get it.[2]

SOURCE: extracts from 'Ben Jonson', published in *The Sacred Wood* (1920) and subsequently included in *Selected Essays*; the revised version of an essay which first appeared in the *Times Literary Supplement*, 13 November 1919; the extracts here are from the text of *Selected Essays*, 3rd edition (1951) pp. 148, 151, 152–4, 155–6, 157, 158–9.

NOTES

1. [G. Gregory Smith, *Ben Jonson* (London, 1919) pp. 86ff.]
2. [For an analysis of Eliot's critical procedure in this influential essay, see J. O. Boyd, 'T. S. Eliot as Critic and Rhetorician: The Essay on Jonson', *Criticism*, XI (1969) 167–82.]

Harry Levin (1938)

Gold is the core of Jonson's comedy, getting and spending are the chains which bind it together, and luxury furnishes the ornaments which cover its surfaces. It is further stipulated, by Volpone himself, that such gold must not be the reward of any productive endeavour. Both *Volpone* and *The Alchemist* hinge upon some monstrous device, a will or the Philosophers' Stone, but Jonson can bring to bear upon almost any situation a suspiciously circumstantial familiarity with all the ruses of craft and quackery. Insofar as it would be the nature of Volpone or Subtle to plot, whether on or off the stage, the motive of chicane becomes the determining factor in the strategy of Jonson's plays. In *Volpone*, perhaps even more than in *The Alchemist*, he has erected his most imposing hierarchies of collusion. In the later play he relaxes the two-edged ironies of fathers who disinherit sons and husbands who prostitute wives, in order to admit a procession of more earth-bound appetites, ranging from the petty desires of a lawyer's clerk to cut a figure, to the intransigent gluttony of Sir Epicure Mammon.

This fat knight is a Falstaff who has suddenly begun to babble like a Faustus. Hankering after fleshpots, his lordly talk is 'all in gold'; 'Silver, I care not for.' Out of the boundless opulence which his insatiate libido has already summoned up, he is even prepared to make an occasional benefaction – 'And now, and then, a church.' The limit of his lust is only measured by his gullibility; he observes Hapsburg and Medici traits in Dol Common, and addresses her in the language which Faustus reserved for Helen of Troy. 'Tis pity she's a whore! Before he takes her upstairs, he is warned not to arouse her fanaticism by introducing topics of biblical controversy. 'We thinke not on 'hem,' he replies. And their departure gives Face and Subtle the excuse to bring experiments to a fiasco and blame it upon Sir Epicure's impatient sensuality. 'O my voluptuous mind!' he cries.

Marlowe consistently presented the voluptuary as a hero; to Jonson, he is always either a villain like Volpone or a dupe like Sir Epicure Mammon. Taking up, at Eliot's suggestion,[1] Sir Epicure's moist-lipped recital of the delights he hopes to enjoy, and placing it alongside Gaveston's announcement of the entertainments he has prepared for Edward II, we can observe in each case a texture woven with equal richness and a comparable barrage of sensuous appeal. Jonson's accumulation of images is even denser and more various than Marlowe's, and its effect is utterly subversive. Jonson could not have expressed his reservations more explicitly, nor hit upon a more elaborate contrivance for turning to dust and ashes all the lovely fruit of the Renaissance imagination. Nothing has been neglected, but the intonation has changed, for he is consciously dealing in illusion. Marlowe to Jonson is as Hyperion to a satyr. Sir Philip Sidney had pimples, Jonson told Drummond, and advanced an appalling explanation of Queen Elizabeth's best-known trait.[2] . . .

Because Jonsonian comedy can only succeed by subordinating parts to whole, its cast of characters is not its outstanding feature. Each has only his characteristic move, as in chess, and the object of the game is to see what new combinations have been brought about. Between the abstract idea of the plot and the concrete detail of the language is a hiatus. Nothing is lacking, but the various components can be distinguished without much trouble. In Corvino's phrase, it is too manifest. After the large masses have been sketched out in baroque symmetry, decoration is applied to the surfaces. What is said, frequently, does not matter, so long as something is said, and then Jonson is at special pains to make what is said interesting for its own sake. Surly's school-book Spanish and Dol's memorized ravings are simply blocked in. But when Mosca reads the inventory, or when Subtle puts Face through the alchemists' catechism, they too are saying something where – in the dramatic economy – they mean nothing, and their speeches take on the aspect of incantation. It is a trick which reaches its logical limit in *Epicoene*, where everything spoken has a high nuisance value and the words themselves become sheer filigree. Beyond that point, they have the force of Molière's comic refrains. Lady Would-be's uncontrollable flow of recipes, prescriptions, literary opinions, and philosophical speculations, at cross-purposes with Volpone, demonstrates how conveniently this talking-machine technique bears out Bergson's theory of laughter.

To linger over the elements of pure design in Jonson's dialogue is to ignore its expressiveness as representation. The language itself is completely idiomatic, uninhibited by the formality of plot and characterization or the complexity of scenes and speeches. Because 'Spenser writ no language',[3] Jonson refused to tolerate him, and he could spare Marston nothing but a prescription to purge unnatural diction.[4] . . .

Graphic speech is the generic trait with which even Jonson's ugliest ducklings are well endowed. The stolid Corvino indulges in unsuspected flights of conceit and the sullen Ananias reveals a flamboyant strain of polemical eloquence. Kitely's jealousy of his wife prompts him to deliver an exhaustive survey of the wiles of amorous deception. To dismiss the threat of punishment, Voltore invokes a swarm of luridly ridiculous tortures upon the prostrate person of his client. In introducing Drugger as an honest tobacconist, Face cannot resist the temptation to add some dozen or sixteen lines covering the various sharp practices of dishonest tobacconists that Drugger utterly eschews. Dramatic action is supplemented by the potential drama of these three speeches. In each instance a set of images picks up the situation where the business leaves off, and projects it to the most extravagant bounds of possibility. Uniformly Jonson's style is stamped with the brilliance of his iconoplastic talents.

The imagery surprises us by being so tangible, by presenting its objects not as fanciful comparisons but as literal descriptions. They are seldom glimpsed through the magic casement of metaphor, through the intervention of rhetoric. The rich jewel in the Ethiop's ear belonged to Juliet only by metaphysical parallel; Jonson would have slashed off the ear, conveyed the jewel to Volpone's coffers, and dangled it before Celia as the price of her virtue. Heaping up sensuous detail in thorough-going Elizabethan fashion, he ordinarily contrives to bring it within the immediate grasp of his tantalized characters. The result is that the theme of his plays and their poetic realization are more closely knit together. Examining the content of Jonson's images, Caroline Spurgeon has discovered that the largest single category is drawn from the usages and conditions of society and that he returns more consistently than any of his rivals to the subject of money.[5] A further consequence of this restriction of materials is a kind of heightening of the commonplace, more proper to the humorous than to the lyrical imagination. Deprived of other figures of speech, Jonson relies much on hyperbole. That is not the only quality of style he shares with Aristophanes and Rabelais.

The poetry of misplaced concreteness and solid specification is an instrument of the satirist; he is adept at mastering the tricks of a trade and enumerating technical data; his swift, disintegrating glance takes in all the ingredients of Goody Trash's gingerbread. A profusion of images is not the best way to communicate feeling. Selection is more likely to produce the poignant response; accumulation bewilders at first and invites analysis in the end. When Jonson's intention is not satirical, his 'wit's great overplus' dilutes the effect of his verse.

SOURCE: extracts from Introduction to *Ben Jonson: Selected Works* (1938) pp. 22–4, 30–1, 33–4.

NOTES

1. [In a part of his essay not extracted above Eliot develops the view that 'Jonson is the legitimate heir of Marlowe'; see Jonas A. Barish (ed.), *Volpone: A Casebook* (London and Basingstoke, 1972) pp. 56–7.]

2. [See Herford and Simpson, vol. I, pp. 138–9, 142.]

3. ['*Spencer*, in affecting the Ancients, writ no Language' – *Discoveries*, ll. 1806–7.]

4. [In *Poetaster*, v iii, Marston, in the character of Crispinus, is given an emetic which makes him vomit up his 'terrible, windie wordes'.]

5. [Caroline F. E. Spurgeon, *Shakespeare's Imagery and What It Tells Us* (Cambridge, 1935) pp. 37–8 and chart IV.]

PART TWO

*Every Man
in his Humour*

1. COMMENT 1667–1950

Samuel Pepys (1667)

. . . very busy late, and then went home and read a piece of a play, *Every Man in his Humour*, wherein is the greatest propriety of speech that ever I read in my life: and so to bed.

> SOURCE: extract from *Diary*, entry for 9 February 1667.

John Dryden (1672)

. . . *Ben. Johnson*, the most judicious of Poets, . . . always writ properly; and as the Character requir'd: and I will not contest farther with my Friends who call that Wit. It being very certain, that even folly it self, well represented, is Wit in a larger signification; and that there is Fancy, as well as Judgement in it; though not so much or noble: because all Poetry being imitation, that of folly is a lower exercise of Fancy, though perhaps as difficult as the other: for 'tis a kind of looking downward in the Poet; and representing that part of mankind which is below him.

In these low Characters of Vice and Folly, lay the excellency of that inimitable Writer: who, when at any time, he aim'd at Wit, in the stricter sence, that is, Sharpness of Conceit, was forc'd either to borrow from the Ancients, as, to my knowledge he did very much from *Plautus*: or, when he trusted himself alone, often fell into meanness of expression. Nay, he was not free from the lowest and most groveling kind of Wit, which we call clenches;[1] of which, *Every Man in his Humour*, is infinitely full; and, which is worse, the wittiest persons in the *Drama* speak them. . . .

Let us ascribe to *Johnson* the height and accuracy of Judgement, in the ordering of his Plots, his choice of characters, and maintaining what he had chosen, to the end. But let us not think him a perfect pattern of imitation; except it be in humour: for Love, which is the foundation of all *Comedies* in other Languages, is scarcely mention'd in any of his Playes. And for humour it self, the Poets of this Age will be more wary than to imitate the meanness of his persons. Gentlemen will now be entertain'd with the follies of each other: and though they allow *Cob* and

Tib to speak properly, yet they are not much pleas'd with their Tankard or with their Raggs: And, surely, their conversation can be no jest to them on the *Theatre*, when they would avoid it in the street.

SOURCE: extracts from 'An Essay on the Dramatic Poetry of the Last Age', appended to *The Conquest of Granada* (1672).

NOTE

1. [Puns.]

Anonymous (1757)

DRURY LANE, March 31, 1757.

This evening was performed, to one of the most numerous and polite Audiences that have been seen this Season (for the Benefit of Mr. Beard[1]) Ben Jonson's Comedy, called, *Every Man in his Humour*. If we consider that this Piece was exhibited in the Year 1598, being near 160 Years ago, it must be allowed that it is a Proof of an uncommon Genius to entertain us at the Time of Day with Ideas and Manners totally obliterated. It shews that the Painter's Pencil must have been faithful to Nature, otherwise we should hardly please ourselves, at present, with Portraits whose Originals are no more; for, excepting the Picture of Jealousy in the Drawing of Kitely, there is not one Personage in the whole Groupe known to our modern Critics. Besides, the Business lies so much in what we call middle Life, or perhaps low Life, and in Parts of the Town disgustful to People of Fashion, such as the Old Jewry, Lothbury, &c. that nothing but the strong Colouring of old Ben could support the Piece. . . .

It may not be improper to take Notice, that according to the modern Acceptation of the Word Humour, this Piece does not by any Means answer the Title. A Critic of these Days would naturally expect a Set of Humourists, or Men deeply tinged with Habits and Oddities discolouring their whole Conduct; instead of which we have but one Character of that Cast, which is Kitely; Old Knowell having no peculiar Mark; his Son and Wellbred being merely young Fellows upon Town; Stephen and Matthew two contemptible Half-fools; and in short, all the rest, excepting Bobadill and Brainworm having no distinguishing Characteristic. Bobadill's Oddities are not strong enough to denominate him an Humourist; he has indeed a ridiculous Affectation of Courage and military Skill; and when he takes a Kicking, he affords us a very laughable Contrast. Brainworm is an impudent notable Fellow, and diverts by the various Appearances he assumes: And Justice Clement is an hearty chearful old Fellow, but has no particular Bias to the Gratification of any prevailing Humour, or whimsical Turn of Mind. The Poet has two Passages, one in this Play, and the other in *Every Man out of his Humour*, which may serve to inform us of what he intended in the Title.

CoB   Nay, I have my rewme, and I can be angrie as well as another, sir.
CASH   Thy rewme, CoB? thy humour, thy humour? thou mistak'st.
CoB   Humour? mack, I thinke it be so, indeed: what is that humour? some rare thing, I warrant.
CASH   Mary, Ile tell thee, CoB: It is a gentleman-like monster, bred, in the speciall gallantrie of our time, by affectation; and fed by folly.
CoB   How? must it be fed?
CASH   Oh I, humour is nothing, if it bee not fed. Didst thou never heare that? it's a common phrase, *Feed my humour*.

In the Play called *Every Man out of his Humour*, he hath the following passage –

> when some one peculiar quality
> Doth so possesse a man, that it doth draw
> All his affects, his spirits, and his powers,
> In their confluctions, all to runne one way,
> This may be truly said to be a Humour.

In this latter passage the Author shews us that he had formed an exact Idea of Humour in the strict Sense of the Word: But we apprehend, when he called the Play now before us *Every Man in his Humour*, he meant to be understood in the former Sense, and intended to shew us a Set of Men following their Affectations. What was usually called Manners in a Play began now, says the above-mentioned ingenious Editor,[2] to be called Humours; the Word was new, and the Use or rather Abuse of it was excessive. We should therefore be inclined to think that Ben Jonson took Advantage of a Phrase in Vogue, and intended merely an Exhibition of Manners or Humours in the loose Sense of the Word, as it was commonly used; and not a Picture of People under the Operation of one strong Foible, not vainly assumed out of Levity, or imitative Folly, but rooted in the Mind, and engrossing all their Thoughts. Kitely indeed is a Character of this latter Class, and his Spirits and Powers all run one Way, which may be said to be a Humour. Thus much we thought proper to remark concerning the general Idea of the Manners and Characters of this Play. The main Action turns on the Jealousy of Kitely: To shew this Foible in ridiculous Appearances, and to hold up a Mirror, where it may see itself, is the Poet's principal Scope; though all the other Characters are busy in their own separate Walks, and have their own subordinate Pursuits. . . .

Mr. Dryden has somewhere compared a well-wrought Comedy to a Country Dance, where two or more lead off, the rest fall in by Degrees, till they all mingle in the sprightly Tumult; then they separate into several petty Divisions; detached Parties are made from the main Body, and at length they all meet together again, and form one entire harmonious Movement. This Remark we think perfectly applicable to the Play now under Examination: We have already mentioned the principal Personages of the Piece, with a short Account of their Manners or Humours. How exquisite is the Poet's Skill in grouping these together! While each Person has his own By-Concerns, he helps forward the main Action, and they are all brought together, and made acquainted with each other by Means probable and natural. Perhaps no Writer had greater Art in the Conduct of his Plots than Jonson: He is always sure to prepare us for every Character worthy our Notice, and this he does, *quasi aliud agens*, as if minding other Business, in the Course of which we receive accidental Notices of the Person, who is afterwards to appear; and thus our Expectation is raised before we see him engaged in any Scene of Action. Old Knowell opens this Play, and the Letter from Wellbred, who lives in Kitely's Family, to young Knowell, gives us, casually as it were, a further Insight into the Business: It promises us more new Characters, and the suburb Humours of Master Stephen are likely to be entertaining, when contrasted by the City Fop. Then again, how judiciously is Bobadill described, and after the Account of his peculiar Oaths and assumed Valour, his mean Condition is nicely touched by his Landlord's saying, 'He owes mee fortie shillings (my wife lent him out of her purse, by sixe-pence a time).' Bobadill's Affectation is finely kept up, and we find too that he is one of Wellbred's Rioters; and he likewise prepares us for the Character of Downright: We are thus let into a Knowledge of all the *Dramatis Personæ*, except Kitely, whose Jealousy being of a secret Nature, that Matter could only come from himself. And how finely is this developed! His Fear of being known to be jealous acquaints us with it; and Wellbred's Followers give Occasion to all his Suspicions. It is observable that Kitely and Othello complain of an Head-ache, when first their Wives come to them, amidst their Suspicions. The Part Brainworm takes in thwarting Old Knowell's Purposes, is diverting, and serves to puzzle Matters till the Business is worked up to a Crisis, which happens from the Rendezvous of Wellbred's Revellers at Kitely's House. . . . Thus very artificially[3] all Parties are brought together; the Denouement is skilfully made out; Kitely is convinced of his Error, and the jolly Temper of the old Justice prevails on them to conclude the Evening in Chearfulness and Good humour. If the Limits of our Paper would permit, we could with

Pleasure review separately the Characters of Kitely and Bobadill, the two conspicuous Figures in this Piece; but this perhaps is unnecessary, as they are both so well performed by Mr. Garrick and Mr. Woodward.[4] The latter, in our Opinion, never conceived a Character better than that of Bobadill, who is the best Braggadocio on the Stage; his Assurance has a Mixture of Modesty, and is heightened by it: While he pretends to be a consummate Master of every Branch of military Knowledge as well as Courage, he protests he has only some small Rudiments of the Science, 'as to know my time, distance, or so'. – When he is sure his Friends will prevent Mischief, he begs them to let his Enemy come on with 'Ile not kill him', and when at last he takes a Beating, he is 'planet-struck', 'fascinated', &c. – All this Mr. Woodward performs with such a Reserve and Gravity, and such a judicious Jeu de Theatre, that he is justly a Favourite with the Audience all through the Piece. Were we to examine Kitely we should find the *Suspicious Husband*[5] to be in some Measure copied from it: The Scenes where both those Characters are tempted to confer with their own Domestics, and are yet afraid to do it, and then continue about it and about it, palpably resemble each other. Were we to give the Preference to either, we should declare the modern to have lopped Excrescences, and to have therefore rendered his Scene a juster Imitation of Nature, where there is nothing too often touched nor nothing overdone. But the former has the Advantage of Mr. Garrick's Performance; in this Actor every Thing has Manners, every Thing has real Life, and whatever his Author may have done, he does not any where exceed thc natural Workings of Jealousy.

SOURCE: extracts from article in the *London Chronicle*, 31 March to 2 April 1757.

NOTES

1. [John Beard (1716?–1791), an actor in Garrick's company.]
2. [Peter Whalley (ed.), *The Works of Ben Jonson*, 7 vols (London, 1756) vol. 1, p. 145.]
3. [Skilfully.]
4. [See below, Arthur Murphy, 'David Garrick as Kitely', n. 1.]
5. [By Benjamin Hoadly; first performed 12 February 1747.]

William Gifford (1816)

It has been invidiously urged that the characters of this drama are not original: as a general observation, this may be allowed to pass, for they were undoubtedly copied from nature, as modified by extraneous

circumstances in the poet's days; but when the enemies of Jonson
descend to particulars, and specify the objects of his imitation, the
absurdity and falsity of every charge becomes immediately manifest.

Jealousy is the *humour* of Kitely, but it is no more the jealousy of Ford[1]
than of Othello: original it neither is nor can be, for it is a passion as
common as the air, and has been the property of the stage from the
earliest times; yet what but a jaundiced eye can discover any servile
marks of imitation? Kitely's alarms are natural, for his house is made the
resort of young and riotous gallants; yet he opens his suspicions with
great delicacy, and when circumstances 'light as air' confirm them, he
does not bribe a stranger to complete his dishonour, but places a
confidential spy over his wife, to give notice of the first approaches to
familiarity. In a word, the feelings, the language, and the whole
conduct of Kitely are totally distinct from those of Ford, or any
preceding stage character whatever. The author drew from nature; and
as her varieties are infinite, a man of Jonson's keen and attentive
observation was under no necessity of borrowing from her at second
hand.

Bobadill has never been well understood, and, therefore, is always too
lightly estimated: because he is a boaster and a coward, he is cursorily
dismissed as a mere copy of the ancient bully, or what is infinitely more
ridiculous, of Pistol; but Bobadill is a creature *sui generis*, and perfectly
original. The soldier of the Greek comedy, from whom Whalley wishes
to derive him,[2] as far as we can collect from the scattered remains of it,
or from its eternal copyists, Plautus and Terence, had not many traits in
common with Bobadill. Pyrgapolonices,[3] and other captains with hard
names, are usually wealthy; all of them keep a mistress, and some of
them a parasite: but Bobadill is poor, as indeed are most of his
profession, which, whatever it might be in Greece, has never been a
gainful one in this country. They are profligate and luxurious; but
Bobadill is stained with no inordinate vice, and is besides so frugal, that
'a bunch of redish . . . and a pipe of *tobacco*, to close the orifice of the
stomach,' satisfy all his wants. Add to this, that the vanity of the ancient
soldier is accompanied with such deplorable stupidity, that all
temptation to mirth is taken away; whereas Bobadill is really amusing.
His gravity, which is of the most inflexible nature, contrasts admirably
with the situations into which he is thrown; and though beaten, baffled,
and disgraced, he never so far forgets himself as to aid in his own
discomfiture. He has no soliloquies like Bessus and Parolles,[4] to betray
his real character, and expose himself to unnecessary contempt; nor
does he break through the decorum of the scene in a single instance. He
is also an admirer of poetry, and seems to have a pretty taste for
criticism, though his reading does not appear very extensive, and his
decisions are usually made with somewhat too much promptitude. – In

a word, Bobadill has many distinguishing traits, and till a preceding braggart shall be discovered with something more than big words and beating to characterize him, it may not be amiss to allow Jonson the credit of having depended entirely on his own resources.

Knowell is a scholar and a gentleman; his *humour* is an over-strained solicitude for the purity of his son's morals, amidst an indulgence of lighter foibles: he is an amiable and well drawn character, and very artfully contrasted with the rude, but manly and consistent Downright.

Brainworm is evidently a favourite of the author; he is sufficiently amusing, and his transformations contribute very naturally to the perplexity of the scene: he is most successful in the mendicant soldier, a character not uncommon in those days either in the streets, or on the stage.

The rest require little notice. The females, as is usually the case, occupy but a small part of the poet's care; yet they are correctly drawn, and probably such as the family of a respectable merchant, in Jonson's time, would readily supply. Dame Kitely is a very natural character; unsuspicious in herself, but, having her fears once awakened, credulous and violent in the extreme. Bridget is merely a sensible young woman; not so vain of the attentions of her poetical lover, as not to sacrifice them to a more rational courtship; won, as was then the case, with little wooing, and easily persuaded to follow her own inclinations. The two young gentlemen fill the parts allotted to them with perfect propriety, and play upon the vanity and imbecility of the other characters with very laughable effect: as for the two gulls, as they are called, they enhance and set off the absurdities of each other; and, as natural deficiency cannot be supplied, are dismissed with a simple exposure, by way of punishment: indeed, nothing can be more admirable, or consonant with justice, than the winding up of this drama, and the various dispensations dealt out to the different characters.

SOURCE: extract from Introduction to *The Works of Ben Jonson*, vol. 1 (1816).

NOTES

1. [In *The Merry Wives of Windsor*.]

2. [P. Whalley (ed.), *The Works of Ben Jonson*, 7 vols (London, 1756). In his Preface, Whalley echoes Dryden in acknowledging Jonson's indebtedness to classical literature, but nowhere suggests this derivation. See, however, Henry Holland Carter's discussion of Bobadill below.]

3. [In Plautus's *Miles Gloriosus*.]

4. [In *A King and No King*, by Beaumont and Fletcher, and *All's Well that Ends Well*.]

A. C. Swinburne (1889)

It must be with regret as well as with wonder that we find ourselves
constrained to recognize the indisputable truth that this first acknowl-
edged work of so great a writer is as certainly his best as it certainly is
not his greatest. Never again did his genius, his industry, his conscience
and his taste unite in the triumphant presentation of a work so faultless,
so satisfactory, so absolute in achievement and so free from blemish or
defect. The only three others among all his plays which are not
unworthy to be ranked beside it are in many ways more wonderful,
more splendid, more incomparable with any other product of human
intelligence or genius: but neither *The Fox, The Alchemist*, nor *The Staple
of News*, is altogether so blameless and flawless a piece of work, so free
from anything that might as well or better be dispensed with, so simply
and thoroughly compact and complete in workmanship and in result.
Molière himself has no character more exquisitely and spontaneously
successful in presentation and evolution than the immortal and
inimitable Bobadill; and even Bobadill is not unworthily surrounded
and supported by the many other graver or lighter characters of this
magnificent and perfect comedy.

> SOURCE: extract from *A Study of Ben Jonson* (1889).

Henry Holland Carter (1921)

In *Every Man in his Humor*, as in Jonson's other plays, the simplest and
most obvious exemplification of classical influence is in the matter of
direct quotations. In the combined two versions occur quotations from
Juvenal,[1] Terence,[2] Virgil,[3] Ovid,[4] and Seneca.[5] Closely allied to these
are paraphrases and close imitations of passages in the classics.
Specimens of these are in evidence from Juvenal,[6] Quintilian,[7]
Martial,[8] Plautus,[9] Terence,[10] Horace,[11] and Aristotle.[12]

A borrowing more deeply ingrained in the present play is that of
characters and situations which have become conventional in Roman
comedy. The most important of these are: the motive of the father and
wayward son; the two-faced intriguing servant; the braggart soldier; the
gull or dupe; mistaken identity; the clandestine marriage; the general
atmosphere of trickery and intrigue; the sudden resolution of plot-
complication at the end of the play.

The father–son motive occurs clearly in eight of Plautus's plays[13]
and in five of Terence's.[14] Its particular form in *Every Man in his Humor* is

that of the fond and indulgent father, himself moral, who fails to detect the deception and dissipation of his son, who, meanwhile, takes pleasure in deceiving his parent, and idling with gay companions. The boy indulges in the excesses of youth, but is not vicious or dissolute. The 'follies, not the crimes of men' are dealt with here, and the comic atmosphere is even and unbroken. The typical father of Roman comedy is of two sorts. The type reflected in Old Knowell may be illustrated by Charmides, in Plautus's *Trinummus*.[15] This wealthy Athenian is thoroughly moral, long-suffering, and forgiving. After his property has been much wasted by his son, he goes abroad. During his absence, the boy, by reckless extravagance, consumes the remainder of his father's resources, and even sells his house. The latter returns in time, is apprised of his son's perfidy, and, at the intercession of a friend, after lamenting his wickedness, forgives him. The father may also be vicious and immoral, abetting his son in his knavery, or practising independent vices of his own.[16] A suggestion of the mingling of the two types in Old Knowell is seen in the ease with which he stills his conscience when he reads his son's letter. There are often two fathers in the plays of Plautus and Terence, troubled by two obstreperous sons.[17] Aside from the definite father–son motive, there is a general lack of respect towards age, and a delight in seeing older men duped by younger, which helped to create the atmosphere upon which Jonson drew for his play.[18] Young Knowell is a less serious offender than most of the young men of the New Comedy. There, many times, the whole gamut of vices is run through. When stripped of the personal characteristics which render him a typical young Englishman, however, and relegated to a type, his general theory and conduct of life place him with those others whose escapades delighted the audiences of Rome. His friendship with Wellbred is also conventional. The Roman youth was almost certain to have a companion in his frolics.

The two-faced, intriguing servant is an indispensable factor in Roman comedy, and no play belonging to it is without him. No obligation or relation is sacred to him. A servant to a father and a son, he may be faithful to one and untrue to the other, aid one to bring about the other's discomfiture, or be untrue to both. If a plot-complication is needed, he stands ready to assume a disguise, conceive and execute a trick, fail to perform a duty assigned him, and thus effect the proper entanglement. If no convenient resolution of a plot is available, the servant, again, may enter with the necessary information and disclosures to make all clear. The manysidedness of his nature must have created an unfailing atmosphere of interest around him, and made the audience regard him with ever-expectant eyes. The variety of his escapades, too, made him a perennial funmaker. In these several capacities, Brainworm is equally as useful a character in *Every Man in his*

Humor. Without him, the slender plot of this play could hardly hold together. The first hint of action in the play comes with Brainworm's juggling with Wellbred's letter to Young Knowell (i i–ii). He next appears disguised as a soldier, and imposes upon Stephen's simplicity by selling him a rapier (ii ii). Shortly after this (ii iii), in the same disguise, he deceives Old Knowell, who takes him into his service. Filled with merriment over his own duplicity, he hastens to the Windmill Tavern (iii i) to tell Ned Knowell and his companions of his latest trick. To complete the father's mystification, Brainworm tells him his son (iv vi) has learned that he has followed him to town, and sends him to Cob's house on a fruitless search for the culprit. Brainworm follows, with a new plan on foot to gull Formal. His services are much in demand, for he is next (iv viii) engagéd by Wellbred, disguised in Formal's clothes, to tell Young Knowell to meet him and Bridget at the Tower. On the way (iv ix) Matthew and Bobadill meet him, and engage him to arrest Downright for assault; this he accomplishes in another disguise (iv xi), at the same time arresting Stephen for stealing Downright's cloak. Finally, the speedy unraveling of the plot in the last act is made possible only by Brainworm's disclosures of his many tricks. Jonson has shown splendid originality in working out the details of Brainworm's character for the present purpose, but its essential elements, and his basic function in the play, are strictly classical.

The boastful soldier has his most complete incarnation in Pyrgopolinices,[19] the Miles Gloriosus of Plautus, although he appears also, in less pronounced form, in Therapontigonus, in *Curculio*, and Stratophanes, in *Truculentus*. The original Miles is a 'bragging, impudent, stinking *fellow*, brimful of lying and lasciviousness, [who] says that all the women are following him of their own accord'.[20] He killed a hundred and fifty men in Cilicia, a hundred in Cryphiolathrona, thirty at Sardis, sixty at Macedon, and five hundred at Cappadocia altogether at one blow.[21] Compare with this Bobadill's boast (iv vii 80):

say the enemie were fortie thousand strong, we twentie would come into the field . . . wee would challenge twentie of the enemie; . . . well, wee would kill them: . . . thus, would wee kill, every man, his twentie a day, that's twentie score; twentie score, that's two hundreth; . . . two hundreth dayes killes them all up, by computation.

Bobadill is the only character which can be definitely paralleled in classical comedy.

Almost as essential to classical comedy as the intriguing servant is the gull or dupe. There must be somebody to fool, and somebody to be fooled. A variety of people may serve in the latter capacity. The father is duped by his son;[22] the wife by her husband;[23] the procurer by the youth who patronizes him;[24] or the parasite is himself sometimes rebuffed.[25]

The degrees of gullibility range from cases where the deception is accomplished only by the inordinate cleverness of the intriguer to those where the butt of the joke is mentally deficient. So, in *Every Man in his Humor*, Old Knowell is deceived by his son, and both the son and father are fooled by Brainworm through the latter's unusual skill in subterfuge, while Stephen is gulled on all sides because of his own stupidity.

Mistaken identity was a device thoroughly familiar to the Latin poets, and made to subserve a number of uses. As in the previous category, the particular importance assigned to this motive may vary in importance. A disguise may be assumed temporarily and for a given purpose,[26] or there may be a genuine mistaken identity, due perhaps to an accident at birth which calls for a recognition-scene and a clearing up of mystery.[27] All the instances of this in *Every Man in his Humor* are of the first sort, and caused by Brainworm's antics. This motive is quite as useful to Jonson as to the classical poets, and he does not neglect his opportunity.

To marry, or intrigue with, a woman secretly is a favorite way for a son to deceive his father.[28] Rather less importance is assigned to this as a structural element in Jonson than would have been the case in either Plautus or Terence. Here it is one among many incidents, and not so much more important than they.

One's general memory of Roman comedy is of a series of tricks performed upon a given set of characters in typical situations; so is it with *Every Man in his Humor*. The play is built upon the broad outlines established by classical tradition. Had Jonson himself been unable to devise the way to tangle a plot so completely that no solution seemed possible, and then suddenly to unravel all by surprising disclosures at the end of the play, he might have learned it from Roman comedy.

The theory implicit in *Every Man in his Humor* is clearly that of the New Comedy. The theme does not concern the State at large, nor does it publicly attack those in authority. It does, however, reveal the life of the time, and the customs and manners of the people. In thus attempting to perceive and reveal the truth about human nature, it naturally discloses the vanity and weakness current in society. This theme could be developed at any time in any country; and Jonson was peculiarly fitted to do it for England.

It must not be assumed, however, that Jonson was a mere copyist, lacking in originality. Technically considered, no one of the Elizabethan poets is more original than he. The last charge which could be brought against him is that of being un-English. It has been seen that an analysis of *Every Man in his Humor* reveals parallels, conscious or unconscious, to the most essential basic elements of Latin Comedy; yet the material and particular treatment are all new. He succeeded surprisingly well, as F. E. Schelling says, 'in picturing, in vivid realism, the absurdities, the eccentricities and predicaments, so to speak, of Elizabethan life in terms of a glorified adaptation of the technique of Plautus'.[29]

SOURCE: extract from Introduction to *Every Man in his Humor* (1921) pp. lxxxviii–xciv.

NOTES

1. Title pages of Q and F.
2. Q, III i 57.
3. Q, II iii 17, v iii 448–9; F, III i 22.
4. Q, v iii 210–12.
5. Q, v iii 236.
6. F, I i 86, II v 5, II v 51.
7. F, II v 14.
8. F, Prologue.
9. F, I ii 122.
10. F, I ii 129–34.
11. F, II v 48–9.
12. F, Prologue, l. 24.
13. *Trinummus, Bacchides, Pseudolus, Asinaria, Mercator, Mostellaria, Epidicus, Truculentus.*
14. *Andria, Heautontimorumenos, Phormio, Hecyra, Adelphi.*
15. Cf. also Micio in *Adelphi.*
16. Demipho in *Mercator*, Simo in *Pseudolus*, and Demaenetus in *Asinaria* are good illustrations.
17. Cf. *Bacchides.*
18. The deception worked upon Hegio, in the *Captivi*, the cheating Euclio of his treasure in *Aulularia*, and the duping the procurer in the *Persa*, are cases in point.
19. See Karl Reinhardstoettner, *Plautus* (Leipzig, 1886) p. 677, and E. P. Lumley, *The Influence of Plautus on the Comedies of Ben Jonson* (New York, 1901) pp. 57 ff.
20. *The Comedies of Plautus*, trans. H. T. Riley, 2 vols (London, 1887) vol. 1, p. 74; cf. *Miles Gloriosus*, ed. Frederick Leo (Berlin, 1895) I ii 8: 'illest miles meus erus . . . gloriosus, impudens, stercoreus, plenus periuri atque adulteri'. Cf. Reinhardstoettner, *Plautus*, pp. 595–680, for a full discussion of the literary history of the 'braggart soldier'.
21. *Miles Gloriosus*, I i 42–5, 52, 53; in *Comedies of Plautus*, trans. Riley, vol. 1, p. 72.
22. *Trinummus.*
23. *Asinaria.*
24. *Pœnulus.*
25. *Stichus.*
26. *Pœnulus, Amphitryon.*

27. *Captivi, Menæchmi, Rudens.*

28. *Bacchides, Pseudolus, Curculio, Phormio.*

29. F. E. Schelling, *English Literature during the Lifetime of Shakespeare* (New York, 1910) p. 231.

William Archer (1923)

The merit of the play, then, lies in its vigorously-drawn, playable caricatures. But by no reasonable canon of art can a mere array of caricatures be said to constitute a good comedy. One other ingredient at least is essential – a clear, more or less ingenious and entertaining, story. Nothing of the sort is to be found in *Every Man in his Humour*. I defy anyone to relate comprehensibly or to make credible the wholly uninspired and uningenious comings and goings and to-ings and fro-ings of which the story consists. The machinations of Brainworm supply its motive force; and, except as vehicles for virtuosity in acting, they are devoid of interest or plausibility. A worse-constructed play could not easily be discovered, outside of Jonson's works. What a masterpiece is *The Merry Wives of Windsor* in comparison with it! Yet how unquestionably one of Shakespeare's poorest plays! Or compare it with *She Stoops to Conquer* or *The School for Scandal*! These are delightful inventions;the mere stories, the situations, enrich our memories. Who ever could, or ever wanted to, recall the story of *Every Man in his Humour*?

SOURCE: extract from *The Old Drama and the New* (1923).

C. H. Herford and P. and E. Simpson (1950)

THE NOTICES OF TIME IN THE PLAY

The action takes place in one day, as Jonson points out with comic pertinacity. The clock ticks audibly in every act. The first scene is early morning, 'A goodly day toward!' (1 i 1), and Edward Knowell 'scarse stirring yet' (1 i 29, 30). In the third scene he is just up, and has received Wellbred's letter, but an hour has passed: 'my father had the full view o' your flourishing stile, some houre before I saw it', he tells Wellbred later (III i 47–9). At 1 iv 58 'It's sixe a clocke'; at 1 v 29 'some halfe houre to seven'. At II ii 45 the bell rings for breakfast at Kitely's house. In III iii 44 it is 'Exchange time, sir'. The quarto version of the corresponding scene (III i) defines minutely: at the beginning of the scene it is 'New striken ten', and at line 37 'Past ten'. Kitely calculates that his business will take him two hours: he will then be either at the Exchange or at Justice Clement's (F, III iii 118–19). The sixth scene finds him at Clement's, i.e. about noon. In IV ii 64 Matthew refers to the verses which he made 'this morning'; in scene vi Knowell left Brainworm with Formal 'betweene one and two' (v i 11). The false message of IV viii 134 was delivered 'After two' (v i 14). In v iii 94 the newly married pair are on the point of ordering their wedding supper; at the end of the act the entire party sup at Clement's house. Six o'clock was the usual hour with Londoners of that class.

In no other play is the day so elaborately mapped out; Jonson must have worked from a time-table.

SOURCE: extract from *Ben Jonson*, vol. IX (1950) p. 343.

2. MODERN STUDIES 1947–74

Freda L. Townsend

'THE UNCLASSICAL DESIGN OF *EVERY MAN IN HIS HUMOUR*' (1947)

'I travell with another objection, signior', complained Mitis to Cordatus – 'That the argument of his *Comœdie* might have beene of some other nature, as of a duke to be in love with a countesse, and that countesse to bee in love with the dukes sonne, and the sonne to love the ladies waiting maid: some such crosse wooing, with a clowne to their servingman.'[1] If in *Every Man out of his Humour* the author's mouthpiece could thus harangue against the author for being so unconventionally bold as to dispense with the common formalities of plot and to be 'thus neere, and familiarly allied to the time', it is the author's critics who must perform the same function for *Every Man in his Humour*. Connecting this first of the folio comedies with *The Case is Altered* because of the presence in both of Plautine elements, the critic seeks to make it conform as exactly as possible with Plautine structural design and plot requirements. Herford ascribes 'the most definite source of the technique of *Every Man in his Humour*' to 'the art of classical comedy'.[2] Young Knowell's shadowy love affair is generally presumed to give the play the superficial structure demanded by classical comedy. Brainworm's espousing of the cause of the son against the father and his manipulation of events so that the son marries the girl of whom he is enamored are felt to be thoroughly Latin.[3]

Yet qualification is almost immediate. Miss E. Woodbridge, one of those who selects the love affair as the main action, concedes that 'the actual bulk of this main action is relatively small. . . . It is scarcely more than a pretext for the author to bring together a set of amusing people, and the greater part of the play is occupied with *episodes* in which Brainworm or the young men are intriguers, or "showmen", and the various *subordinate* characters are in turn victims.'[4] 'Very little plot', notes Baskervill,[5] and an editor of the play observes that however true it is that to marry or intrigue with a woman is a favorite way for a son to deceive a father in Roman comedy, 'rather less importance is assigned to this as a structural element in Jonson than would have been the case in either Plautus or Terence. Here it is one among many incidents, and not so much more important than they.'[6] Disapproving of Jonson's failure to build his play on traditional lines and labelling the procedure 'plot disintegration', Herford names the plan 'a complex of several actions, ingeniously tangled together'.[7]

Perhaps one of the most effective ways of illustrating how foreign are classical standards to this first of the Humour plays is to indicate how an eighteenth-century 'improver' attempted to refashion the comedy. *Every Man in his Humour*, as R. G. Noyes points out, 'depended on its force as a realistic picture of an epoch, resembling a Dutch painting, with a large group of characters representing different passions or humours'. Its weakness lay, continues Noyes, in its 'slight centrifugal control' and the 'danger of diffuseness'. These Garrick, retaining the 'spirit of the original' and yet presenting 'a really improved stage piece', eliminated by emphasizing the most promising emotional possibility of the comedy – Kitely's jealousy.[8] Verbal omissions were made generously throughout; scenes dealing only with characters who seemed to distract from what Garrick wished to make the main interest either were greatly reduced or entirely displaced.[9] Although he did not actually eliminate any character, Garrick reduced the parts of Cob, Bobadill, Matthew, and Clement so substantially as to cut in half their appearances on stage. Cob was the heaviest sufferer in this respect, Garrick ruthlessly using the blue pencil on his account of his lineage (i iii), his 'humourous' conversation with Cash (iii iv), his aspersions on tobacco (iii v), his soliloquy on 'vineger, and mustard revenge' (iii vi); his appeal to Justice Clement for redress for the beating received from Bobadill (iii vii). Bobadill's part was also so shortened as to be virtually mutilated. Gone, for instance, is his boasting about his prowess in fencing (I vi; I V vii), his eulogy on tobacco (III v). Other blue-pencilings included numerous contemporary allusions, proverbs, and oaths; Matthew and Bobadill on *The Spanish Tragedy* (I v); the elder Knowell's lines on education in the good old days (II v); those of young Knowell on sonnet-writing (III i); Kitely and Cash on cuckoldry (III iii); the crowded and witty scene I V ii; the cross-purposes scene v i. On the other hand, Garrick expanded wherever possible the rôles of Kitely and Dame Kitely, particularly in Acts IV and v, where episodes were so manipulated as to give Kitely a continuous appearance on stage, lines were so altered as to heighten his jealousy, and a scene between him and his wife was added. After this climactic scene, Garrick had ended his Act IV; Jonson had continued the act for three further scenes, scenes devoted in the main to Bobadill, Matthew, Brainworm, Stephen, Downright, Cob, and Tib. Jonson's scene v i was abridged in such a way as to make Kitely appear more prominently, Garrick adding a few lines for Clement in which he advises the jealous and irate husband to give quiet and serious thought to the tricks which had been played on him.

It becomes easily apparent that Garrick's revision not only destroyed the original structure of the play, which had been calculated to give importance equally to several actions, but cut away much of the material for which Jonson was anxious to find dramatic form. Such materials as comments on poetry and drama, on various social customs, on fencing and cuckoldry, the elaborate word-play, the indiscriminate trickery, had been contrived to fit into the capacious frame. Only the deliberate playing down of certain characters, the playing up of others, could secure the single action; and when such single action is secured, the spirit of the original seems, indeed, to be very slightly retained. One feels great sympathy with Theophilus Cibber's suspicion that Garrick gave his original to his cat, and 'What Puss claw'd off, the Actor left out.'[10] Unity for the sake of variety has been sacrificed to unity alone.

By the end of Jonson's first act, there are four major intrigues under way: (1) the deception of the elder Knowell by his son; (2) the gulling of Stephen; (3) the trials of Cob; (4) the gulling of Matthew and Bobadill. With Act II, the fifth complication, the Kitely affair, begins. Other characters are successively presented, and always in such a way as to involve them in intrigues already begun, just as characters already active in one intrigue become auxiliaries in another. Thus Downright is involved both with the escapades of his brother, Wellbred, and with the discomfiture of Bobadill. Cob, besides having his own humour, is brought into the Kitely situation, and is involved with Bobadill and Matthew. Young Knowell and Wellbred do much more than gull respectively father and brother, for they pipe the tunes to which Stephen, Matthew, and Bobadill dance. Brainworm, not content with helping young Knowell to outwit his father, involves in his network of tricks Kitely, Dame Kitely, Stephen, Cob, Tib, Downright, Bobadill, and Matthew. The climax of Brainworm's machinations occurs at the end of the fourth act, when he successively sends to Cob's house the elder Knowell, Kitely, Dame Kitely, Justice Clement; and then, disguised as Formal, he jubilantly issues warrants to Bobadill and Downright. Justice Clement's separate dealing with the various cases brought before him emphasizes the separate nature of these intrigues:

Come, I conjure the rest, to put of all discontent. You, Mr. DOWNE – RIGHT, your anger; you, master KNO'WELL, your cares; master KITELY, and his wife, their jealousie. . . . Master bridegroome, take your bride, and leade; every one, a fellow. Here is my mistris. BRAYNE-WORME! to whom all my addresses of courtship shall have their reference. Whose adventures, this day, when our grandchildren shall heare to be made a fable, I doubt not, but it shall find both spectators, and applause.

(v v 69–91)

Clement's laughing tribute to the chief machinator, Brainworm, may seem to point to a Latin model, but no wily slave ever had so many strings to his bow, nor so many gulls to make sport of.

SOURCE: extract from *Apologie for Bartholmew Fayre: The Art of Jonson's Comedies* (1947) pp. 42–5

NOTES

1. *Every Man out of his Humour*, Grex after III vi.
2. Herford and Simpson, vol. I, p. 338.
3. C. R. Baskervill, *English Elements in Jonson's Early Comedy* (Austin, Tex., 1911) p. 107.
4. E. Woodbridge, *Studies in Jonson's Comedy* (Boston, 1898) p. 48. Italics mine.
5. Baskervill, *English Elements*, p. 107.
6. [Henry Holland Carter; see above, Part Two, section 1.]
7. Herford and Simpson, vol. I, p. 336.
8. R. G. Noyes, *Ben Jonson on the English Stage 1660–1776* (Cambridge, Mass., 1935) p. 258.
9. See *Every Man in his Humour. Written by Ben Jonson. With Alterations and Additions* (London, 1752). Detailed comparisons of the alteration with the original are to be found in Franz Krämer, *Das Verhältnis von David Garrick's 'Every Man in his Humour' zu dem gleichnämigen Lustspiel Ben Jonson's* (Halle, 1903); Heinrich Maass, *Ben Jonsons Lustspiel 'Every Man in his Humour' und die gleichnämige Bearbeitung durch David Garrick* (Rostock, 1903); Noyes, *Jonson on the English Stage*, pp. 258–65.
10. *Dissertations on Theatrical Subjects as They Have Several Times Been Delivered to the Public* (London, 1756) pp. 34–5.

Jonas A. Barish

RHETORIC'S TINKLING BELL (1960)

With *Every Man in his Humour*, Jonson takes a huge step forward. The uncertainty stamped on nearly every page of *The Case is Altered* has almost vanished; only an occasional clumsiness, an infrequent breach of decorum, betray the hand of the apprentice. Each character now possesses his own idiom, and is revealed by it: Jonson bids his creatures speak, and they tell us what they are. When he came to revise the play for inclusion in the folio of 1616, he found much to add, but little to change.

Prose predominates over verse in *Every Man in his Humour* (quarto version of 1601) in a ratio of three or four to one, and thus becomes the staple language from which verse is a deviation. Only two major characters, Thorello the *jaloux* and Lorenzo Senior the Terentian elder, normally speak verse, the one standing somewhat outside the events of the plot, the other possessed by a passion so fierce that Jonson may have felt unequal, at this time, to rendering it without the assistance of meter. Even so, he has not troubled to maintain anything like exact consistency, and one must confess, once and for all, that though one can often discern rough criteria governing the alternations between prose and verse, these can never be regarded as absolute. Jonson changes them or departs from them at his pleasure, for reasons of momentary convenience that often can better be guessed at than explained.

The prose of *Every Man in his Humour* is both more incisive and more dynamic than that of *The Case is Altered*. Jonson has learned to write dialogue that can annihilate its object and transfix its speaker at one and the same time, as in Cob's description of Matheo:

He useth every day to a Marchants house (where I serve water) one M. *Thorellos*; and here's the jest, he is in love with my masters sister, and cals her mistres: and there he sits a whole afternoone sometimes, reading of these same abhominable, vile, (a poxe on them, I cannot abide them) rascally verses, *Poetrie, poetrie*, and speaking of *Enterludes*, 't will make a man burst to heare him: and the wenches, they doe so geere and tihe at him; well, should they do as much to me, Ild forsweare them all, by the life of Pharaoh, there's an oath: how many waterbearers shall you heare sweare such an oath? oh I have a guest (he teacheth me) he doth sweare the best of any man christned. . . .

(I iii 63–75)

This excerpt from Cob's opening monologue illustrates the associational movement, as one may term it, of much of Jonson's dramatic prose. Cob's unflattering account of Matheo courting his 'mistres' turns unpredictably into a loud bray of scorn against poetry and *'Enterludes'*. The recollection of Matheo surrounded by his giggling wenches provokes a silly and pointless brag as to how he, Cob, would behave in such circumstances; the idea of 'forswearing' reminds him of a fine oath he has just learned, 'by the life of Pharaoh', and the oath in turn reminds him of its inventor, his guest Bobadilla, who now becomes the object of an admiring eulogy. Cob's unstable train of thought starts and stops and jolts crookedly from one detail to another without the least attention to logical exposition: neither he nor the audience knows that he will interrupt his reminiscences of Matheo in order to vent his abhorrence of poetry, or that his fantasied rejection of the wenches will spill over into a panegyric on Bobadilla. The process reveals a mind myopically in pursuit of the object nearest it, unable to hold more than one thing at a time, streaked by the kind of coarse skepticism that can perceive the quackery in Matheo without being able to tell this apart from the real thing, and by the credulousness that falls victim to Bobadilla's suaver pose. The speech, in short, combines self-revelation with formal exposition in a masterly way.

The characteristic winding involutions of the loose period make their first appearance in this play, but they have an occasionally unfortunate tendency to wind around their subject so long that they strangle it with detail. Lorenzo Junior confides to Prospero that Musco's disguise as a soldier has completely fooled him:

> Fore God . . . I might have been joind patten with one of the nine worthies for knowing him. S'blood man, he had so writhen himselfe into the habit of one of your poore *Disparview's* here, your decaied, ruinous, worme-eaten gentlemen of the round: such as have vowed to sit on the skirts of the city, let your Provost & his half dozen of halberders do what they can; and have translated begging out of the olde hackney pace, to a fine easy amble, and made it runne as smooth of the toung, as a shove-groat shilling.
>
> (III ii 7–16)

Here the typically fused manner of the loose style, which does not stop to survey or articulate its parts – the offhand way, for example, in which, after the digression on the Provost and his halberders, the 'and' introduces two unexpected long clauses concerning the gentlemen of the round – seems to lead Jonson astray. The description of the Disparviews, which commences merely as an account of Musco's disguise, turns into such a minutely engraved satiric vignette that we all but forget about Musco. Much of it, then, remains undigested observation, picturesque but encumbering. And it illustrates what was to remain a cardinal temptation for Jonson: his fascination with the picturesque, over and above the strict demands of plot and character.

In the language of the butts of this play Jonson scores his first solid triumph. The styles of the country gull Stephano, the town gull Matheo, and the *miles gloriosus* Bobadilla are rendered with an exquisite attention to minute degrees of folly. The crudest of the three, Stephano, betrays a grasp of sequence as weak as Cob's, whether he is advertising his own gentility or indulging in fits of childish sulkiness. Encountering Matheo and Bobadilla, he is spurred to instant emulation by the sound of their rich, fruity diction and bizarre oaths. Matheo, who has moved for some time in Bobadilla's orbit, has already been working hard to deform his own speech by imitating Bobadilla's. Bobadilla himself, the fountainhead of eccentricity of this group, has evolved his own style, partly through an eclectic use of cant terms from dueling and 'polite' locutions, partly through his coinage of strange oaths. 'Wantonnesse of language',[1] it may be noticed, is here linked firmly to social aspiration and moral slackness. Stephano and Matheo, the mimics, have almost literally no minds of their own, but automatically soak up the attitudes of their associates, preferably such companions as Bobadilla, whose manner offers a suitably flamboyant object of imitation. The moment they are confronted with moral choices, they collapse into meanness, as in Stephano's theft of the dropped cloak, or Matheo's plagiarisms. Bobadilla, who has worked up the language of the duello from books and learned to cause a stir by swearing picturesquely, uses the first as a cloak for cowardice and the second as a badge of singularity. A far more accomplished fool than his pathetic satellites, he becomes contemptible in direct proportion to the skill and effort he expends on his impostures.

Less obviously than by his affected singularity, Bobadilla proclaims his insatiable self-absorption at every moment by his fixation on the first-person pronoun, as in his verdict on *The Spanish Tragedy*: 'I would faine see all the Poets of our time pen such another play' (I iii 129–30); his rebuff to Matheo for his clumsy fencing technique: 'I have no spirit to play with you, your dearth of judgement makes you seeme tedious' (I iii 214–16); his appraisal of Stephano's new sword: 'A Fleming by *Phoebus*, ile buy them for a guilder a peece and ile have a thousand of them' (II iii 147–8); his judgment on Giuliano: "I hold him the most peremptorie absurd clowne (one a them) in Christendome: I protest to you (as I am a gentleman and a soldier) I ne're talk't with the like of him' (I iii 165–8). Bobadilla's mode of expression manages to imply that his every sentiment is a matter of the keenest interest to others: 'I professe my selfe no quack-salver' (III ii 84), 'I delight not in murder: I am loth to beare any other but a bastinado' (IV ii 48–50), 'I love few wordes' (II iii 75). Insistent disclaimer thus becomes a covert form of self-eulogy.

Bobadilla's language at one point shows another kind of wantonness; Jonson is beginning to grope toward the effects implicit in traditional rhetorical schemes. After the beating administered to him by Giuliano, Bobadilla replies to a question from Matheo by losing himself in a forest of asyndetic clauses, stiffened by anaphora, that suggest the extent to which he can 'bewitch' himself with his own rhetoric:[2]

MATHEO I but would any man have offered it in *Venice*?

BOBADILLA Tut I assure you no: you shall have there your *Nobilis*, your *Gentelezza*, come in bravely upon your reverse, stand you close, stand you ferme, stand you fayre, save your retricato with his left legge, come to the assaulte with the right, thrust with brave steele, defie your base wood. But wherefore do I awake this remembrance? I was bewitcht by Jesu: but I will be revengd.

(IV iv 10–17)

The parisonic members, hardened by alliteration, set up a kind of incantation which permits Bobadilla to forget his recent humiliation and triumph once more in fantasy. His repeated use of the impersonal 'your' heightens the effect of complacency. The fantasy, no doubt, becomes choreographic as well as verbal: with each phrase, Bobadilla thrusts, lunges, parries, retreats, miming with his whole body the gratifying victory that his cowardice has in fact denied him. Years of poring over books on the duello have ended in his being able to mesmerize not only Matheo and Stephano but himself into a belief in his own valor.

A similar use of balanced language creeps into the begging pleas of the disguised Musco:

you seeme to be gentlemen well affected to martiall men, els I should rather die with silence, then live with shame: how e're, vouchsafe to remember it is my want speakes, not my selfe: this condition agrees not with my spirit.

(II i 50–3)

Where Bobadilla's chanting represented a species of self-delusion, Musco, in his role as mendicant soldier, adopts the antithetic turn and the sophistical distinction in order to deceive others, and with a certain malicious pleasure in the smoothness of his own tongue. But in each case the elaborately logical structure implies fraud, falsity of language directed toward the falsification of truth. And we shall find other occasions on which Jonson uses this pat logicality to signal moral deficiency.

So much, perhaps, will serve to demonstrate the remarkable gain in stylistic control of *Every Man in his Humour* over *The Case is Altered*. The rather slapdash linguistic portraits of Juniper and Onion have been refocused into a series of precisely discriminated fools, each with his particular syndrome of folly, each with his linguistic deformities to match. Every effect that Jonson can command is now lashed firmly to the dramatic context. Nevertheless, as the revision will serve to indicate, Bobadilla is probably the only character whose language already fully and consistently fills in the outlines predicated for it by the action. The final realization of the other creatures, fools and wise men alike, awaits the hand of the reviser a dozen years later. . . .

The distribution of prose and verse remains nearly the same in the new version. Four odd lines of verse of Lorenzo Junior's in I ii 11–14 have been struck out, as well as his fervent metrical defense of poetry in Act v.[3] These excisions leave Lorenzo's counterpart, Young Knowell (we shall henceforth use chiefly folio nomenclature), an exclusively prose-speaking character and very much more of a piece than before. Old Knowell's complaint of his son's poetical leanings is irrelevant even in the quarto until the sudden interchange on the subject between his son and Justice Clement in Act v. In the folio, the complaint is preserved, but it is now wholly irrelevant. Young Knowell is simply the witty young gallant about town, unafflicted, so far as we can see, with poetical symptoms. By removing most of the serious remarks on poetry and by dismissing Matthew's plagiarisms more casually, Jonson reduces to its strictly comic aspects the war between good and bad poets he had explored so strenuously in the comical satires. The lighter sentences accorded Matthew and Bobadill now resemble the indulgent treatment of Sir John Daw in *Epicoene*. The whole exhausting question of the antagonism between Poetry and Humor is thus momentarily shelved, or at least soft-pedaled, and this tends to set the revised *Every Man in his Humour* apart from the trio of plays that precede it.[4] On the other hand, as we shall see in a moment, revisions of a different sort tend to emphasize the resemblances.

Setting aside the occasional clarifications of verse rhythm or prose rhythm, and the orthographic changes that contribute to a more phonetic realism, one might classify the folio changes roughly into three groups: first, those that heighten the vividness or precision of the dialogue without actually affecting character; then, those that correct flaws in decorum or fill in more exactly the outline of character as premised in the quarto; finally, those that transform character or add a fresh dimension to it.

The first group demonstrates most plainly Jonson's fascination with detail, since this kind of change does not spring from any need to clarify motive or illuminate action, but simply embroiders on what was already blocked out in the quarto. In some cases Jonson merely particularizes more fully a statement from the quarto:

By this good ground, I was faine to pawne my rapier last night for a poore supper, I am a Pagan els: sweet Signior.

(Q, II ii 58–60)

by this good ground, I was faine to pawne my rapier last night for a poore supper, I had suck'd the hilts long before, I am a pagan else: sweet honor.

(F, II v 89–92)

Elsewhere, the substitution of a more concrete or specific term for a general one infuses new vitality into the language:

(as Gods my judge, they should have kild me first)

(Q, IV i 35)

(as I protest, they must ha' dissected, and made an *Anatomie* o' me, first, and so I told 'hem)

(F, IV vi 36–7)

Or Jonson may replace a simple literal statement with a metaphoric one, or vitalize it by subjoining a simile to it:

he is come to towne of purpose to seeke you.

(Q, II iii 206–7)

he has follow'd you over the field's, by the foot, as you would doe a hare i' the snow.

(F, III ii 46–8)

oh that my bellie were hoopt now, for I am readie to burst with laughing.

(Q, II ii 101–3)

O that my belly were hoopt now, for I am readie to burst with laughing! never was bottle, or bag-pipe fuller.

(F, II v 133–5)

Changes such as these, to be sure, are not wholly without effect on character. If nothing else, they imply Brainworm's increased slyness and self-confidence, his sharper powers of observation. Still one feels that the impulse behind them is less psychological than decorative: the desire to fill every nook and cranny with its appropriate bits of design, over and above the bare necessities of narrative.

A larger group of changes involves clear considerations of character. In the first place, there is a crescendo of courtly jargon in the speeches of Bobadill and Matthew. Where the original Bobadilla summoned the hostess to 'lend us another bedstaffe here quickly' (Q, I iii 195–6), his later counterpart commands her to 'accommodate us with another bedstaffe here, quickly: Lend us another bed-staffe. The woman do's not understand the wordes of *Action*' (F, I v 126–8), thus replacing the simple 'lend us' with the high-flown verbal phrase 'accommodate us', and retranslating it back into plain English so as to be able to plume

himself on his smart vocabulary and rebuke the hostess for her
ignorance at the same time. Similar touches heighten Bobadill's already
evident egoism. His original impatience with Matthew was sufficiently
self-preoccupied: 'Why you do not manage your weapons with that
facilitie and grace that you should doe, I have no spirit to play with you'
(Q, I iii 213–15). The folio makes the self-reference even more
pronounced: 'Why, you doe not manage your weapon with any
facilitie, or grace to invite mee: I have no spirit to play with you' (F, I v
146–8). On the other hand, Bobadill's manner toward Downright, at
the moment of the beating, becomes more obsequious and cowardly.
Instead of 'Signior heare me! . . . Signior, I never thought on it till now'
(Q, IV ii 109–11), he tries to conciliate his antagonist with flattery:
'Gentleman of valour, I doe beleeve in thee, heare mee . . . . Tall man, I
never thought on it, till now' (F, IV vii 122–5).

Bobadill's vocabulary of cant and his elegant periphrases, amplified
in the folio – '*chartel*' (F, I v 111) for 'challenge'(Q, I iii 184),'the fume of
this simple' (F, III v 81) for "Tabacco" (Q, III ii 74) – infect his pupil
Matthew, who strives more zealously after the lordly tone and the
arcane manner in the folio than in the quarto. For 'beautifull' (Q, I iii
159), Matthew now says 'peremptory-beautifull' (F, I v 82–3); for 'verie
rare skill' (Q, I iii 191) he coins the grotesque superlative 'un-in-one-
breath-utter-able skill' (F, I v 121); for 'O Gods mee' (Q, I iii 138) he
devises an oath of his own, 'O, the *Muses*' (F, I v 61). The edict against
blasphemy in the Act of Assizes forced Jonson to suppress a good many
oaths in the revision, or to find less offensive ones, but he turned the
handicap into a triumph. The new oaths are more weirdly appropriate
to their speakers than the old ones, and the gulls now show a tendency to
grope more palpably after their oaths. Master Stephen, raging over a
fancied insult, exclaims in the quarto, 'Well I will not put it up, but by
Gods foote, and ere I meete him –' (Q, II iii 157–8). Jonson had to
retrench the blasphemous allusion to God's foot, but he did so with a
stroke of genius: 'Well, I will put it up, but by – (I ha' forgot the
Captaynes oath, I thought to ha' sworne by it) an' ere I meet him –' (F,
III i 176–8), thus replacing a bit of straightforward mimicry with a piece
of pathetic would-be mimicry, and so exchanging a single comic effect
for a double one.

Stephen's fatuousness is heightened throughout by small mutations
in the folio. Greeting a messenger, he exclaims foolishly enough in the
quarto:

Welcome good friend, we doe not stand much upon our gentilitie; yet I can
assure you mine uncle is a man of a thousand pounde land a yeare; hee hath but
one sonne in the world; I am his next heire, as simple as I stand here, if my cosen
die: I have a faire living of mine owne too beside.

(Q, I i 81–5)

The folio expands this slightly:

Nay, we do' not stand much on our gentilitie, friend; yet, you are wel-come, and I assure you, mine uncle here is a man of a thousand a yeare, *Middlesex* land: hee has but one sonne in all the world, I am his next heire (at the common law) master STEPHEN, as simple as I stand here, if my cossen die (as there's hope he will) I have a prettie living o' mine owne too, beside, hard-by here.

(F, I ii 2–8)

It should perhaps be explained that the phrase 'we do' not stand much on our gentilitie' is an idiotic echo of the advice his uncle has just finished giving him concerning his social pretensions. The rest of the speech, in both versions, underscores the extent to which the advice has been wasted. In the folio, every new stroke heightens the pointlessness of his boasting. By placing 'you are wel-come' after the disclaimer of pride in his gentility, Stephen contrives to suggest that there is some connection between them, that the messenger is welcome in spite of the fact that Stephen does not stand much on his gentility – a stunning piece of illogicality. Of the two added parentheses, the first is a vain display of parts, the second a stroke of monumental imbecility, considering that the uncle who stands beside him, and whose wealth he expects to inherit, is also the father of the 'cossen' whose death he is complacently hoping for. The pleased self-identification 'master STEPHEN' and the change from 'faire' to the more simpering word 'prettie' complete the effect of infantine self-congratulation. Similar alterations elsewhere in Stephen's dialogue produce similar results.

In a few cases Jonson rectifies lapses from decorum, usually by substituting a colloquial phrase for a pedantic one. Cob's too mincing stream of grateful epithets, 'O divine Doctor, thankes noble Doctor, most dainty Doctor, delicious Doctor' (Q, III iii 119–20), at the end of his scene with Justice Clement, has been cut short and made more appropriate to Cob: 'O, the Lord maintayne his worship, his worthy worship' (F, III vii 79–80). Brainworm now says 'remov'd' (F, III ii 37) instead of 'sublated' (Q, II iii 198), 'drum extraordinarie' (F, III ii 35–6) instead of 'God *Mars* extraordinarie' (Q, II iii 106–7), and Young Knowell, 'Ile be gelt' (F, I iii 62) for 'Then will I be made an *Eunuch*' (Q, I ii 58). At the same time, Jonson does not hesitate to replace a common word with an elegant one if the situation prompts it. Brainworm as Brainworm speaks a saltier lingo than the original Musco, but Brainworm as skeldering soldier tends toward preciosity, and this is intensified rather than toned down in revision. Finally, one must observe that in two or three spots the attempt to expunge minor improprieties dulls the effect. Downright, vowing retaliation against the poetasters, declares in the quarto, 'Ile marre the knot of them ere I sleepe perhaps: especially signior *Pithagoras*, he thats al manner of shapes' (Q, III iv 173–5). But the folio, doubtless in order to remove a learned allusion from the aggressively philistine Downright, transmutes the cuttingly Jonsonian 'signior *Pithagoras*, he thats al manner of shapes' into the much weaker, tamer 'Bob, there: he that's all manner of shapes' (F, IV iii 16–17).

The third group of changes, not always absolutely distinct from those so far discussed, produces actual extension or enlargement of character. At least three of the dramatis personae – Downright, Brainworm, and Young Knowell – emerge as more substantial and complex creations than their quarto prototypes.

Downright, the choleric humor, becomes more choleric, but a fresh thread has been woven into the texture of his language. This is signaled to us in advance in Bobadill's disdainful description, much enlarged in the folio:

I protest to you (as I am a gentleman and a soldier) I ne're talk't with the like of him: he ha's not so much as a good word in his bellie, all iron, iron, a good commoditie for a smith to make hobnailes on.

$$\text{(Q, I iii 167–70)}$$

I protest to you, as I am a gentleman, and a souldier, I ne're chang'd wordes, with his like. By his discourse, he should eate nothing but hay. He was borne for the manger, pannier, or pack-saddle! He ha's not so much as a good phrase in his belly, but all old iron, and rustie proverbes! a good commoditie for some smith, to make hob-nailes of.

$$\text{(F, I v 92–8)}$$

Aside from such inevitable nuances as the replacement of 'talk't' by the affected 'chang'd wordes', the new details add little to our knowledge of Bobadill, but they introduce us more adequately to Downright, whose new attribute is precisely his habit of larding his speech with 'rustie proverbes'. 'It will never out o' the flesh that's bred i' the bone' (F, II i 71–2), 'counsell to him, is as good, as a shoulder of mutton to a sicke horse' (F, II i 73–4), 'as he brewes, so he shall drinke' (F, II ii 34), 'he has the wrong sow by the eare, ifaith: and claps his dish at the wrong mans dore' (F, II i 78–9). In a sense Jonson has merely realized more concretely a pattern already clear in the quarto. Downright is perhaps not so much changed as he is substantiated, but this in itself amounts to a change of some importance, since his substantiality is the very thing that sets him in contrast to the anemic Bobadill and the scarce-existent Matthew. On the one hand the pseudo soldier and would-be gentleman lisping exotic oaths; on the other the plain-spoken bourgeois, whose language smells of the stable and market place. On the one hand the chirping little plagiary; on the other hand the gruff philistine to whom verses are 'worse then cheese, or a bag-pipe' (F, IV ii 21–2). The vividness of these confrontations depends to a large extent on the greater solidity of Downright's language in the revision.

The metamorphosis of Musco into Brainworm and of Lorenzo Junior into Young Knowell, however, not only substantiates these characters, it reorients them: both come to resemble the satiric expositor of the comical satires. Exposure of humors, in the comical satires, required not merely that a fool exhibit his folly, but that he be held up to ridicule by a commentator provided for the purpose, as Asper, Crites, Macilente, Carlo Buffone, Mercury, or Cupid. The folio text of *Every Man in his Humour* remodels Brainworm and Young Knowell so as to make them perform this function more clearly; they now flout the gulls more openly and so deflate them more emphatically. The scene in Q, I ii 28–52, as an instance, where Musco and Stephano confer over the latter's boot, undergoes a marked shift of tone in F, I iii 14–55. Brainworm's formerly unfocused verbal high spirits now turn into an instrument of irony directed steadily at Stephen. His silly quibble on 'boot' in the quarto is transferred to Stephen, and now figures as one more item in Stephen's long inventory of folly. Brainworm's reiterated 'master STEPHEN' this, 'master STEPHEN' that, ends by itself becoming a form of sly ridicule. His deferential praise of Stephen's leg in the quarto is banished in the revision; the folio allows Stephen to introduce the commendation of his own leg, 'How dost thou like my legge, BRAYNE-WORME', to which the reply, ostensibly judicious, is now sardonic, 'A very good leg! master STEPHEN! but the woollen stocking do's not commend it so well.' Finally, Musco's parting words in the quarto, 'You have an excellent good legge, sir: I pray you pardon me, I have a little haste in' (Q, I ii 51–2), completely lack the suave mockery of Brainworm's speech at the same point: 'You have an excellent good legge, master STEPHEN, but I cannot stay, to praise it longer now, and I am very sorie for't.' Brainworm's dry raillery not only draws the attention of the audience more sharply to Stephen's stupidity, it heightens that stupidity itself, since Stephen does not grasp the fact that he is being laughed at, and this affords a further contrast with those occasions on which, quite gratuitously, he takes it into his head to imagine that he *is* being laughed at.

In the case of Young Knowell, there is a sadistic rasp to many of his speeches in the folio, where the prevailing tone in the quarto was one of playful banter. His grandiloquent exhortation to Stephen, good-natured in the first version, is full of concealed barbs in the later one:

why cousin, a gentleman of so faire sort as you are, of so true cariage, so speciall good parts; of so deare and choice estimation; one whose lowest condition beares the stampe of a great spirit; nay more, a man so grac'd, guilded, or rather (to use a more fit *Metaphor*) tinfoyld by nature, (not that you have a leaden constitution, couze, although perhaps a little inclining to that temper, & so the

more apt to melt with pittie, when you fall into the fire of rage) but for your
lustre onely, which reflects as bright to the world as an old Ale-wives pewter
againe a good time; and will you now (with nice modestie) hide such reall
ornaments as these, and shadow their glorie as a Millaners wife doth her
wrought stomacher, with a smoakie lawne or a blacke cipresse? Come, come, for
shame doe not wrong the qualitie of your desert in so poore a kind: but let the
Idea of what you are, be portraied in your aspect, that men may reade in your
lookes; *Here within this place is to be seene, the most admirable rare & accomplisht worke
of nature*; Cousin what think you of this?

(Q, I ii 94–112)

A gentleman of your sort, parts, carriage, and estimation, to talke o' your turne
i' this companie, and to me, alone, like a tankard-bearer, at a conduit! Fie. A
wight, that (hetherto) his every step hath left the stampe of a great foot behind
him, as every word the savour of a strong spirit! and he! this man! so grac'd,
guilded, or (to use a more fit *metaphore*) so tin-foild by nature, as not ten house-
wives pewter (again' a good time) shew's more bright to the world then he! and
he (as I said last, so I say againe, and still shall say it) this man! to conceale such
reall ornaments as these, and shaddow their glorie, as a Millaners wife do's her
wrought stomacher, with a smokie lawne, or a black cypresse? O couss! It
cannot be answer'd, goe not about it. D R A K E s old ship, at *Detford*, may sooner
circle the world againe. Come, wrong not the qualitie of your desert, with
looking downeward, couz; but hold up your head, so: and let the *Idea* of what
you are, be pourtray'd i' your face, that men may reade i' your physnomie,
(*Here, within this place, is to be seene the true, rare, and accomplish'd monster, or miracle of
nature*, which is all one.) What thinke you of this, couss?

(F, I iii 108–28)

Among other things, the new version clarifies the sense a good deal by
breaking up the long intricate period into a series, by reducing the
jugglery with modifying phrases and trailing clauses, and by readdress-
ing itself at regular intervals to the subject and object, Stephen. The
exclamatory outbursts that punctuate the series, and afford further
clarification, also heighten the bombast of the mock encomium. 'One
whose lowest condition beares the stampe of a great spirit' in the quarto
is ironic, to be sure, but 'one whose every step hath left the stampe of a
great foot behind him, as every word the savour of a strong spirit' caps a
ludicrous bathos with a still droller pun on brandy-tainted breath, the
ambiguities producing an irony more complex and more cutting than
that of the quarto equivalent, which is ironic chiefly by courtesy of
context. At length emerging from behind the cloud of grandiose
comparisons under cover of which he has been mocking his cousin,
Knowell ends by exchanging for the implied sarcasm of '*admirable rare
& accomplisht worke of nature*' the open derision of '*true, rare, and
accomplish'd monster, or miracle of nature*'.

    The folio regularly transforms Knowell's colorless gestures of polite-
ness into caustic rejoinders, often altering other speeches so as to make

room for such rejoinders. Bobadill's revised speech of self-introduction now ends with the announcement, 'I love few wordes', so as to draw a sardonic answer from Young Knowell, 'And I fewer, sir. I have scarce inow, to thanke you' (F, iii i 84–6). Later, when Bobadill has dismissed Stephen's sword as a mere Fleming, Matthew, unexpectedly contradicted by his idol, is forced to reverse his own previous judgment and declare that on closer view it must be a poor Fleming after all: 'Masse I thinke it be indeed' (Q, ii iii 154). The folio amplifies at this point – 'Masse, I thinke it be, indeed! now I looke on't, better' – so as to draw another wicked gibe from Knowell: 'Nay, the longer you looke on't, the worse' (F, iii i 172–4).

Where the quarto text already contains mockery of the gulls, the folio frequently adds to it. In the former, Wellbred compares Stephen 'to nothing more happely, then a Barbers virginals; for every one may play upon him' (Q, ii iii 184–5). In the latter, he likens him, more devastatingly, 'to nothing more happily, then a drumme; for every one may play upon him'. To which Young Knowell makes a further correction: 'No, no, a childes whistle were farre the fitter' (F, iii ii 23–5). A barbershop virginal can be played by many, but not by all; it requires a certain minimum of training and skill. But absolutely anyone can bang on a drum, and the drum is hence a more degrading comparison. But a drum produces loud booming noises, whereas Stephen emits mainly high-pitched squeaks, so that the child's whistle becomes the final and most accurate figure of analogy.

Young Knowell in his new incarnation is thus a quite different figure from the Lorenzo Junior of the quarto. Having cast off his poetical fervor, he ceases for the most part to be a spokesman for Jonson's ethical view of poetry. Having acquired, on the other hand, a mastery of ambiguous insult, together with his equally changed companion Brainworm, he becomes the satiric expositor engaged in the unmasking of fools. As Knowell and Brainworm now stand out more clearly than ever in the ranks of the witty, so the gulls recede further into the dim legions of the witless. The sentence against them may well be lighter this time, the penances of fasting and recantation removed, since through their own language and through the mordant commentary of their associates they have been so much more pitilessly exposed. The formal penalties and rewards, distributed by a justice more clement than ever, now take on the emblematic nature of the punishment of Tucca;[5] the fools need no more crushing retribution, and the wits no further public sanctification. Folly has finally become its own worst punishment, as the wit of a Brainworm its own reward.

SOURCE: extracts from *Ben Jonson and the Language of Prose Comedy* (1960) pp. 98–104, 130–41.

NOTES

1. [*Discoveries*, ll. 954–8: 'Wheresoever, manners, and fashions are corrupted, Language is. It imitates the publicke riot. The excesse of Feasts, and apparell, are the notes of a sick State; and the wantonnesse of language, of a sick mind.']
2. A point made earlier in A. H. Sackton, *Rhetoric as a Dramatic Language in Ben Jonson* (New York, 1948) p. 61.
3. Even if one shares the extravagant opinion of Swinburne, *A Study of Ben Jonson* (London, 1889) p. 12, that this defense 'is worth all Sidney's and all Shelley's treatises thrown together', one may still feel that Jonson acted wisely in cutting it from the folio version.
4. [*Every Man out of his Humour* (1599), *Cynthia's Revels* (1600), and *Poetaster* (1601).]
5. [Captain Pantilius Tucca, the wordy and double-dealing swaggerer of *Poetaster*, who is gagged and has a pair of masks placed on his head, 'That he may looke *bi-fronted*' (v iii 435).]

Gabriele Bernhard Jackson

'THE PROTESTING IMAGINATION' (1969)

When Ben Jonson placed *Every Man in his Humor* at the head of his collected works and alluded to it in his dedication as his first-fruits, both position and allusion were symbolically appropriate, as he was no doubt fully aware. He had earlier dramatic writing to his credit, including at least one full-length comedy; but unlike what had come before, this springtime production held all the flavors of the mature harvest. All Jonson's characteristic concerns, values, turns of mind and phrase, dramatic techniques, structural designs – all are here, ready to be selected, developed, recombined. The very copiousness is, from the point of view of dramatic consistency, this play's disability: it offers too much simultaneously, sometimes contradictorily. It exceeds itself, and so displays its author better than almost any single later play. It is quintessential Jonson.

Jonsonian comedy is the comedy of non-interaction. In the characteristic Jonsonian plot, a group of personages in a state of chronic

introspection is brought together by a central action which loosely
unites them, or rather, brings them into proximity. Each character,
though responsive in his own way to outside stimuli, acts essentially
alone; he moves along the line of force directed by his nature, and comes
into collision, when time or a manipulator decrees, with another
character moving along an intersecting line. It follows that Jonsonian
plot is not plot in the ordinary sense. It does not develop outward from a
coherent center, but moves inward from widely separated points to an
accidental, as opposed to essential, meeting point – accidental in terms
of action, though at its best essential in significance. For this reason, the
plot of a Jonson comedy is peculiarly hard to recall; we remember
individual characters and confrontations, as though the story were a
means to achieve certain juxtapositions. These moments of intersection
constitute characteristic Jonsonian comedy; the design is not organic
but geometric.

   A Jonsonian comic plot is a group of subplots collected in one place.
How deeply this comedy of non-interaction differs from comedy of
interaction is evident if we think of Shakespeare's comic plots: where
subplot and main plot meet, they merge into one another, each
clarifying the other: the moment of meeting is the moment of
resolution – consider the confrontation of Portia and Shylock, the Duke
and Malvolio, Oliver and Orlando, or Theseus joined in celebration with
the midsummer-night's lovers and the workmen. The motto for
Shakespeare's comedy could well be taken from this last play: 'All the
story of the night told over, / And all their minds transfigured so together,
/ . . . grows to something of great constancy.' In Jonson there is no
together; each mind is transfigured separately. If these separate transfigur-
ations are simultaneous, their crisscrossing only exhibits more strik-
ingly the need to avoid gullibility. They teach, perhaps, the source of
transfiguration and the means of escaping it, but the condition itself
contains nothing valuable. No mutual element of great constancy can
be deduced from the interweaving of confusions. On the contrary, the
moment when Jonson's subplots coincide is a moment of chaos; instead
of merging, they rebound from one another; instead of clarifying, they
confound. The chaos is funny to the observer, who, aware of all the
motivations which compose it, laughs at the disparities he, but not the
characters, can perceive – for the audience, too, is detached. This
comedy of non-interaction is what Theseus expressly rejects; when his
master of ceremonies predicts that he will enjoy the workmen's botched
play only if he 'can find sport in their intents', he rebukes him: 'Our
sport shall be to take what they mistake.' In Jonson the sport of those
who play audience is all in the performers' intents; as Wellbred says
when he has aroused Dame Kitely's jealousy, 'this may make sport
anon'.

Furthermore, the coming together of plots in Shakespeare is a moment of resolution and merging because the plots are already organically connected by the relationships between their central figures. Oliver and Orlando are brothers; the Duke and the midsummer lovers are court and courtiers, and besides the Duke's group includes Hermia's father; Olivia and Malvolio are two halves of a household; Portia defends her husband's best friend. When the plots make contact we experience relief and release, for what has been artificially fragmented is reassembled. It is what we have been waiting for. In Jonson, on the other hand, although families do exist, they occupy the same subsection of plot to begin with, so that the meeting of two or more plot lines has no reason to bring a sense of fitting union. The separate subplots are not interconnected by previous personal relationships. Corvino and Corbaccio happen to be fellow citizens, and the Would-bes happen to be visiting their city; Drugger and Dapper and Sir Epicure Mammon happen to encounter Face at different times; Cokes (or Wasp) happens to choose John Littlewit to draw up a marriage license. Of course, in these great plays the characters are brought together by a far more subtle relationship than that of family ties: they have similar complexions of soul. The 'something of great constancy' which transfigures their minds is a capacity for similar evil (or folly – which Jonson always sees as weak evil). But since the evil is invariably such as to cut them off from other men, what metaphorically unites them actually divides them.

Now I do not think that Jonson was yet aware, when he wrote *Every Man in his Humor*, that his great comic genius lay in documenting and exploring this division; nor could he possibly foresee that the triumphs of that genius would be reserved for a time when he would find dramatic correlatives for his ultimately metaphysical belief that, while pursuit of an absolute good leads to unity and a constructive ordering of society, pursuit of evil leads to fragmentation and absolute isolation. But in *Every Man in* he is already attempting to introduce such a dramatic correlative in the debate about poetry; he sees, though perhaps but hazily, the direction in which he will have to move. The debate about poetry frames the play, whether one begins with the dedication to Camden, with the Prologue, or with Knowell's opening speech. Its settlement at the end by Clement, whose word is in every sense law, immediately precedes the proper ordering of society metaphorically ('I will doe more reverence, to him [a true poet], when I meet him, then I will to the Maior') and in fact (in the arrangements for rewards and punishments). General unification follows: Clement exhorts each participant to put off his divisive humor, to enjoy the symbolically unifying banquet; and he insists on a final procession properly emblematic of unity: 'every one, a fellow'. (The occasion, of course, is a wedding.) So the identification of a metaphysically valid ideal, poetry, is forced into linkage with constructive organization of society – forced, because the society has no more than the most tangential concern with poetry and seems unlikely either to be constructive or to remain, under pressure, organized. Clement has to push and shove to make them 'put of all discontent': 'You, Mr. DOWNE-RIGHT, your anger; you, master KNO'WELL, your cares; master KITELY, and his wife' – this is hard work. The picture of a society in the process of being constructively organized is always the weakest part of Jonson, and in his most satisfying plays he cuts it down to a minimum. In his least satisfying, *Catiline* and *Cynthia's Revels*, he makes it, alas, the major part of the proceedings. In these two plays and in *Poetaster* he tried again to use poetry as the ideal which could unite society, in all three works making eloquence a centrally important part of the plot, whereas in *Every Man in* it is very lightly dealt with in the action, though given disproportionate symbolic weight to bear. The relationship between the value of a society and the position of poetry within it was a theme dear to Jonson, but perhaps too indirectly dramatic to make a really great play, since poetry itself is still only a symbol for the moral and spiritual qualities it embodies.

That Jonson had not yet clearly perceived the drift of his own creativity is plain in his attempt to superimpose an organic unification on the arbitrary unification demanded by Justice Clement. The marriage between Edward and Bridget literally makes the 'worthwhile' characters one big family. Even Cob and Tib are worked in as household retainers, with their allotted place in the buttery. Clement, who might be considered an exception, has his special role above and outside of the action, sanctioning and repairing family ties and providing the family mansion and the family dinner. Only Matthew and Bobadill remain literally unrelated on either side of the family; their position is evidently intended to correspond to their moral state, for they are specifically excluded from humanitarian concern as unsalvageable ('these two, have so little of man in 'hem, they are no part of my care'). Since they do not share in the communion of humanity they get no organic dinner, either. But while this gesture toward a discriminating interactive comedy provides an agreeable and symbolically correct ending to the played-out action, it is utterly mechanical. The marriage, a most unconvincing piece of work patched up by Wellbred ('Hold, hold, be temperate', the fortunate bridegroom begs him), is as much of a contrivance as Clement's final procession. Clement dedicates 'This night . . . to friendship, love, and laughter' as though he were articulating the elements of the action, three motivations joined to bring about the final success. But major laughter in *Every Man in*, when connected with these two emotions at all, is based – as laughter typically is in Jonson – on perversions or negations of love (Kitely's for his wife,

Knowell's for his son, Matthew's courtship of Bridget) and friendship
(Kitely's suspicions of Cash, Brainworm's deception of Knowell, Edward's baiting of Stephen, and Wellbred's of Bobadill and Matthew).
Clement is asking for the simultaneous celebration of effects opposed at
the very root. All Brainworm's laughter-making talents have been
dedicated, as talents in Jonson always are, to the pleasant task of self-
aggrandizement, which separates father from son, brother from sister,
husband from wife (with the false message delivered to Kitely), master
from servant (Formal from Clement as much as Brainworm from
Knowell), for as long as the laughter is able to continue.

To be sure, there is not much separation needed; as in the great
comedies, all that is wanted is judicious intensification of a spiritual
state that already exists. And Clement's conjunction of friendship, love,
and laughter is only unconvincing, not, as it might be, offensive, for
Brainworm is not yet Mosca or Face, the non-understanding between
Knowell and Edward is not yet the deadly opposition of Corbaccio to
Bonario, Kitely's treatment of his Dame is not Corvino's treatment of
Celia, Brainworm's deception of Knowell is not Mosca's betrayal of
Volpone, and to counterfeit a London Justice's warrant is not to pervert
the Venetian courts. But as folly is a weak evil, so *Every Man in* is an
incipient *Volpone* or *Alchemist.* The situations are basic to Jonsonian
humanity: bonds of relationship are always denied by separation of
spirit.

Clement, thus circumscribed by human nature itself, can only create,
as family relationships do, a tenuous physical pairing. The characters
Jonson would like, in *Every Man in*, to present as 'fellows' are incapable
of fellowship. Can there be anywhere in literature a more tedious pair of
friends than Edward and Wellbred? Their sterile interchange of
witticisms is outgone only by the silence of the stony young lovers, who
exchange not a single remark either before or after marriage. The place
for emotional activity is in soliloquy; there old Knowell can protest his
paternal affection, but confronted with his newly-married son he does
not address a word to him, until the opportunity to mock Edward's
poetic inclination unseals his lips. His one disagreeable sentence is the
sum total of communication between them. Kitely, even more lavish of
passion in soliloquy, dredges up four direct remarks to his wife (one is
'How now? what?'), of which the last seems promising: 'kisse me, sweet
heart'; but his final pronouncement, *'When ayre raynes hornes, all may be
sure of some'*, does not augur well for the harmony of his union. Indeed,
the quarto text, continuing to the very end Kitely's suspicious
questions – intermixed with his assurances that he is cured of jealousy –
makes explicit the rocky future of his marriage.

The natural conclusion of Jonsonian comedy is complete fragmentation, coupled with (since this is comedy and not tragedy) an arbitrary

reconstitution of some kind of society – the ending of *The Alchemist*, *Volpone, Bartholomew Fair*. It is the conclusion of *Every Man in*, too, but here the fragments are unstably glued together in the hope that the traditional judgment, marriage, and banquet may retain their face value. . . . The great Jonsonian ending is a parody of the traditional ending of interactive comedy: its symbols of unity become affirmations of fragmentation. On a large scale as on a small (Volpone's morning hymn, Face's catechism), Jonson is a master of revelation through ironic form.

Although in *Every Man in* Jonson composes not ironically but straightforwardly, as if he were writing comedy of temporary, not permanent, non-interaction, the special nature of his characters and plot already exhibits itself everywhere. From the moment Knowell strikes the keynote in his opening lines by making Brainworm the bearer of his own paternal authority, each major character conducts his important relationships through a go-between. Brainworm shuttles back and forth between Knowell and Edward; Edward's courtship is conducted by Wellbred; Kitely sends his reprimand to Wellbred through Downright, whom he also uses as a stand-in at the connubial breakfast table; Kitely makes Cash his informant about his wife – and Cash delegates the position to Cob; Bobadill attacks Downright through a law clerk, whom he approaches through Matthew, and serves the resulting warrant by intermediary; even Justice Clement deals at one remove with the petitioner standing before him:

> CLEMENT   Tell OLIVER COB, he shall goe to the jayle, FORMALL.
> FORMALL   OLIVER COB, my master, Justice CLEMENT, saies you shall goe to the jayle.

. . . The need to interact is a challenge Jonson's characters cannot meet, and it is just this disability which really interests Jonson.

The successful pursuit of this interest raises formal problems of coherence in the play as artifact, which Jonson solves by the strictest economy and unity of structure. What he erects in the Prologue into a universal creed is really the intuitive perception by an individual artist of the form he needs. The formal Unities take over the role which in interactive comedy is played by motivation, while motivation performs the splintering which in interactive comedy can be accomplished by separation in time and space. The implications as to what is the essence and what the accident in human behavior are, of course, precisely opposite. The frequent presence of a manipulator like Brainworm serves exactly the same purpose. Not only does his puppeteer-like control of the disparate actions tie them into an artistic whole – his feverish sleight-of-hand, without which there would be no plot at all, em-phasizes the artificiality of simultaneous motion.

The characters themselves cohere by contrast – not only the general, and therefore structurally loose, contrast between a Downright and a Matthew, but the detailed and therefore structurally unifying contrast between, say, Matthew and Stephen. Whether or not the characters have met is immaterial; what is important is that Jonson, through parallels in their situations, puts them conceptually side by side. They throw psychological and moral light on one another by means of this non-personal unification, which in interactive comedy may reinforce the personal unification of emotional relationship, but in Jonsonian comedy replaces it. Jonson's balanced pairing sets off against one another those who seem identical and links those who seem opposite. Only when we meet the town gull, aping the fashion just coming in (rapier dueling) and praising the configuration of a friend's leg in a boot, can we comprehend the full idiotic pathos of the country gull, aping the fashion just going out (hawking) and praising the configuration of his own leg in a woolen stocking. Only beside his carefree 'double' Wellbred can Edward be clearly seen as his father's serious-minded son, urging upon his counterpart temperance, abstention from oaths, and the gravity of their situation; Edward's sexual purity – or indifference – which keeps him from ever making an indecent remark stands out against Wellbred's penchant for bawdry as the latter seizes every opportunity for playing a heavy-handed Mercutio to Edward's anemic Romeo.

More telling still, because they reveal not so much character as the ultimate significance of character, are those surprising juxtapositions of the apparently unconnected or antithetical which pinpoint a character's position in a universal pattern. In the great plays such unifying contrast is a major source of ironic illumination. Consider Corbaccio, the old man who obsessively pretends that he is young and vigorous, target of scorn for Volpone, the young man who obsessively pretends that he is old and impotent. Or Tribulation Wholesome, whom Subtle the Alchemist wittily baits for serving a false and self-seeking religion. Or Trouble-all and Quarlous, Bartholomew Fair's real and pretended madmen, of whom the real seeks a 'warrant' for his every action and the pretended does whatever self-involvement directs. In Every Man in, Jonson is already intrigued with the structural balance to be obtained through such mirror images, but, as I have noted before, his sense of irony is not yet equal to his intuitive perception of ideal form. Whatever ironic insight could be provided by identification of Brainworm (the fake fake soldier) as a version of Bobadill (the real fake soldier) is denied by the straightforward view of Brainworm we are required to take; and Bobadill as a version of Brainworm is either obvious or untrue. What we do already get from this doubling is a forceful sense – forceful because of the surprise with which we recognize the likeness – that the play operates in a unified world, where the bases of unification lie in the realm of disguise and deception. The unexpected conjunction of Brainworm and Bobadill jolts us into the characteristic universe of Jonsonian comedy, though it is not yet, as by later conjunctions, brilliantly particularized.

Yet there are certain kinds of particularity and invitations to evaluate in this comedy which are in essence the same as the structural interplay of later work. These characters, while going about their unrelated business, parody one another's behavior in as effective, if not as far-reachingly significant, a way as they do in the great plays. Not only is Cob, in his jealousy, a burlesque of Kitely; both are travesties of the troubled, spying Knowell, distorted mirror images which come together in the grand superimposition before Cob's house. Further, Knowell's acquaintanceship with the eccentric and easygoing Clement, the worried father's only reassurance, is an exact replica of the source of his worries: Edward's acquaintanceship with Wellbred – which is in its turn caricatured by that of Matthew with Bobadill (for Edward 'is, almost, growne the idolater / Of this yong WELL-BRED'). The cautious and unimaginative will always attach themselves respectfully to Pharaoh's foot. And so Stephen, who is even more cautious and less imaginative than Matthew, joins the pattern by giving his allegiance to that gentleman, and via him to Bobadill – for which Edward very rightly scoffs at him; while Edward's father muses in disbelief over Wellbred's letter, 'Is this the man, / My sonne hath sung so, for the happiest wit, / The choysest braine, the times hath sent us forth?' Everything depends on where one stands.

Knowell himself, despite his name, does not stand in the position of final authority. Personally he is appealing: the archetypal fond parent ('but why does he pick such inferior friends?'), he gives careful thought to his son's upbringing, exercises restraint and psychological insight in his discipline, puts himself to a good deal of trouble to follow his paternal course; a kindly and humane master, he risks an obviously poor investment in the begging Fitzsword, then forgives him immediately when he turns out to be Brainworm making a laughing stock of his employer; he is human enough in his customary moralism to stretch a moral point ('This letter is directed to my sonne: / Yet, I am EDWARD KNO'WELL too . . .'), human enough in his customary generosity to be stung by the imputation of pettiness ('Why should he thinke, I tell my Apri-cotes?'), and generous enough to recognize spontaneously that he deserves tricking, 'to punish my impertinent search; and justly'. But when he is placed in perspective, now with regard to this piece of similar behavior, now with regard to that, his actions lose their individuality and their coherence; he becomes depersonalized. The effect is just the opposite of that in interactive comedy, where the more links a character forms with others, the more personal qualities he displays. Knowell is instead subjected again and again to partial re-evaluation through people he has never met. His kinship with Kitely and Cob forces his reasoned solicitude to fall under the shadows of irrationality and possessiveness; his benign incomprehension of Brainworm's character must take its overall place beside Kitely's malign incomprehension of Cash's; his understandable outburst at Stephen's idiocy, 'fore heaven, I am asham'd / Thou hast a kinsmans interest in me', is qualified by Downright's excessive outburst over Wellbred's pranks: 'I am griev'd, it should be said he is my brother, and take these courses' – an unpleasantly similar refusal of indulgence on the grounds of personal dignity. Indeed, though Knowell has never set eyes on any member of Kitely's household, what he thinks he is doing is constantly compromised by what we know they are doing. How can we retain faith in his admirable theory of discipline when we hear it parroted by futile Kitely to incompetent Downright? Here is Knowell's original:

> I am resolv'd, I will not . . .
>   practise any violent meane, to stay
> The unbridled course of youth in him. . . .
> There is a way of winning, more by love,
> And urging of the modestie, then feare . . .
>   [he will]
> By softnesse, and example, get a habit.

And an act later, here is Kitely:

> But, brother, let your reprehension (then)
> Runne in an easie current, not ore-high
> Carried . . .
> But rather use the soft perswading way,
> Whose powers will worke more gently, and compose
> Th'imperfect thoughts you labour to reclaime:
> More winning, then enforcing the consent.

We know how to value Downright's 'I, I, let me alone for that, I warrant you'; and Knowell's psychological validities are integrated into a pattern of useless educational theory. These implied equivalences between Knowell and others – particularly his major counterpart, Kitely – produce an interesting complication of value judgment. We are forced to look at a piece of behavior first in isolation and then all over again in juxtaposition. The positive values projected by a Knowell seen as complete in himself are as true as, but no truer than, the negative values acquired by a Knowell divided into spiritual parts with matching doubles. Who would not live in kindly, generous, soft-hearted

Knowell's household? And yet all over London men like him are misunderstanding their servants, denying their relatives, failing their juniors, and beating their wives.

This dramatic guilt by association is not yet the glittering web of corruption woven by characters in the great plays, but it displays the identical complex of personalities, totally disparate in type, unconnected by emotional relationship, yet held together by a single spiritual disorder. But whereas *Volpone*, *The Alchemist*, and *The Silent Woman* are tightly constructed, each around one central spiritual disease, *Every Man in* resembles *Bartholomew Fair* in its multiplicity of aberrations, without a connecting character like the latter's Trouble-all to raise one overreaching question with his refrain, 'Have you a warrant?' Instead, Jonson here strings the characters together like beads, on thematic threads which hold a few at a time. So the central question of use and misuse of poetry is touched upon by everyone except Wellbred and Brainworm; Stephen, Matthew, Kitely, Edward, and Cob are, each in his own way, ineffectual lovers; Stephen, Matthew, and Cob are foolishly concerned with lineage, on which Knowell has the deciding say; Stephen, Kitely, and Matthew all affect melancholy; and book-learning is honored and dishonored by Knowell, Cob (who likes to bring Roger Bacon and King Cophetua into the conversation), Edward, Matthew, and Stephen – each of the three last being, in his special sense, 'at his booke'. Jonson, who dedicated this first product of his own muse to Camden, the paragon of true learning, must have enjoyed writing the mischievous counterpoint in scene i:

KNO'WELL   My selfe was once . . .
Dreaming on nought but idle *poetrie* . . .
But since, time, and the truth have wak'd my judgement (*Enter*
    STEPHEN)
And reason taught me better to distinguish,
The vaine, from th'usefull learnings. Cousin Stephen!

– as gratifying in its way as 'the heaven's breath / Smells wooingly here: . . . The air is delicate. (*Enter* LADY MACBETH).'

Distortion of education, of poetry, of love, of social status – Jonson's favorite issues are all here; like the pairing of characters and the unities of time and place, they tie together the action in a delimited realm where the same problems come up over and over again. Taken together, they amount to an enumeration of abuses similar to that formed by the aggregate of Juvenal's satires, or, contemporaneously, Marston's. Jonson, who drew liberally on Juvenal in *Every Man in*, had in mind a similar anatomizing of a diseased society, though here the disease is so mild as to be merely the common cold. As Juvenal devotes one satire to dramatizing one vice, and Marston follows suit with one central representative character in each such satire, Jonson here assembles a sub-group of his characters around each separate folly and connects the groups into a play. The sum of all the parts is Society, or, more correctly, Humanity in a specific microcosm, built up out of a multitude of local references until the existence of the characters in time and place becomes indisputable.

This definition of an ethical whole by adducing all possible parts is the characteristic additive technique of Jonson's comedy. In *Every Man in* he still makes some use of the iterative technique favored by interactive comedy, in which a subplot repeats the situation of the main plot, but in the mature comedies he abandons it. Even here the iteration (Cob's and Kitely's jealousy, Edward's and Wellbred's images in their elders' eyes) is subordinate to the introduction of more and more individual examples of varied human folly. Characteristically, instead of a proliferation from one original source – of absurd passions, say, as in *A Midsummer Night's Dream*, or of hopeless adorations as in *Twelfth Night*, or of rulers and usurpers as in *The Tempest* – Jonson gives us one fox, one fruit-fly, one vulture, one crow, one raven, one parrot-turtle, and adds them together into a definitive summation of human animal life. The play's significance grows inductively, not deductively.

In *Every Man in* this typical profusion of unlike examples coheres structurally but not essentially. The absence of that pervasive symbolic imagery (e.g. of gold, of alchemy) so integral to the great plays is indicative of the absence of a pervasive metaphysical concern; the play lacks an ethical center. The attempt to make this center a loose, and moreover a practical, concept, society, is not artistically satisfying. Venice, Bartholomew Fair, an alchemical workshop – these set certain symbolic limits on the meaning of 'society'; they postulate a select *kind* of society. The appearance in these settings of an apparently random sample of personages ceases to have sociological significance and instead becomes interpretable much as an emblem with separate constituents is interpretable. 'Society' becomes a warped construct of warped spirits, and the accepted temporal values are so many clues to the eternal, world-controlling values which have been flouted. But London is a neutral setting in which society means merely a collocation of varied types; it cannot offer a hard ethical core. The constant insistence upon the locale, by providing a conceptual center, goes some way toward disguising the lack of an evaluative center, but it is no substitute.

In addition to this more or less artificial centralization, Jonson provides a tentative ethical norm in Justice Clement, which with sufficiently ingenious acting might prove palatable in performance. In theory Jonson is proposing a synthesis between excessive devotion to imagination (Brainworm, Wellbred, Kitely) and excessive devotion to practical concerns (Knowell, Downright) as the ordering principle in society. Clement, the orderer, is himself an older man of practical understanding, successful in the world of affairs, who recognizes the desirability of becoming 'a stay'd man' but also sympathizes with youthful energy and excess (thus joining the two generations divided in the rest of the play), and both values and exhibits 'mirth', eccentricity, and nimble wit – not to mention the nominal spiritual criterion of the play, poetry. He is the man of judgment as well as imagination. But Clement is only abstractly a satisfying character. His merry tricks are not among Jonson's happiest strokes. It is hard to be much tickled by his donning armor to meet Bobadill or by his natty scatological quatrain. His treatment of supplicant Cob borders on mild sadism ('I but feare the knave'), and his mechanical invocations of a drink of sack (four times), to signify that jollity has yet again conquered all, have the quality of slightly dipsomaniac reflex. As always, the supposedly constructive norm is by far the weakest part of Jonson's play.

The inadequacy of Justice Clement is typical of Jonson's drama because at bottom his plays are neither satire nor normative comedy, though they utilize some of the devices of each and Jonson believed them to be both. Satire, and especially social satire, constantly invokes the desirable norm whose violation it portrays. . . . But upon what conceptual norm does the funniness of Bobadill, or even of Stephen, depend? Only upon the broad assumption that human beings behave with a degree of moderation, rationality, and adherence to fact. Even Jonson's powerfully irradiated metaphysical norms operate only as beacons from which to measure the distance to a character's actual location. They illuminate grandly but generally. So Volpone's religious invocation to his gold and Subtle's catechism of Face impart to these characters' actions the thrill of blasphemy, but make them infinitely culpable without instilling any corresponding sense of the desirability of conventional worship or, indeed, of any particular mode of behavior except the avoidance of what we see. Jonson's success, in such moments, is the combination of shudder and laugh.

Just as Jonson's greatest strokes are independent of the support of any precisely defined norm, so it is impossible to deduce a specific norm from them by contrast, as [in the 'Epistle to Dr Arbuthnot'] one can deduce Pope from the negation of Atticus, Bufo, and Sporus. This definition of a norm by contrast is a technique satire shares with normative comedy. From *Twelfth Night*'s Duke and Olivia we can deduce the ideal of Viola; from the midsummer-night's lovers, Theseus; from the couples in the Forest of Arden, Rosalind. But Celia and Bonario are not delineated by their opposition to the other characters except insofar as good is the opposite of bad – rather too broad a contrast to serve for integrated dramatic structure. It is not just that Celia and Bonario are unsuccessfully characterized, as Justice Clement is unsuccessfully characterized.

True, they are bores, and Justice Clement is a bore, and Crites in *Cynthia's Revels* is a bore – but so, at times, is Milton's God, without invalidating his normative function. What is peculiar about Jonson's normative characters is that they are extraneous to the real dramatic activity of the play. They are not engaged in the same type of action as the others in a more desirable way (like Viola, Theseus, and Rosalind) – they are simply not engaged in the same type of action. The nature of Jonson's comedy precludes the integrated normative character. Justice Clement is a try at it; but he, too, remains dramatically irrelevant, though his eccentricity is certainly an attempt to show him behaving like the others in a more desirable way. He is intractably extraneous to Stephen and Matthew, if not to Brainworm and Wellbred, and, what is much worse, hopelessly extraneous to the chief ornaments of the play, Kitely and Bobadill. Jonson's attempt to proffer him symbolically as a normative version of Bobadill by making him dress up as a soldier is only embarrassing.

The truth is that Jonson's greatness is not the greatness of satire at all, except in the supremely general sense in which all great comedy is satire because it exposes neglected truths about human behavior. Nor is it the greatness of normative vision. Jonson, in his numerous manifesto-like utterances, has himself been the most diligent obfuscator of his creation. Evidently he regarded himself, and wished to regard himself, as a writer of corrective comedy and satire. Indeed, his compelling moral and ethical bias caused him to punish all his highly imaginative characters for deviation from spiritual and social equipoise – perhaps a form of self-flagellation for his own zest in portraying their feats. But no amount of beating or imprisonment can convince us that Bobadill is less worthwhile than Justice Clement, or that Bonario should have been a model for Volpone. Jonson's devotion to the ideals of correction and satire pulls in a direction contrary to his bent for pure comedy, and creates an unevenness in the progress of his work. His social satire is by turns brilliant, dull, and incandescent: brilliant when it constitutes a beautifully composed aria; dull when it affords merely 'an Image of the times' (Cob on fasting days); incandescent when it plays into Jonson's comedy of solipsism by giving his characters recognizable objects of obsession. When it is incandescent it is not at all corrective. To lampoon the affectations of fencing or the popularity of tobacco is no more the real point of Bobadill than to decry the disproportionate concentration of wealth among the aristocracy is the point of *Volpone*. The road of normality from which Bobadill and Volpone have diverged is lost to view, and well lost, behind the picturesque landscape of the territory in which they have arrived.

On the grounds of successful presentation of a comic norm, we would have to give the palm to *Poetaster*, since Horace, if not lovable, is at least deducible. But this evaluation is manifest nonsense. It is evident that Jonson is writing a different sort of comedy: non-normative comedy. Jonson's success is invariably to be gauged by the strength of the anti-norm. His greatest plays succeed not by enforcing a concept of balance but by impressing upon us the overwhelming force of imbalance. So *Every Man in* succeeds not insofar as Justice Clement suceeds but insofar as Bobadill and Kitely succeed. For Jonson is not writing about common agreement on the outside world at all. He is writing about diverse and unmergeable inner worlds, about the impossibility of common agreement, about the psychological artificiality of a commonly defined outer world, even when it is a moral necessity. We recognize him as a writer of genius when he exchanges the mandatory optimism of satire for the deep pessimism of comedy.

Jonson's comedy is of the type afforded by a really thoroughgoing marital quarrel or a United Nations debate. It is the comedy of minds which never touch, of confinement within an insurmountable point of view. Jonson's so-called humor characters and his later elaborations upon them are human beings whose minds have become (or have been from the beginning) rigid in a certain position – a phenomenon by no means uncommon. In fact it is the frustrating familiarity of the immovable mind in ordinary life that makes its objectification on the stage so welcome. Anyone who has been much concerned with logical demonstration – anyone who has taught – has bowed to the inert strength of Stephen's type of mind, as pliable and as resilient as rubber. Give him your best twenty-five lines on the social, moral, and logical impossibility of standing upon gentility, and he will yield you the following harvest:

Nay, we do' not stand much on our gentilitie, friend; yet, you are wel-come, and I'assure you, mine uncle here is a man of a thousand a yeare, *Middlesex* land: hee has but one sonne in all the world, I am his next heire (at the common law) master STEPHEN, as simple as I stand here . . . though I doe not stand upon my gentilitie neither in't.

But it is not only specific types of fixity that we recognize in Jonson. It is the inherent capacity of every mind to retreat, as it does in extreme joy or extreme pain, deep into itself, and there to relate every event to its own pleasure or suffering. It is the impulse which upheld for thousands of years the natural assumption that the sun revolves around the earth. It is the impulse which convinces us that the automobile turning at the same corner with us contains guests for the party to which we are going. When Knowell before Cob's house absurdly mis-sees Kitely ('Soft, who is this? 'Tis not my sonne, disguisd?') – when, unregenerately solipsistic in the very utterance which proclaims his supposed comprehension, he nods wisely, 'I doe tast this as a trick, put on me, / To punish my impertinent search; and justly: / And halfe forgive my sonne, for the device' – he is the exact comic equivalent of Lear on the heath mis-seeing Edgar: 'Didst thou give all to thy two daughters? And art thou come to this? . . . Nothing could have subdu'd nature to such a lowness, but his unkind daughters. . . . Judicious punishment!' They are both upholding a sense of personal significance and mental control in the face of a universe suddenly incomprehensible. Since both have chosen to define themselves by their relationships to their children, if they are to see themselves as centrally important they must see outer events as similarly defined. Lear responds to Kent's 'He hath no daughters, sir,' with 'Death, traitor!' while Knowell reacts to Clement's 'Your sonne is old inough, to governe himself' with total deafness. Who can bear to be tangential?

Jonsonian comedy constantly plays upon its participants the cosmic joke of encouraging each to think himself central, while its author knows that they are every one tangential. This is exactly the joke Wellbred and Edward play upon Matthew and Stephen, Volpone and Subtle upon their visitors, Mosca and Face upon Volpone and Subtle, and Jonson upon Mosca and Face. Furthermore, since the characters, being non-interactive, are all tangential to one another, the action is a continual revelation that centrality is delusion. *Volpone* and *The Alchemist* play out the joke most perfectly, for here Jonson produces with inexhaustible copiousness another and yet another variation on the deluded figure of The Chosen, within a situation itself dependent upon the concept. Each of Volpone's dupes believes that 'Onely you / (Of all the rest) are he, commands his love', just as Volpone believes this in regard to Mosca; each dupe believes that the inheritance 'is yours, without a rivall, / Decree'd by destinie', just as Mosca believes this for himself. Each of Subtle's gulls believes not only that Subtle is an initiate, but also that he himself is uniquely selected to share in supernatural benefits, as long as he does not 'cause the blessing leave you'. The paradigm case is certainly Dapper, persuaded that 'a rare starre / Raign'd, at your birth' and made him nephew and favorite of the Queen of Fairies; the really important action crowds him into the privy, to drop utterly out of memory for an act and a half. The audience itself becomes an accomplice in the existential joke; we forget him, his gag, his blindfold, his hopes, his illusions – and his sudden return into our consciousness, sick to his stomach, totally irrelevant, unwaveringly committed to his long-obsolete centrality, makes his *cri de coeur*, 'For gods sake, when wil her *Grace* be at leisure?', one of the great triumphs of comedy.

The essence of Dapper is already incarnated in *Every Man in*: in Stephen, 'a wight, that (hetherto) his every step hath left the stampe of a great foot behind him, . . . *the true, rare, and accomplish'd monster, or miracle of nature*'; in Matthew, exemplar of 'some peculiar and choice spirits, to whom I am extraordinarily ingag'd'; in Bobadill, singled out for persecution by the multitude 'because I am excellent, and for no other vile reason on the earth'; all bear willingly the burden of unique importance. And the tangential privy is present, too, in the form of the buttery and courtyard to which these indispensable spirits are consigned – Matthew and Bobadill fasting, like Dapper, and urged to 'pray there, that we may be so merrie within, as to forgive, or forget you'.

Jonson's unwillingness or unreadiness to see his own implications in *Every Man in* makes him conceal the necessary ending of his joke behind the comforting charade of mutual centrality arranged by Justice Clement for the 'worthy' characters; but though he is not yet prepared to admit that Clement himself, in a non-interactive universe, must be tangential in his attempt to impose order (an admission finally made in Justice Overdo of *Bartholomew Fair*), he is already drawing characters of stature whose claim to dignity is the degree of their delusion. For to accept tangentiality can only be a source of stature when the inner self is so strong and spiritually resourceful that it can afford to secede from what it has come to recognize as centrality, and to rely wholly on itself, or itself in combination with its few spiritual allies. It declares the central principles of the universe tangential to something of greater value which it possesses in itself. This is the condition of Lear in his final address to Cordelia, in which he welcomes their prison as a reflection of the tangentiality he desires. Jonson's 'humor' characters counterfeit this condition of spiritual independence by ignoring the central principles of the universe and erecting whatever psychological principle is most crucial to their own inner lives into an objective truth or criterion of value. Having eschewed any painful confrontation with reality, they are subject to have their scheme of values destroyed by its intrusion, as Lear no longer is. Reality, in the very act of destroying what is dearest to Lear, can only confirm its importance. In destroying the humor character's psychological treasure, however, reality would simultaneously wipe out its significance. Consequently there is almost no limit to the amount of delusion Jonsonian characters are willing to accept or invent for themselves to fend off what would be – and in the end often is – psychological annihilation.

This clinging to a subjective construct is much closer to what most men do in real life than the behavior of Lear. Very few of us are willing to die and be born again; we would rather live with all our imperfections on our heads – preferably regarded as special versions of perfection. Who has not marveled at the extraordinary inner jugglings and compromises that human beings prefer to what an observer, with the smugness of detachment, can call 'facing the facts'? Such self-

delusion is the instinct of self-preservation dictating to the mind; despite
all self-righteous superiority, we must recognize survival as victory –
and especially survival with *panache*. Who could do other than applaud
Bobadill's virtuoso recovery from the brutality of fact:

MATTHEW   ... but what can they say of your beating?
BOBADILL   A rude part, a touch with soft wood, a kind of grosse batterie
us'd, laid on strongly, borne most paciently: and that's all

or refuse to admire that gallant vision of an ideal world constructed
especially for him:

MATTHEW   I, but, would any man have offered it in Venice? as you say?
BOBADILL   Tut, I assure you, no: you shall have there your *Nobilis*, your
Gentelezza, come in bravely upon your *reverse*, stand you close, stand you firme,
stand you faire, save your *retricato* with his left legge, come to the *assalto* with the
right, thrust with brave steele, defie your base wood! But, wherefore doe I awake
this remembrance?

Nessun maggior dolore che ricordarsi del tempo felice nella miseria[1] – as they say
in Venice.
  This saving imbalance which invents its self-centralized Utopia –

KNO'WELL   When I was yong, he liv'd not in the stewes,
    Durst have conceiv'd a scorne, and utter'd it,
    On a grey head; age was authoritie
    Against a buffon

KITELY   See, what a drove of hornes flye, in the ayre, ...
    Watch 'hem, suspicious eyes, watch, where they fall.
    See, see! on heads, that thinke th'have none at all!

– this imbalance was fitly imaged by contemporary medicine as
physical incompatibility with the elements of the universe. The universe
being, to the Elizabethan view, a balanced composition of the four
elements – earth, air, fire, and water – the little world of man formed a
corresponding amalgam of the four 'humors', earth appearing as bile or
melancholy (cold and dry), air as blood (hot and moist), fire as choler
(hot and dry), and water as phlegm (cold and moist). Predominance of
one element produced physical and thus psychological unbalance – the
condition of a humor character. It is easy to see how this well-known
medical theory would be symbolically suggestive for Jonson, interested
as he was in the predominance of one element of the inner self and the
ensuing lack of correspondence between the makeup of an individual
and the makeup of his surroundings. It is equally easy to see how the
simplistic concept of four humors would rapidly become inadequate for
dramatic representation of mental convolutions in a character engaged
in preserving his psychological existence. So even in *Every Man in* only

Kitely is a true humor character, suffering from a recognizable medical condition of head-melancholy, while in the others 'melancholy' is already a metaphor for a spiritual stance, and 'humor' shorthand for 'identifying aspect of self'.

Jonson's cosmic joke is the disparity between the psychological need of human beings for this kind of significant identification and the inexorable demands of the universe or society. Refusing reduction of their unique selves to a balanced component of the impersonal universe; refusing the moral equivalent, a Christian self-abnegation for the common salvation; refusing the psychological analogue, yielding up a portion of the self to relationship with another human being – Jonson's comic characters revel in their delusion of freedom. Their solipsistic conviction of centrality renders them infinitely gullible and creates Jonson's special comedy of mutual deception. Sundered from the outside world by urgent attention to an inner clamor, these characters meet in a congenial setting (which fosters their illusions of a reality constructed around their needs) to assume the roles of dupe and manipulator-dupe. For the manipulators are merely solipsists with talent. Perceiving in their superior intelligence that other human beings render themselves cosmically ridiculous by a rigidity calculated as monumentality, they seek their escape into significance by way of volatility. Instead of one mask of self the manipulator assumes many, as though this were a difference in kind. But his varied masks prove to be only alternative ways of making a single statement about himself, for disguises in Jonson's mature plays are always as ironically revelatory of hidden springs of motivation as are the self-presentations of the dupes. The manipulator, though gifted with more consciousness of his surroundings than the people he manipulates, is still rigid in acting out his conviction that he defines the universe, that only the creations of his intellect are really real, and that events are arrangeable for his exclusive benefit. In the end his line of force, too, crosses another, and the collision overthrows him; he discovers that the action to which he is central is itself tangential to another which he did not comprehend. This is the fate of Brainworm. His disguises as manipulator, like the other typically Jonsonian elements in the play, are not ironically exploited, but they are already ironic in their deceptive offer of freedom. Not only is Brainworm entrapped by his disguise into the final accounting, but he has himself had to recognize at the outset – when he was less self-enamored – that disguise is a ruse by which the tangential character renders himself apparently central: 'now I, . . . to insinuate with my yong master (for so must we that are . . . men of hope and service doe . . .) have got me afore, in this disguise'. Whether he be nominally dupe or nominally manipulator, the Jonsonian character is ultimately confronted with the fact that every man's action involves him in, and

subordinates him to, the action of others – whereupon Jonsonian man
ceases to function.

This active and passive solipsism produces those moments of collision
which, together with the inspired portrayal of self-delimited character,
are the glory of Jonsonian comedy. Seen from without, a moment of
collision is a point at which two (or more) consciousnesses, like billiard
balls of different colors, touch surfaces with a perceptible click and part.
One might take as its type this interchange between Mosca and
Volpone:

> MOSCA   You lothe, the widdowes, or the orphans teares
> Should wash your pavements; or their pitious cryes
> Ring in your roofes; and beat the aire, for vengeance.
> VOLPONE   Right, MOSCA, I doe lothe it.

The pleasures of Volpone's reply are manifold. One is simply the
neatness of the collision itself, like a well-executed shot at billiards.
Beyond this lies the sudden perception that what appears to be
communication is only self-propulsion. Beyond this still, the intellectual
pleasure of recognizing, in one sharp instant, the source of the collision,
the gap between the ruthless, bored aristocracy of Volpone the
Magnifico and the essentially conventional, bourgeois orientation of
social-climbing Mosca. And just as the points at which moving objects
collide with a stationary one define the outer limits of the latter, so this
collision defines the outer limits of Volpone's human comprehension.

The defining collision is already one of the aural satisfactions of *Every
Man in*:

> BRAYNE-WORME [Disguised as a soldier.]   I assure you, the blade may
> become the side, or thigh of the best prince, in *Europe*.
> EDWARD   I, with a velvet scabberd, I thinke.
> STEPHEN   Nay, and't be mine, it shall have a velvet scabberd, Couss,
> that's flat. . . .

Here are fewer overtones, no doubt – less resonance; but that is in the
nature of the body struck. Kitely gives off a deeper sound:

> KITELY   if thou should'st
>   Reveal it, but –
> CASH   How? I reveale it?
> KITELY   Nay,
>   I doe not thinke thou would'st; but if thou should'st:
>   'Twere a great weakenesse.
> CASH   A great trecherie.
>   Give it no other name.
> KITELY   Thou wilt not do't, then?

CASH   Sir, if I doe, mankind disclaime me, ever.
KITELY [*Aside.*]   He will not sweare, he has some reservation.

Here the *non sequitur* bears more clearly the identifying marks of such a moment of collision. Seen from within, it is a point at which one human being (often, though not here, himself the fantasy hero in his own world) enters the delusion of another in a supporting role – a moment when the nearness of outer reality, in the shape of an independent presence, only lights up the cavernous reaches of the deluded self. . . .

In the Jonsonian world incomprehension becomes the only basis of relationship. All important relationships in the plays could be seen as collisions drawn out into the semblance of interaction.

The converse is also true: a moment of collision occurring within what passes itself off, to either or both of the participants, as a relationship reveals its essence, and heralds the inevitable disintegration of its bonds. But it is a failed revelation. It is the moment we remember in retrospect and understand when acrid experience has confirmed it. Jonson's entirely external representation of it shifts the burden of comprehension from actor to observer: as audience, we pre-experience what the speaker may never come to feel. Kitely, who fears nothing so much as pseudo-relationship, is revealed in this moment as doomed to its creation; in his mental deflection from contact with Cash we can foresee the whole unraveling, from

> He is a jewell, brother . . .
> > in his place so full of faith,
> That, I durst trust my life into his hands

to

> > oh, that villaine dors me. . . .
> Shee's gone a'purpose, now, to cuckold me,
> With that lewd raskall, who, to win her favour,
> Hath told her all.

We can foresee it because, as in Volpone's reply, we have heard Kitely fix the limits of his comprehension. 'Full of faith' can have no practical meaning for a man himself constitutionally incapable of faith. Clement dimly perceives Kitely's plight when he offers his truism: 'Hornes i' the mind are worse than o' the head'; but Kitely never understands his disability at all, and so preserves his inner construct against the assault of Clement's good sense. Similarly, Stephen remains as impervious to Edward's indirect as to Clement's direct sarcasm, and to the implications of his final allotted place (with Cob and Tib in the buttery) for his gentlemanly pretensions. All his connections are laid open as false; but to Stephen the revelation does not signify, for he is equally happy with relationship or pseudo-relationship – a position self-sufficient in its irony, and typically Jonsonian. Self-absorption is the source of all vital energy; relationship must crumble before it. . . .

Such collisions are undoubtedly the most ironic; yet there is another group of collisions which shares all their basic principles and is even more purely comic – those between people utterly unrelated to one another. Here the disparity between apparent intimate connection and actual indifference is absolute. Here the sole justification for a belief in connection is the construct of the individual mind. So intense is the craving for personal centrality that perception simply gulps down whole anyone who walks into range. One thinks of jealous Lady Would-be 'unmasking' Peregrine as a harlot, or of pugnacious Kastril, interrupted in a deliberate breach of the peace – his attempt to start a fight with Surly – when Ananias brings Subtle the news of the Puritan capitulation to alchemy: 'ANANIAS   Peace to the houshold. . . . Casting of dollers is concluded lawfull. KASTRIL   Is he the Constable?' Here the hopelessness of relationship is not grounded in personal difference; it appears rather as a category of experience. Out of the chaotic happenstance of ordinary life the mind constructs an orderly set of relationships – painful perhaps, but also full of meaning. By the end of this latter scene, the accidental convergence of a number of unrelated customers upon the Alchemist's house has been satisfactorily arranged into significant pattern in the mind of each – in each mind, a different significant pattern.

In these collisions the hopelessness of relationship and the mind's circumvention of it are represented dramatically in the sudden encounter between disparate actions. The great example in *Every Man in* is the scene before Cob's house, the play's climax. The fantasy of interaction can go no further than the mutual 'recognition' of Kitely and Knowell, begun when Knowell identifies Dame Kitely ('O, this is the female copes-mate of my sonne! / Now shall I meet him straight'), continuing with Knowell's assimilation of Kitely into his private world as Edward, and culminating in the moment of actual collision, as Kitely literally turns around and assimilates Knowell:

> This horie-headed letcher, this old goat, . . .
> O, old incontinent, do'st not shame,
> When all thy powers inchastitie is spent,
> To have a mind so hot?

This is the very parody of Aristotle's 'discovery and peripeteia', the conjunction by which tragic action becomes meaningful to its protagonist. If action has no inherent meaning, but is only a product of individual bent or of manipulation, then pattern in events is the product of the mind's illusion. And under the circumstances coexisting before

Cob's house, the logic of delusion is at least as persuasive as the real explanation. We have a choice, momentarily, only between the crazy conclusion of Kitely ('KNO'WELL   What lunacie is this, that haunts this man?') and the obsessive insistence of Knowell ('TIB   The constable? the man is mad, I thinke'), wherein either derangement is aesthetically far more satisfying, in its imaginative unity, than the truth. Is it not wholly natural to prefer the organically meaningful, internally consistent plot of either of these imaginary actions to the forced, meaningless machinations of Brainworm? and to prefer to see oneself as the hub of the one rather than a cog in the other? The moment is uniquely Jonsonian in inducting us into the satisfactions of imaginative delusion. The characters have successfully escaped epiphany. Like chaotic *Bartholomew Fair*'s Trouble-all, also haunted by lunacy and also calling for the official representative of law and order, they preserve faith in the 'warrant' behind action by retreat into the self. The moment of collision, with its proffer of reality, is a dangerous invitation refused.

The ultimate importance of collision, then, is that it provides the occasion upon which the self is enabled to confirm its refashioning of reality. At these moments the deluded mind ties together events in the outside world, and ties itself to the world by the illusion of human relationship. Since neither connection really exists, commitment to them means further and further progress into fantasy – the typical mode by which action in Jonsonian comedy advances.

Though Jonson professed himself to be writing in the spirit of the ancients, and cited Greek authority for his belief that 'The parts of a Comedie are the same with a *Tragedie*, and the end is partly the same' (*Discoveries*, ll. 2625–6), the premises of his comedy are directly anti-Aristotelian. Aristotle recommends the choice of incidents which have 'an appearance of design as it were in them; as for instance the statue of Mitys at Argos killed the author of Mitys' death by falling down on him . . .; for incidents like that we think to be not without meaning. A Plot, therefore, of this sort is necessarily finer than others' (*Poetics*, l. 1452a). But this sort of fine plot is limited to the imaginations of Jonson's characters. In Jonson's own plot coherence is formal and symbolic, but never personally meaningful. If final coherence is established, it is imposed from without in the name of ethically necessary order – a process not inherently different from manipulation, or from the imposition of psychologically necessary order, but aimed away from, rather than toward, individual freedom. The need for bondage is also very strong. Jonson's comic action appeals to the aspiration for significance; his moral endings, to the conviction of mediocrity – the belief that real strength is social strength, that real meaning is the meaning of the group, the company, the university, the church. Without these saving structures we would live, in a Jonsonian universe, in the midst of the comedy of non-interaction forever. With them, we can join in composing a harmonious balance of which each element is equally unimportant.

Committed to both its comic action and its ending, *Every Man in* provides conflicting answers to that most basic Jonsonian question: is non-interaction the cause or the effect of the characters' delusions? Jonson the critic and satirist would like us to deduce that it is effect: that a beneficent universe is distorted by, then rescued from, abnormality. But Jonson the comic genius deduces for us, rather, from the premises of an indifferent universe, splendid abnormalities of the protesting imagination.

SOURCE: extracts from Introduction to *Every Man in his Humor*, The Yale Ben Jonson, vol. v (1969) pp. 1–34.

NOTE

1. ['There is no greater pain; when one is unhappy, than remembering happy times.']

J. W. Lever

'THE SOCIAL COMEDY OF *EVERY MAN IN HIS HUMOUR*' (1971)

. . . the 'life of the play'[1] takes shape in terms of social comedy, a theme of unflagging interest to English audiences. Plautus and Terence had focussed almost exclusively on personal or domestic relationships: Jonson left the conventions of family life unquestioned, to concentrate on the absurdities of social climbing. Snobbery is the universal folly derided in *Every Man in his Humour*, whose real key word is not 'humour' but 'gentleman'. Through all the class gradations of its characters, from squire's nephew to shopkeeper's son, from seedy gallant to small clerk and semiliterate water-bearer, the aspiration to gentry typifies the fool. The fashionable cults of the day – hunting, duelling, tobacco-smoking, vociferous oaths – are ridiculed chiefly because they are practised as short cuts to the status of a gentleman. Stephen's eagerness to learn 'the sciences of hawking, and hunting' springs from his conviction that 'a gentleman mun show himselfe like a gentleman'. Matthew practises fencing in hope of acquiring 'a more sweet comely gentleman-like guard'. Cob is ironically rebuked by Clement for speaking against tobacco; whatever its ills, it is 'receiv'd in the courts of princes, the chambers of nobles, the bowers of sweet ladies, the cabbins of souldiers'. Bobadill's oaths are admiringly copied by Stephen, who longs for the right to swear 'as I am a gentleman, and a souldier'; even by Cob, in the belief that this raises him above the common run of water-bearers. Social ambition is the real impulse behind the cultivation of pseudo-humours. Stephen flourishes his melancholy as a passport for admission into the company of gallants. For Matthew, the son of a 'worshipfull fish-monger', melancholy and poetry go together as means to 'creepe, and wriggle into acquaintance with all the brave gallants about the towne'.

Braggarts and gulls were the stock-in-trade of Elizabethan authors; Jonson's individual contribution was to trace in minute detail their unending quest for social status. Stephen, while parroting his uncle's warning not to stand on his gentility, is so sensitive to possible slights that he vulgarly bullies Wellbred's servant for an innocuous remark. Edward Knowell retaliates by derisive play on Stephen's own phrase, 'I speake, to serve my turne':

Your turne, couss? . . . A gentleman of your sort, parts, carriage, and estimation, to talke o' your turne . . . like a tankard-bearer, at a conduit!

Cob implicitly burlesques such pretensions by his claim to fetch his pedigree from 'the Harrots bookes', being descended from '*Herring* the King of fish'. A mixture of shrewdness and naivety, he despises Matthew's gentlemanly affectations, his poeticizing and talk of '*Enterludes*', but is impressed by Bobadill's verbal flourishes. In turn, Bobadill and Matthew agree to despise Downright for his blunt language and rejection of shams, declaring that he lacks 'any gentleman-like part' and fails to 'carry himselfe like a gentleman of fashion'. While gull and gallant are portrayed in terms of their sobbery, the rogue succeeds by appealing to the common weakness. Brainworm's patter as a begging ex-soldier is laced with appeals to his victims' social vanity. 'I am a poore gentleman, a souldier. . . . You seeme to be gentlemen, well affected to martiall men.' Stephen's desire to obtain a Spanish sword at a low price is whetted by Brainworm's deferential 'you are a gentleman, give me what you please'. Even old Knowell is not impervious. Brainworm's obsequiousness gradually melts his caution; having enjoyed the satisfaction of delivering a moral lecture, he is willing to take the counterfeit soldier on trust. After Knowell, the lawyer's clerk Formal is easy game, happy to pay good money for the privilege of hearing a military man's discourse.

Unlike satire, comedy functions through a system of checks and balances. Instead of upholding a norm of good sense against foolish aberrations, it offsets one extreme by another, leaving the norm to build itself in the minds of the spectators. Old Knowell represents not exemplary wisdom but a limited degree of knowledge – the knowledge of his own generation, which borders on complacency as that of his son's generation tends to frivolity. Clement, the arbiter of other men's fortunes, is himself a random *deus ex machina*, who rewards Brainworm's rascality by making him partner at the evening's festivity. To infer a bitter scorn for authority, comparable with that shown in *Volpone*, would be unwarranted here; balanced scepticism is an attitude more fitting to comedy. Downright growls his contempt for Bobadill and Matthew, to be rebuked for intemperance by Kitely, whose own intemperance is presently shown. Each character undercuts the absurdities of the other, to be exposed for his own failings in turn. At the bottom of the scale, Cob is no mere target for laughter, but has the active function of burlesquing his superiors, mocking Stephen's pretensions through boasts of his royal lineage, and parodying Kitely's jealous outcries with his stage rant 'Revenge: vineger revenge: vineger, and mustard revenge.' All through the play the pattern of comic interaction weaves back and forth.

Standing out from the more type-cast figures are Bobadill and Kitely, whose inner vitality gives the appearance of existence 'in their own right'. Yet both are organically related to their wider setting. In a line of descent from Plautus's *miles gloriosus*, the Italian Signor Capitano, and Shakespeare's Falstaff, Bobadill's distinct personality has emerged from the overall theme. His peculiar trait is neither his boasting nor his cowardice but his craving for social esteem. The cherished image of himself as a soldier and a gentleman is projected in a jargon of rhetorical clichés, fencing terms, and army slang. Behind this verbiage he seeks to defend himself against the many slights and humiliations inflicted by life. His first appearance, drunk in the morning on a bench behind the curtain, reproduces that of Falstaff in *1 Henry IV*. But while Falstaff's natural buoyancy keeps him unperturbed in the presence of the king's son, Bobadill suffers acute dismay at the encounter with Matthew, son of a London fishmonger. Groping for his verbal armory he desperately struggles not to lose face. The threadbare lodgings become a convenient 'Cabbin', chosen to avoid unwelcome publicity. His great love is for privacy, 'above all the tumult, and roare of fortune'. At last he regains his poise in a flow of Italian duelling terms and through a fencing lesson improvised with bedstaffs. Unlike the braggart soldier of tradition, Bobadill hedges his boasts with genteel modesty. He has 'no skill i' the

earth', only 'some small rudiments', practised 'for noblemen, and
gentlemens use'. Concerning past exploits he is ostentatiously careful
not to claim sole credit for himself. True, he was the first to enter the
breach at Strigonium; but only after seven hundred resolute gentlemen
had lost their lives in the attempt. The enemy gunner whom he shot at
point-blank range was 'a man of no meane skill, and marke'. His plan to
save the nation from war involves the training of a team of nineteen
other gentlemen 'till they could all play very neare, or altogether as well
as my selfe'. Unfortunately no venture of Bobadill's is secure from other
men's ungentlemanly conduct – treason in war, hailshot in a duel,
Downright's beating with a stick. Somewhere there must be a place
where Bobadill's dream status as a soldier and a gentleman would be
accepted: in Venice, no doubt – 'you shall have there your *Nobilis*, your
Gentelezza'. At home, justice, embodied in the thick-skinned personality
of Clement, laughs at his claims. Declared a sham, he is excluded from
the company at supper and sent with his poor disciple Matthew to fast it
out in the courtyard. Harsher punishments were laid on him in the
quarto version; by the time of the revision Jonson realized that the worst
disgrace for Bobadill was the fate of an outsider.

Kitely too is part of the social comedy. It is important to recognize
that his jealousy is differently motivated from that of the stock domestic
cuckold. Kitely is not in fact deceived by his wife and sister; he only
deludes himself into a belief in his own cuckoldry; and the delusion has
grown up in the conditions of his life as a merchant. With a realism
comparable to Middleton's, the daily routine of the Elizabethan
business man is carefully sketched in – the bustle of transactions,
impending deals, appointments at the Exchange – set against the
enigmatic feminine confines of breakfast-room and parlor, and the alien
roistering of gallants in the warehouse. Kitely's insecurity originates in
his merchant's fear of seditious elements within his cherished domains;
only gradually does it come to center upon the morals of his womenfolk.
He worries as much about his business reputation as his marital peace.
Should Cash reveal his secret, he will be 'gone, / Lost i' my fame for
ever: talke for th'Exchange'. The comic situation is fully exploited, with
Kitely's dashings on and off stage, his misconstructions of his wife's most
innocent words, his sudden conviction that he has been poisoned. But in
its unfolding the comedy takes on a psychological dimension. Freudian
symbols and psychopathic beliefs need not be teased out of Kitely's
quite usual Elizabethan idioms.[2] What he undoubtedly manifests is a
state of abnormal anxiety. It appears in his overcautious, circuitous
mode of address with both Downright and Cash; in his tortuous
introspection; in his loss of capacity to make simple decisions. When not
overcome by jealousy he is a kindly, intelligent figure, considerate
towards his manager Cash, proud of Wellbred's accomplishments,

mildly reproachful of Downright's outbursts, which ironically he seeks
to restrain by an appeal to reason. His fears for his wife are voiced in
grave reflections on the vulnerability of beauty; in his analysis of his own
mental state he is dispassionate and well informed in the psychology of
his time. As the play mounts to a farcical climax outside Cob's house,
Kitely is manipulated, like the other characters, into the role of a
puppet, to be jerked back into sanity by Clement's commonsense
advice. He remains nevertheless a character of intrinsic interest, called
into being by the social context of the play, yet fully individualized by
Jonson's imaginative grasp.

The eighteenth-century theater, devoted to character acting, found
the sole justification of *Every Man in his Humour* in Kitely and Bobadill.
Garrick's production cut out whole scenes of the play while expanding
Kitely's part by an extra 270 lines written for the occasion. Without
minimizing Jonson's achievement in creating these characters, our own
age is more likely to recognize the worth of the drama as a whole, with
its tight construction, its development of all the latent comedy in the
social scene, its deep yet unsentimental understanding of diverse
attitudes in men of disparate conditions and ages. Many years of
experiment lay ahead before Jonson's genius came into full flower, but
this first mature work may stand in its own right as a fully realized
dramatic creation.

SOURCE: extract from Introduction to *Every Man in his Humour*
(1972) pp. xv–xx.

NOTES

1. [Referring to Eliot's comment that in Jonson 'the life of the character is
inseparable from the life of the drama'; see Part One.]
2. As in M. Seymour-Smith's comments on 'mine eye ejects', 'erection', etc.
(II iii 31, 71, and elsewhere) – New Mermaid edition (London, 1966).

Jonas A. Barish

FEASTING AND JUDGING IN JONSONIAN COMEDY (1972)

The impulse to judge – to sift, to grade, weigh, and evaluate –
culminates characteristically in Jonsonian comedy in a judgment scene
in which scores are settled, penalties prescribed, and rewards bes-
towed.[1] Along with our judicial sense, such scenes satisfy our aesthetic
sense; they bring all the strands of the plot into a close weave; they pass
its elements in review and formulate a conclusive attitude toward
them – one with which we may not always agree.

'Poetic justice', whether in life or art, implies that a person receives
his 'just deserts', often by some stroke of luck, some unexpected or even
magical turn of events. According to Miss Prism in *The Importance of
Being Earnest*, the good end happily and the bad end unhappily, and
'that is what fiction means'. That is also, in essence, what poetic justice
means. It brings about a truer justice than the more prosaic sort. It fits
punishment more perfectly to crime; it satisfies our desire to see order
prevail, and our wish to allow appropriate mitigations and exceptions.
It may, on occasion, confirm the world's coarser judgments, but usually
it also refines on them. The fact that Jonson's plays frequently end with
court scenes affords clear evidence of his concern for justice, but equally
notable is the fact that these scenes trade so heavily in fantasy: they
imaginatively allude to, rather than literally reproduce, the processes of
actual courts. Their verdicts preserve a mysteriously self-validating
quality not to be found outside such archetypes as the judgment
of Solomon or the decrees of Daniel. They feed our craving for equity
with small reference to mere law, for which Jonson shows increasingly
scant respect.

Jonson, as critics have noticed, was haunted throughout his career by
the problem of authority: who has the right to administer justice, and
how does he acquire that right?[2] Each play grapples anew with the
question and propounds its own experimental answers. Glancing over
Jonson's output as a whole, we can perceive a gradual abandonment of
the attempt to embody justice in figures of authority or public
institutions, and an increasing reliance on the happy conjunctions of wit
and chance. We discover also a rough inverse correlation between

severity of judgment and feasting. Where judicial stringency prevails,
the festive element tends to remain tentative and muted. Where the
festive note is strongly struck, judgment tends toward leniency. . . .

In *Every Man in his Humor* (1598), Jonson begins to experiment with a
more explicitly judicial finale, in which a spokesman for law presides
over the disentangling of the plot and the distribution of deserts. Justice
Clement is at once a properly constituted magistrate, 'a Justice here, an
excellent good Lawyer, and a great scholler', in Wellbred's reassuring
credentials, but also 'the onely mad, merrie, old fellow in *Europe*!' (F, III
v 53–5), whose whimsical humors insure that his justice will be anything but cut and dried. And so it proves. Clement holds court with a
nice sense of theater. He illustrates his fitness to judge an announced
soldier (Bobadill) and a supposed poet (Matthew) by donning armor to
receive the one, and reciting a sample of his own muse before hearing
the verse of the other. Discovering Brainworm to be at the root of the
day's confusions, he is prompted by Brainworm's happy skill in disguise
to renounce all rigor; twice he exuberantly toasts the offender. Then
comes the unorthodox sentence: 'Pledge me. Thou hast done, or assisted
in nothing, in my judgment, but deserves to bee pardon'd for the wit o'
the offence' (F, v iii 112–14). Brainworm's virtuosity in jest and his
theatrical talent thus call forth the judge's own vein of mirth; judicial
correction gives way to festive invitation. Keeping the promise of his
name, Clement proceeds to play the peacemaker with the rest as well,
urging them to drop their mutual grievances. Only two claimants seem
to warrant some stringency: Matthew, whose verses are burned in a fiery
sacrifice to the muses, and Bobadill, whose suit against Downright is
stingingly spurned. The sentence on these two is unorthodox in a new
way:

Well now my two Signior Out-sides, stand foorth, and lend me your large eares,
to a sentence, to a sentence: first you signior shall this night to the cage, and so
shall you sir, from thence to morrow morning, you signior shall be carried to the
market crosse, and be there bound: and so shall you sir, in a large motlie coate,
with a rodde at your girdle; and you in an olde suite of sackcloth, and the ashes
of your papers (save the ashes sirha) shall mourne all day, and at night both
together sing some ballad of repentance very pitteously, which you shall make
to the tune of *Who list to leade and a souldiers life*.

(Q, v iii 355–65)

The most striking feature of this penance is that for all its intricacy it
possesses only poetic validity. Clement, a fantast of a justice, imposes a
justice that is itself a fantasy. For neither Matthew nor Bobadill has
broken the law. Doubtless it is immoral to be a coward, as it is shameful
to pillage other men's verses, but to these as to multitudes of other
delinquencies the law does not extend. Clement ignores, at the same

time, offenses genuinely subject to statute and for which warrants have been issued, such as Stephen's theft of the cloak or Bobadill's beating of Cob. The punishments contemplated for Bobadill and Matthew – the one to dress in motley with a rod at his girdle, the other in sackcloth and in the ashes of his burnt poems, both to stand first in a cage, then in the marketplace, bound, mourning all day prior to singing a ballad of repentance at night, with the tune carefully specified – these recall hallucinations by Bosch or Brueghel more than they do the proceedings of courts of law. The whole device aims to turn the culprits into emblems of themselves, transfixing them with shame, and us with recognition, at this revelation of their natures.

In the folio, Clement explains why his corrective hand falls so heavily on Bobadill and Matthew after brushing the rest so lightly: 'Only these two, have so little of man in 'hem, they are no part of my care' (F, v v 2–3). This confirms our sense that the two are being punished not for what they have done but for what they are. What they are is unmanly: imposture, especially the forging of false credentials of valor or letters, constitutes a dereliction of manhood. Clement is chastising most stingingly the faults Jonson finds hardest to forgive, momentarily excluding these characters from the ranks of men, while letting the rest pass unreprimanded. But even the scorned pair receive gentler shrift in the folio:

> to dispatch away these, you signe o' the Souldier, and picture o' the *Poet* (but, both so false, I will not ha' you hang'd out at my dore till midnight) while we are at supper, you two shall penitently fast it out in my court, without; and, if you will, you may pray there, that we may be so merrie within, as to forgive, or forget you, when we come out.

> (F, v v 48–54)

The twain will not, this time, have to drink the cup of humiliation to the dregs; they will not have to parade in public as allegories of themselves; they will simply be barred from the general mirth. Stephen, Cob, and Tib are to be segregated in the buttery and provided with napkins and trenchers – Jonson leaves it uncertain whether he means this as a social or a moral segregation. The rest march off to a feast, at which the guest of honor, for his inventiveness in sport, will be Brainworm, invested (in the quarto version) in the very robes of justice. Somewhat like a boy bishop or a king of fools, he will preside for the duration of the feast in the magisterial chair itself. . . .

By the time Jonson's career was under way, Shakespeare had also written a number of comedies terminating in judgment scenes, in which a Duke or Prince presides over the reuniting of splintered families or sundered lovers, sometimes accompanying his acts with appropriate moral reflections. But Shakespeare tends to shun sentencing and

punishing. The closing lines of *Much Ado About Nothing* expressly refuse
to entertain punitive designs against the play's chief mischief-maker, for
to do so would mar the spirit of festivity, while the judicial fourth act of
The Merchant of Venice is followed by a fifth filled with terrestrial and
celestial music, as if to tease us out of all remembrance of legalism,
punishment, and crime.

To Jonson such Shakespearean casualness did not come easily.
Questions of justice seemed to demand careful accounting rather than
offhand theatrical dispatching. Shakespeare scarcely concerns himself
with the legitimacy of his dukes and princes; he simply assumes it.
Jonson tends to ponder the credentials of his judges and magistrates,
investing them with legal power but not necessarily equivalent moral
authority. In *Every Man in his Humor* Judge Clement possesses the official
status of a justice of the peace, but also the madcap personality of a
Simon Eyre [in *The Shoemakers' Holiday*]. It is the former that allows him
to settle the confusions among the dramatis personæ, but the latter that
confers on his judgments their humanity and corrective wisdom. . . .

It is evident that when we speak of justice in Jonsonian or any
comedy, we refer not merely to the legal forms for rendering judgment,
or even to the morality behind the decisions, but to an ordering
principle which conducts the characters to destinations appropriate to
their dramatic journeys. Justice decrees that a play play itself out to the
end, that it stabilize and equilibrate its various elements before taking
leave of them. Early in his career Jonson prefers the formal scene of
arraignment, which permits him to pass character and event in review
and sentence them – that is, assign meanings to them. We find that the
major comic successes occur when he balances a skeptical treatment of
legal process against an imaginatively conceived distribution of reward
and punishment. The comical satires, with their overpowering tri-
bunals, leave us slightly oppressed beneath the weight of so much
machinery; so, in a different way, do the savage parodies of due process
in *The Devil is an Ass* and *The Staple of News*. In the one case the law is too
worshipfully invoked as a salvation, in the other too furiously repudiated as a cheat and a delusion; in the last plays of all it is too wearily
disregarded. In the great middle comedies we find plenary justice
executed through spirited improvisations on normal procedure, according to a logic of the spirit no actual court could even approximate. Such
justice fosters our festive responses as well as our judicial approval; it
enables us to relish the follies of the fools and the peculations of the
knaves without making us feel that we are endorsing the inadmissible.

SOURCE: extracts from essay in *Renaissance Drama*, new ser., v
(1972) 7–8, 9–12, 13–14, 34–5.

NOTES

1. See the paragraphs on this subject by Harry Levin, 'An Introduction to Ben Jonson', in *Ben Jonson: A Collection of Critical Essays*, ed. Jonas A. Barish (Englewood Cliffs, N.J., 1963) pp. 48–9; originally published as Introduction to *Selected Works of Ben Jonson* (New York, 1938).

2. The fullest treatment of this theme to date appears in John J. Enck, *Jonson and the Comic Truth* (Madison, Wis., 1957), especially in the passages indexed under 'Justice'.

A. Richard Dutton

THE SIGNIFICANCE OF JONSON'S REVISION OF *EVERY MAN IN HIS HUMOUR* (1974)

A number of major changes marked the development of Jonson's career as a dramatist, but none is more striking than the difference of tone and approach between *Volpone* (1605) and *Epicoene* (1609). Professor Harry Levin neatly summed up what has come to be the general attitude to this change in saying: 'As [Jonson's] powers of realistic depiction came into full play, he gradually relinquished his loudly proclaimed moral purposes.'[1] This interesting assertion – based upon a fanciful analogy between the supposed 'metempsychology' of Pythagoras's soul, described in *Volpone*, I ii 1–62, and the equally supposed mellowing of Jonson's satiric temper after that play – sees the conflation of two popular lines of thought on Jonson's career: Jonson the realist, the journalist-depictor of the foibles of his age, and Jonson the satirist who grew to be more tolerant and indulgent with age. Both are in their various ways myths, and to some extent they feed on each other, as may be evident in the words of one of their most enthusiastic, but least critical proponents, John Palmer. Regarding *Epicoene*, for instance, he states that 'there are no intensities, and the moralist is silent . . . There is none of the satire which in *Volpone* bites into the substance of human nature, but a merry confounding of impostures and eccentricity.'[2] Merry confounding, indeed. 'Volpone,' he continues, 'playing upon his dupes for the love of the game, is a moral portent. The rogues whom we meet in *The Alchemist* have no such significance. Livelihood is the beginning and end of their endeavour, and the play ends merrily with the ablest villain of the pack successfully outwitting the rest and making his peace with authority.'[3] Ends merrily, indeed. 'Jonson is nowhere more tolerant, open of mind and sense than in this play [*Bartholomew Fair*]. It is a fit expression of the merry England which was passing.'[4] Merry England? This picture of open-minded, avuncular amiability in the plays of the middle period leaves much to be desired – almost as much as Edmund Wilson's antithetical, pseudo-Freudian picture of a morose Ben Jonson.[5] Nevertheless, the suggestion that the plays after *Volpone* are somehow more indulgent, less satirically wounding, remains widely held, so that even Jonas Barish thinks in terms of 'the geniality and relaxed moral temper of the later plays, as typified by *Bartholomew Fair*'.[6]

Of course, *something* does happen to the tone and character of the plays. We have lost the in-jokes and the back-biting of the plays belonging to the so-called War of the Theatres; there is none of the virulence of a Macilente, or the complacent smugness of a Crites – or, if they do appear, it is only to be parodied in a Surly or a Justice Overdo. No later play creates the same sense of insistent moral corruption as *Volpone*. But impressionistic accounts of a change of heart in Jonson himself are hardly adequate to explain the complex alteration of aims and techniques which produce the great plays of the middle period. The apparent strength of Professor Levin's statement hinges upon a genuinely acute observation – that the supposed change of 'tone' or 'attitude' in the plays after 1605 coincides with Jonson's adoption of fully-realized, contemporary London settings for his comedies. But the process of cause and effect is surely more involved than he suggests. Traditionally, of course, Jonson is, with Dickens, the quintessential London writer, but it is important to bear in mind that his earlier plays are not on the whole located in London. The obvious exception to that statement is *Every Man out of his Humour*, which is incidentally set in London; one scene is marked 'The Middle Aisle of St Paul's', and another 'A Room in the Mitre', but Jonson can scarcely be said to capitalize on these settings, and the prevailing tone of the play is set by the stylization of the characters, which is quasi-Italian. With this exception, none of Jonson's plays to which we can fix a definite date was located in London until 1609, when *Epicoene* appeared. After that date, all the plays (excepting only *Catiline*) were unmistakably set in contemporary London, though this does become more nominal in the very late plays. The fact remains that Jonson had already written one masterpiece, *Volpone*, before making what appears to have been a deliberate and calculated switch to recognizably Jacobean London settings. The notion that Jonson gradually developed a talent for

realism hardly seems to fit the facts. It was Swinburne who complained
that: 'There is nothing accidental in the work of Ben Jonson';[7] and it is
as if Jonson deliberately appointed himself as playwright to the city, just
as he had effectively become masque-maker to the Court at this period.
No one appears to have commented much on this fact; Brian Gibbons,
for instance, rather glosses over it when he includes Jonson's plays in the
'genre' of 'city comedy'.[8] It seems to me important, and it lends
particular significance to the revision of *Every Man in his Humour* – the
revised version of which was deliberately placed at the beginning of the
1616 folio.

The date of the revision of the play is one of the more vexed problems
of Jonsonian scholarship. Percy Simpson argues a strong case for 1612/
13 in his edition of the play;[9] more recent editors, like G. B. Jackson and
J. W. Lever[10] outline the difficulties more fully. The evidence is
confusing and circumstantial, and conclusions can only be tentative,
but there would seem to be good reason for supposing that the revision
might occupy some of the time that Jonson was off the public stage, after
Volpone (1605) and before *Epicoene* (1609). This does not preclude the
possibility of further revision for the 1616 folio, for which the prologue
was obviously written. But the timing of the revision, though intriguing,
is not crucial; what matters here is that we have an unparalleled
opportunity to study the writer in his maturity (the period 1606–13–
the accepted terminal dates of the argument – is certainly within the
time of Jonson's best and most original dramatic writing) reassessing
material he had already used much earlier in his career. Whatever date
we choose, there can be no doubt that the revision is linked with the
impulse which led Jonson to set his other plays in London. Certainly, no
one who has deliberately compared the two texts of *Every Man in his
Humour* could doubt but that the change of locale was a thoroughly
calculated move. The London 'colouring' is neither casual nor
incidental, but comes as it were in strategic bursts, where it is most
telling, most notably in the opening scenes; for instance, the idiotic
Stephen grows pompous: 'Because I dwell at *Hogsden*, I shall keepe
companie with none but the archers of *Finsburie*? or the citizens, that
come a ducking to *Islington* ponds?' (F, 1 i 47); 'mine uncle here is a man
of a thousand a yeare, *Middlesex* land' (F, 1 ii 3). The former passage is a
completely original insertion; in the latter, the word 'Middlesex' is
interpolated in a bald line of the quarto (1 i 82–3). One effect is precisely
to define Stephen's milieu and the nature of his pretensions to the
audience that Jonson was writing for; familiarity makes for ease of
communication. On a very basic level, the local insertions act as clearer
strokes of the pen in a rather blurred original picture: 'over the fields to
More-gate' was obviously much easier for Jonson's audience to con-
ceptualize than a bare 'to *Florence*'. On this level, they are no more

significant than Jonson's obvious efforts to clarify the sister/sister-in-law/
brother/half-brother relationships complex, which is needlessly vague
and confusing in the quarto, or than the tightening-up of the
denouement in the last act. We expect this kind of care from a
professional.

Swinburne and others have seen more to it than that:

Translated from the imaginary or fantastic Italy in which at first they lived and
moved and had their being to the actual and immediate atmosphere of
contemporary London, the characters gain even more in lifelike and interesting
veracity or verisimilitude than in familiar attraction and homely association.
Not only do we feel that we know them better, but we perceive that they are
actually more real and cognisable creatures than they were under their former
conditions of dramatic existence.[11]

Herford and Simpson (vol. 1, p. 359) are similarly enthusiastic about
the Balzacian depiction of contemporary London manners:

Ben Jonson knew too little of Italy for effective realism, even had this been his
aim. The transfer to London liberated his vast fund of local knowledge. The
London of the Folio is crowded with precise localities which have only vague
equivalents in the Florence of the Quarto. It acquires a distinct physiognomy
and atmosphere, as Florence never does.

The emphasis in both these accounts seems questionable: the former
sees the revision in terms of a move towards a rather naïve, nineteenth-
century form of verisimilar realism, while the latter gives a faintly
condescending impression of Jonson as a frustrated urban folk-lorist.
Either of these accounts is surely misleading if taken in isolation, and not
related to Jonson's art as a whole. And does the London of the folio
really acquire a 'distinct physiognomy'? Although the play is recognizably located in London, the setting is essentially passive and
incidental to the story. By comparison with Lovewit's house and
Bartholomew Fair it is a feeble outline, in spite of the care that has been
lavished on it. The revision points the way in which Jonson's technique
improved and intensified, but it is not up to the standard of the best
plays (even though Swinburne exalted it as virtually *the* best play). This
is not simply a question of quantity – of how much realistic material is
included – but of function; the setting of the revised play is adequate
and a distinct improvement on the original, but it is not so integral to
the drama as to form the basis of a completely new dimension to the
satire, as I shall shortly suggest is the case in the best plays.

There would be little point in compiling a painstaking list of all the
alterations; the general principles are agreed upon, even though
interpretations of them differ. Jonson did not simply alter the locale of
his play; we find ourselves short of differentiated terms to describe the
kind of improvements in the characterization, the style of prose and

verse, even, ultimately, the shape of the play – all of which contribute to what is generally recognized as the greater 'realism' of the folio version. A number of key passages reveal a thorough revision, affecting even basic word-style; Wellbred's intercepted letter, for instance, the main-spring of the action, is almost completely rewritten. There is less in the grandiose manner about Apollo and the Muses, which is part of a general toning-down of references to poets and poetry throughout the play, including the excision of the much-praised and often-quoted speech by Lorenzo Junior (Q, v iii 312–43). The early play smells very much of Jonson the young Renaissance poet, flexing his new-found muscles and glorying in his traditional powers, perhaps at the risk of identifying too readily with Lorenzo Junior. Although the function of the poet is implicitly a key issue in all Jonson's plays,[12] it has little direct bearing on the action of this play and is properly deleted. It is perhaps the surest sign of Jonson's maturity in the revision that he had the heart to cut it out, in spite of its intrinsic merit. In place of the sententiousness of the original, the folio letter captures much better the bantering wit of the young man-about-town, revealing a closer attention to the type-veracity of the characters: *'Doe not conceive that antipathy betweene us, and* Hogs-den; *as was betweene* Jewes, *and hogs-flesh'* (F, ɪ ii 74). The style is still affected and 'clever' (this is part of Wellbred) but the idiom is snappier and more convincingly spontaneous (less 'literary') in its flow of ideas than the original, and this makes Knowell Senior's suspicious misunder-standing all the more credible. *'Leave thy vigilant father, alone, to number over his greene apricots, evening, and morning, o' the north-west wall'* (F, ɪ ii 75). This is taken up by the slow-witted and literal-minded Knowell Senior: 'Why should he thinke, I tell my Apri-cotes?' (F, ɪ ii 103). The result of such a tiny detail is a very neat and credible demonstration of old and young minds working on different wave-lengths – which is perhaps the central theme of the play. It sets old Knowell off on the chase.

It is notable how integrated the improvements are; the local and verbal realism – familiar settings, topical allusions, and a wider use of colloquial idioms (for example the pun on Hogsden) – all contribute to what we might call an increased psychological realism. This is basically a technical improvement, rather than a fundamental change in Jonson's style; he is not attempting to achieve, for instance, a Shakespearian 'roundness'. On the contrary, what takes place is a closer and more precise definition of Jonson's personal idiom – a development of something already there in the quarto. The changes in old Knowell's lines reveal his increasing grasp of character-decorum, and his ability to capture the quality of an eccentric, even deranged, personality. There is a greater terseness to imply his suspicious and impatient mind. His lines are re-cast to seem less studied and 'balanced': for example, 'Go to, you are a prodigal, and selfe-wilde foole' (Q, ɪ i 46), becomes 'You are a

prodigall absurd cocks-combe: Goe to' (F, 1 i 54). The sense of the line is
scarcely altered, but the quarto has no life in it at all, while the folio
builds with indignation, giving a genuine stab to the 'Goe to' at the end.
Stilted and artificial formulae, like the following advice to Stephano,
are simply omitted from the folio:

> Cosen, lay by such superficiall formes,
> And entertaine a perfect reall substance.[13]   (Q, 1 i 74)

The net result of such changes is to achieve a harsh, realistic style of
verse, analogous to the baroque, anti-Ciceronian prose, so well analysed
by Jonas Barish.[14] Knowell Senior's reaction to the letter, which in the
quarto is pathetically tame: 'Well, it is the strangest letter that ever I
read . . .' (1 i 176) explodes in the folio at the signature, 'From the windmill':

> From the *Burdello*, it might come as well;
> The *Spittle*: or *Pict-hatch*.   (1 ii 92)

Once again, the psychological actualization and the London setting
merge perfectly and reinforce one another. Old Knowell is not simply
an abstract 'humour' – he is a manifestation of the London in the play,
where suspicious, rather cynical old age is out of tune with regenerative
nature and society, represented here by the playful vitality of the young
men.

There is a parallel example of more concrete and particularized
dialogue in the case of Kitely. A comparison with Thorello quickly
reveals Jonson's improved command of one of the fundamentals of his
art: the precise definition and speech-depiction of an obsessively closed
and fixed state of mind. Kitely's jealousy is embodied in the nervous,
erratic qualities of his speech; his own description of the way his mind
works, for instance, is adapted in such a way that it expresses, rather
than merely announces, the inner tension. The mellifluous, Shakespearian metaphor:

> my imaginations like the sands,
> Runne dribling foorth to fill the mouth of time
>
> (Q, III i 43)

becomes a less 'poetic', but more anxious:

> my' imaginations runne, like sands,
> Filling up time.   (F, III iii 50)

Kitely's anxiety is acted out at length in this ludicrous scene, when he
debates with himself whether to confide in Thomas or not. The basic
idea, in the quarto, is conveyed with a wild logic, which is obviously to
the point, but it has little definition or dramatic sense; in the folio, the

insight becomes clearer, shrewder, and more explicit. When, for instance, he imagines some prevarication on Thomas's part about taking an oath of secrecy, he reflects:

> He is no puritane, that I am certaine of.
> What should I thinke of it?   (Q, III i 80)

In the folio, this sober, abstracted reflection takes on new definition and concrete dimensions; this is achieved jointly by an infusion of realistic detail and a disjointed word pattern, which is helped by the over-running of the lines:

> H'is no precisian, that I am certaine of.
> Nor rigid *Roman*-catholike. Hee'll play,
> At *Fayles*, and *Tick-tack*, I have heard him sweare.
> What should I thinke of it?   (F, III iii 88)

The deranged running-together of ideas adds far more weight to the question, and creates a much more convincing evocation of the jealous man.

By almost every criterion, in fact, the revised *Every Man in his Humour* is an improvement on the original; the diffuse plot is made slightly clearer, the denouement is shortened, made more straightforward and intelligible, while the characterization and the setting are more fully realized. But do the composite improvements constitute an essentially different kind of play? It would be a mistake to see the new psychological realism as an end in itself, the whole point of the changes, just as it was misguided of Swinburne and others to see the 'verisimilar' realism of time and place as an end in itself. The fact is that Jonson's personal style and growing competence have stamped themselves on the revised version of the play; and with these qualities comes a fuller realization of his mature preoccupations. The commitment behind his writing is more surely engaged, and while that may express itself through psychological and verisimilar realism, these are only means to an end.

The most significant improvements in the later version of the play remain improvements within Jonson's own terms, and there are those who find these terms inadequate, however competently they are executed. Interestingly, it is Swinburne, who had a love–hate relationship with Jonson's writing, who best sums up the most deeply-felt objection: 'it is difficult to believe that Ben Jonson can have believed, even with some half-sympathetic and half-sardonic belief, in all the leading figures of his invention'.[15] However true the characters are to their age, however laboriously accurate Jonson is in their delineation, they lack 'the sympathetic faith of the creator in his creatures', 'the vital impulse of the infallible imagination'. In short, they are not alive in the sense of suggesting the full complexity of persons in real life. The unspoken figure of Shakespeare stands in the background, and Jonson has suffered much for neither being, nor pretending to be, Shakespeare. A study of the revision emphasizes that Jonson never pretended to depict the 'full humanity' of his subjects; for all the increase in realism, his concern for human life and values manifests itself in other ways. The act of creation for Jonson is also an act of judgement. There is a paradox in all his plays, which must lie behind Swinburne's doubts, between the patient effort which goes towards the solid depiction of his characters, and the structural logic of the drama, which is invariably reductive, bent on questioning and often destroying what he has created. He reveals a fully-engaged concern for humanity, for a sane and rational society, in his determination to ridicule and destroy manifestations of folly, which he regards as socially divisive and morally degenerate. Kitely and Knowell Senior are simple examples of typical Jonsonian characters; Justice Clement – an uncomplicated *deus ex machina* of right-thinking and social harmony – arraigns them and bids them put off: 'you, master KNO'WELL, your cares; master KITELY, and his wife, their jealousie' (F, v v 71). At this point, in complete reversal of the care which we have seen Jonson taking to present them, they cease to have any significance; they cease to have any existence, dramatic or otherwise. This has nothing to do with Jonson's alleged lack of 'the sympathetic faith of the creator in his creatures'; it is the working-out of the moral and humane principle that lies at the heart of Jonson's drama. The realism that matters to Jonson is neither verisimilar nor, ultimately, psychological – though these are pieces of the pattern, means to an end – but moral.[16]

The 'characters', Kitely and Knowell Senior, are manifestations of folly, embodiments of a diseased condition which is more than merely psychological and attacks the fabric of natural social harmony.[17] The common distinguishing feature of such folly is that the afflicted creatures have lost touch with 'reality', creating private worlds of fantasy and illusion in its place. It is in the tension between the supposed and the actual 'reality' that Jonsonian drama is generated. We can see it as a function of the realism of the London settings to act as one of the terms of reference for what is real and true, in sharp contrast to the illusions that flourish among them. Bobadill, for instance, lets the ease of his bragging façade get the better of him, and he inadvertently slips into the truth when he mentions: '*Turne-bull, White-chappell, Shore-ditch*, which were then my quarters, and since upon the *Exchange*' (IV vii 44). The sordid reality of brothels and doss-houses suddenly appears, incongruously, in his fanciful bravado. This is only a small example, and the London setting in *Every Man in his Humour* does not really work consistently or cohesively enough in this way to advance the tension.

Old Knowell, Kitely, Bobadill and the rest are splendidly executed cameos, but the London setting does not give sufficient focus to suggest that they are all manifestations of a common condition; this, coupled with the fact that the action is too episodic, prevents the drama from achieving the inclusive, portentous quality of the best plays. It remains an indictment of follies, rather than an insight into human nature. G. B. Jackson makes a similar point: 'London is a neutral setting in which society means merely a collocation of varied types; it cannot offer a hard ethical core. The constant insistence upon the locale, by providing a conceptual center, goes some way toward disguising the lack of an evaluative center, but it is no substitute' [see Miss Jackson's essay above]. This judgement is made in implicit contrast with Volpone's Venice, True-wit's London, Lovewit's house, and Bartholomew Fair, each of which constitutes, in her terms, 'an evaluative center' – they are the stable realities against which the private follies which pass through them are measured.

This is true, but it is only a partial solution to what sets *Volpone*, *Epicoene*, *The Alchemist*, and *Bartholomew Fair* above the early 'humour' plays (including the revised *Every Man in his Humour*, for all its improvements) and also above the so-called dotages. In these plays, Jonson comes closest to resolving the tensions which are ever-present in his art – the divergent aims of creation and destruction being one – by compounding them with those of the dramatic medium itself; that is, he equates the moral reality, which is expressed in the tension between the supposed and the actual, with the ambiguous reality of the dramatic illusion itself. He self-consciously plays around with what is real on stage and what only seems to be real. The role of Peregrine in *Volpone*, and the English elements generally (together with the subsequent parodying of the satirist-figures – Surly, Overdo, etc. and their privileged relationship with the audience); the double illusion of the boy-actor in *Epicoene*; the special resilience of Face in his 'masters worships house, here, in the *friers*', which depends on his ability to be all things to all men, including the audience – as his closing address to them slyly hints; and the whole business of the contract between the author and the audience, coupled with the puppet-show climax, in *Bartholomew Fair*: each of these is a function of what is real and what is illusory in the dramatic art itself. These are not merely technical tricks or embellishments, but underlie a serious intensification and growing sophistication in Jonson's art. In the early plays – and, in this respect, *Every Man in his Humour* remains an early play, for all its mature touches – the audience remained essentially outside the dramatic illusion, passing judgement upon it; the relationship between the play and the audience was essentially static, and the moment of dissolution, where someone with the role, if perhaps not the manner, of a Justice Clement finally ostracized the follies, left a vacuum in which the satirist seemed, all too patly, to have cured the ills of the world. The self-conscious and largely explicit playing with the dramatic illusion, which is a crucial feature of the best plays, helps to break down the formal barriers; it introduces a flexibility which is analogous to the moving camera in cinematography. It seems plausible to suggest that the strong contemporary flavour and the London settings of the plays after 1609 further help to break down the barrier between the stage and the audience, implicating the latter far more strongly *within* the process of recognizing and exposing folly. There are perhaps two major results of this shift: one is to involve the audience in such a way that, from being passive judges, they become agents within the satiric process, if not themselves objects of the satire; the second is to remove the bland finality of the early plays – the solutions of the plays are far more ambiguous, leaving essential problems, unresolved, in the laps of the audience.[18]

Perhaps the most significant feature of the revision of *Every Man in his Humour*, then, is how limited, for all the neatening, tightening, and contemporary flavour, the revision actually is. There is nothing to suggest that Jonson's basic aims have altered, or that his moral conscience is any the less stringent. On the contrary, an investigation of what the revised play lacks in comparison with the 'realistic' plays of its own period suggests that the superiority of those plays is a matter of organization and of manipulation of the medium, rather than a thinning of the satiric impulse. With its episodic structure and the simplistic dismissal of its foolish characters, the folio *Every Man in his Humour* remains an early play, its 'moral purposes' self-evident to the on-looking audience. But it is a sign of maturity, and not geniality, that these are less 'loudly proclaimed' when Jonson's attention shifts from the characters within his plays to their mirror-images in the audience. Jonson's 'powers of realistic depiction' do not portend a decline of moral fervour, but an ironic recognition of the actual powers of the satirist, which are limited by the capacity of the audience to recognize their own shortcomings when they see them. If Jonson does undergo a 'metempsychosis' after 1605, it is not an indulgent frame of mind that he acquires, but the skills and wiles of the old Fox that he 'mortifies' at the end of *Volpone*.

SOURCE: essay in *Modern Language Review*, LXIX (1974) 241–9.

NOTES

1. Harry Levin, 'Jonson's Metempsychosis', *Philological Quarterly*, XXII (1943) 239.

2. John Palmer, *Ben Jonson* (London, 1934) p. 176.

3. Ibid., p. 184.

4. Ibid., p. 199.

5. Edmund Wilson, 'Morose Ben Jonson', in *The Triple Thinkers* (New York, 1948).

6. Jonas A. Barish, 'Ovid, Juvenal and *The Silent Woman*', *PMLA*, LXXI (1956) 213.

7. A. C. Swinburne, *A Study of Ben Jonson* (London, 1889) p. 9.

8. Brian Gibbons, *Jacobean City Comedy* (London, 1968).

9. *Every Man in his Humour*, ed. Percy Simpson (Oxford, 1919).

10. *Every Man in his Humor*, ed. G. B. Jackson, The Yale Ben Jonson (London and New Haven, Conn., 1969) Appendix 2; *Every Man in his Humour*, ed. J. W. Lever, Regents Renaissance Drama Series (London, 1972) pp. xi–xii.

11. Swinburne, *Study of Jonson*, p. 13.

12. He frequently referred to his plays as 'poems', particularly when he was standing on his dignity: see the epistle dedicating *Volpone* to 'the Most Noble and Most Equal Sisters, The Two Famous Universities'.

13. It is, of course, always possible that Jonson realized now naïvely self-revelatory of his own artistic theory that advice is.

14. Jonas A. Barish, *Ben Jonson and the Language of Prose Comedy* (Cambridge, Mass., 1960).

15. Swinburne, *Study of Jonson*, p. 39.

16. There is a parallel here with the scrupulous historical 'realism' of the tragedies, particularly *Sejanus*. They are painstaking monuments of scholarship and accuracy, and yet their authenticity is ultimately a sham; what emerges from the close attention to historical 'fact' and realistic detail is an interpretation of the given sources which amounts to moral propaganda.

17. See J. D. Redwine Jr, 'Beyond Psychology: The Moral Basis of Jonson's Theory of Humour Characterisation', *Journal of English Literary History*, XXVIII (1961) 316–34.

18. This last paragraph is, of necessity, only the outline of a theory, which I hope to have the opportunity of substantiating at a later date.

3. REVIEWS OF PRODUCTIONS
1751–1937

Arthur Murphy

'DAVID GARRICK AS KITELY' (1801)

Having by his performance of *Abel Drugger*, made the *Alchymist* a
favourite play, he chose to bring forward the comedy of *Every Man in his
Humour*. Having carefully retouched the play in several passages, he
added an entire scene in the fourth act between himself and *Dame Kitely*.
To disguise his suspicions, he assumed an air of gaiety, but under that
mask the corrosions of jealousy were seen in every feature. Such was the
expression of that various face, that the mixed emotions of his heart were
strongly marked by his looks and the tone of his voice. . . . *Dame Kitely*
tells [*Justice Clement*], that *Cobb's* house is a place of ill fame; and that she
went thither in quest of her husband. '*Did you find him there?*' says the
Justice. In that instant *Kitely* interposes, saying, in a sharp eager tone, '*I
found her there*.' He who remembers how Garrick uttered those words,
slapping his hand on the table, as if he made an important discovery,
must acknowledge, trifling as it may now be thought, that it was a
genuine stroke of nature. . . .

It must be added, that a comedy, so completely acted, was hardly
ever seen on the English stage. Garrick, Woodward in *Bobadil*, Yates,
and Shuter, and indeed all the performers were so correct and natural,
that the play drew crowded audiences, and kept possession of the stage
during the manager's life.[1]

SOURCE: extracts from *The Life of David Garrick*, vol. 1 (1801).

NOTE

1. [Garrick revived *Every Man in* frequently between 1751 and 1776, when he
retired from the stage. He acted Kitely ninety times. The performances of
Henry Woodward, Richard Yates (Brainworm), and Edward Shuter (Stephen)
were also highly acclaimed. See the anonymous *London Chronicle* article above,
Part Two, section 1, and the discussion of the stage history of the play in the
Introduction.]

William Hazlitt

'EVERY MAN IN HIS HUMOUR AT DRURY LANE' (1816)

Mr. [Edmund] KEAN had for his benefit at Drury-Lane Theatre, on Wednesday, the Comedy of *Every Man in his Humour*. This play acts much better than it reads. It has been observed of BEN JONSON, that he painted not so much human nature as temporary manners, not the characters of men, but their *humours*, that is to say, peculiarities of phrase, modes of dress, gesture, &c. which becoming obsolete, and being in themselves altogether arbitrary and fantastical, have become unintelligible and uninteresting. Brainworm is a particularly dry and abstruse character. We neither know his business nor his motives; his plots are as intricate as they are useless, and as the ignorance of those he imposes upon is wonderful. This is the impression in reading it. Yet from the bustle and activity of this character on the stage, the changes of dress, the variety of affected tones and gipsey jargon, and the limping, distorted gestures, it is a very amusing exhibition, as Mr. [Joseph] MUNDEN plays it. Bobadill is the only actually striking character in the play, or which tells equally in the closet and the theatre. The rest, Master Matthew, Master Stephen, Cob and Cob's Wife, were living in the sixteenth century. But from the very oddity of their appearance and behaviour, they have a very droll and even picturesque effect when acted. It seems a revival of the dead. We believe in their existence when we see them. As an example of the power of the stage in giving reality and interest to what otherwise would be without it, we might mention the scene in which Brainworm praises Master Stephen's leg. The folly here is insipid, from its seeming carried to an excess, – till we see it; and then we laugh the more at it, the more incredible we thought it before.

The pathos in the principal character, Kitely, is 'as dry as the remainder biscuit after a voyage'. There is, however, a certain good sense, discrimination, or *logic of passion* in the part, which Mr. KEAN pointed in such a way as to give considerable force to it. In the scene where he is about to confide the secret of his jealousy to his servant, Thomas, he was exceedingly happy in the working himself up to the execution of his design, and in the repeated failure of his resolution. The reconciliation-scene with his wife had great spirit, where he tells her, to

shew his confidence, that 'she may sing, may go to balls, may dance',
and the interruption of this sudden tide of concession with the
restriction – 'though I had rather you did not do all this' – was a master-
stroke.[1] It was perhaps the first time a parenthesis was ever spoken on
the stage as it ought to be. Mr. K EAN certainly often repeats this artifice
of abrupt transition in the tones in which he expresses different passions,
and still it always pleases, – we suppose, because it is natural. This
gentleman is not only a good actor in himself, but he is the cause of good
acting in others. The whole play was got up very effectually.
Considerable praise is due to the industry and talent shewn by
Mr. [John] H ARLEY, in Captain Bobadill. He did his best in it, and
that was not ill. He delivered the Captain's well-known proposal for
the pacification of Europe, by killing twenty of them each his man a day,
with good emphasis and discretion. Bobadill is undoubtedly the hero of
the piece; his extravagant affectation carries the sympathy of the
audience along with it, and his final defeat and exposure, though
exceedingly humorous, is the only affecting circumstance in the play.
Mr. H ARLEY's fault in this and other characters is, that he too
frequently assumes mechanical expressions of countenance and bye-
tones of humour, which have not any thing to do with the individual
part. Mr. [Richard] H UGHES personified Master Matthew to the life:
he appeared 'like a man made after supper of a cheese-paring'.
M UNDEN did Brainworm with laudable alacrity. [William]
O XBERRY's Master Stephen was very happily hit off; nobody plays the
traditional fool of the English stage so well; he seems not only foolish,
but fond of folly. The two young gentlemen, Master Wellbred and
Master Edward Knowell, were the only insipid characters.

SOURCE: article in *The Examiner*, 8 June 1816.

NOTE

1. [A loose paraphrase of a speech inserted into IV viii in Garrick's
adaptation – *Every Man in his Humour* . . . *With Alterations and Additions* (London,
1752) p. 46 – which was the version Hazlitt saw.]

Anonymous

'WILLIAM CHARLES MACREADY AS KITELY' (1838)

A singular proof of the masterly skill of [Macready] consists in his excluding from Kitely every particle of sympathy or pity. We laugh at him, and are glad that his business suffers such serious interruptions from his jealousy. That is all. Such an effect is more surprising in Mr. Macready's hands, since it is the characteristic of his acting to idealize his characters, and venture everything, even to a fault now and then, for the sympathies of his audience. – And we are really, after all, not sure that a remote touch of pity did not cross us, when, in the closing scene of the third act with Cob, after that worthy person had asked – 'By my troth, sir, will you have the truth of it?' – Kitely was made to drop his voice with fear, and falter out with an agonized effort to seem calm and ready to hear – 'Oh I, good Cob: I pray thee, heartily.' Yet this was a subtle touch of nature, which we could not wish away.

SOURCE: extract from article in *The Theatrical Examiner*, 29 July 1838.

Charles and Mary Cowden Clarke

'CHARLES DICKENS AS BOBADILL' (1878)

The way in which Charles Dickens impersonated that arch braggart, Captain Bobadill, was a veritable piece of genius: from the moment when he is discovered lolling at full length on a bench in his lodging, calling for a 'cup o' small beer' to cool down the remnants of excitement from last night's carouse with a set of roaring gallants, till his final boast of having 'not so much as once offer'd to resist' the 'coarse fellow' who set upon him in the open streets, he was capital.[1] The mode in which he went to the back of the stage before he made his exit from the first scene of Act II, uttering the last word of the taunt he flings at Downright with a bawl of stentorian loudness – 'Scavenger!' and then darted off the stage at full speed; the insolent scorn of his exclamation, 'This a *Toledo*? pish!' bending the sword into a curve as he spoke; the swaggering assumption of ease with which he leaned on the shoulder of his interlocutor, puffing away his tobacco smoke and puffing it off as 'your right *Trinidado*'; the grand impudence of his lying when explaining how he would despatch scores of the enemy, – 'challenge twentie more, kill them; twentie more, kill them; twentie more, kill them too'; ending by 'twentie score, that's two hundreth; two hundreth a day, five dayes a thousand; fortie thousand; fortie times five, five times fortie, two hundreth dayes kills them all up, by computation', rattling the words off while making an invisible sum of addition in the air, and scoring it conclusively with an invisible line underneath, – were all the very height of fun.

It was noteworthy, as an instance of the forethought as to effect given to even the slightest points, that he and [John] Leech (who played Master Matthew) had their stage-wigs made, for the parts they played in Ben Jonson's comedy, of precisely opposite cut: Bobadill's being fuzzed out at the sides and extremely bushy, while Master Matthew's was flat at the ears and very highly peaked above his forehead. In the green-room, between the acts, after Bobadill has received his drubbing and been well cudgelled in the fourth act, and has to reappear in the first scene of the fifth act, I saw Charles Dickens wetting the plume of vari-coloured feathers in his hat, and taking some of them out, so as to give an utterly crest-fallen look to his general air and figure. 'Don't take out the *white* feather!' I said.

SOURCE: extract from *Recollections of Writers* (1878).

NOTE

1. [Dickens first performed the role in 1845. The performance referred to here, his last, was given at the Haymarket in 1848. For further details, see Introduction.]

Anonymous

COMIC COCKNEYS: *EVERY MAN IN HIS HUMOUR* AT STRATFORD (1937)

Ben Jonson recommends his comedy, the first under a new plan, because it is not like Shakespeare's absurd histories but consists of

> deedes, and language, such as men doe use:
> And persons, such as *Comœdie* would chuse.

It was an excellent idea, but at the present time the result must seem to us highly paradoxical. For it was Jonson's pedantry – the influence of the classical drama is responsible for the precision and probability of this comedy – that led him towards low life, towards the conversation of commonplace Londoners rather than the speeches of legendary kings. And at no other time can one imagine such a conjunction of scholarship with quick and close observation of everyday affairs; if a learned man were to attempt such a thing to-day it could only be with overt condescension.

We cannot, of course, be sure that Jonson's listeners did not detect some such condescension, and the consequent artificiality, in his dialogue, though it seems unlikely that this racy profusion of language could ever have rung false. But for a modern audience his diction has only one drawback: it is altogether too authentic. All Jonson's figures are like those minor and comic cockneys who serve to fill an occasional gap in a modern play when a respite from action is wanted; they enlarge their characters in talk which is only loosely connected with the progress of the plot. Nowadays we have no such appetite for humours, keeping them only for incidental decoration, and here this decoration is continuous and, in addition, so thoroughly in character, so authentically Elizabethan, that it requires a constant reference to glossary and notes.

Nevertheless, a performance of the play is thoroughly justified, for all these characters have one quality which is sadly lacking in the diminished humours of the modern stage. They are all incredibly eloquent, expressing the follies of the moment not only in the slang and catchwords of their time but in language of wonderful richness and variety. And such eloquence can never have its full effect in the reading;

to be really impressive it must combine with action, hurry the listener past all obscurities and topical allusions, and serve as the expression of a state of mind which is clearly represented before his eyes.

Without unduly prolonging any situation or labouring any joke, this production makes every incident lucid, and brings out many diversions half hidden in the text. Where the characters spend so much time in apparently aimless wandering, and where so much that they do is apparently casual, even the invention of action is justified, especially when it is as tactfully managed as here. There is no burlesque, and nothing that does not spring easily from the words of the play. The actors have evidently worked as hard as the producer, and it is surprising how real many of these types of a vanished age become. The jokes of the water bearer are certainly odd, and his mysterious claims to be descended from a herring cannot possibly be quite as amusing as they no doubt were in the past, but they do not seem unnatural in Mr. Dennis Roberts's capable hands. Captain Bobadill, the boastful soldier, is certainly a more universal character, and always extremely funny, but Mr. Donald Wolfit managed to contribute many excellent touches of his own to his portrait. The jealous man, Kitely, seems to belong to a rather different world and has a more abstract and classical humour, but with the aid of the verse in which he speaks Mr. Godfrey Kenton made him thoroughly convincing.

The performance was the first of four arranged to celebrate the tercentenary of Jonson's death.

SOURCE: article in *The Times*, 7 August 1937.

PART THREE

The Alchemist

Margaret Cavendish, Duchess of Newcastle (1662)

Likewise my Playes may be Condemned, because they follow not the Antient Custome, as the learned sayes, which is, that all Comedies should be so ordered and composed, as nothing should be presented therein, but what may be naturally, or usually practiced or Acted in the World in the compass of one day; truly in my opinion those Comedies would be very flat and dull, and neither profitable nor pleasant, that should only present the actions of one day; for though *Ben. Johnson* as I have heard was of that opinion, that a Comedy cannot be good, nor is a natural or true Comedy, if it should present more than one dayes action, yet his Comedies that he hath published, could never be the actions of one day; for could any rational person think that the whole play of the Fox could be the action of one day? or can any rational person think that the Alchymist could be the action of one day? as that so many several Cozenings could be Acted in one day, by Captain *Face* and *Doll Common*; and could the Alchymist make any believe that they could make gold in one day? could they burn so many Coals, and draw the purses of so many, or so often from one person, in one day? and the like is in all his Playes, not any of them presents the actions of one day, although it were a day at the Poles, but of many dayes, nay I may say some years.

SOURCE: extract from Preface to her *Plays* (1662). For further comment by Margaret Cavendish, see extract from Herford and Simpson below.

John Dryden (1671)

'Tis charg'd upon me that I make debauch'd persons (such as they say my Astrologer and Gamester are) my Protagonists, or the chief persons of the *Drama*; and that I make them happy in the conclusion of my Play; against the Law of Comedy, which is to reward virtue and punish vice. I

answer first, that I know no such law to have been constantly observ'd in
Comedy, either by the Ancient or Modern Poets. Chærea is made happy
in the *Eunuch*, after having deflour'd a Virgin: and *Terence* generally
does the same through all his Plays, where you perpetually see, not only
debauch'd young men enjoy their Mistresses, but even the Courtezans
themselves rewarded and honour'd in the Catastrophe.[1] The same may
be observ'd in *Plautus* almost every where. *Ben. Johnson* himself, after
whom I may be proud to erre, has given me more than once the
example of it. That in the *Alchemist* is notorious, where Face, after
having contriv'd and carried on the great cozenage of the Play, and
continued in it without repentance to the last, is not only forgiven by his
Master, but inrich'd by his consent, with the spoiles of those whom he
had cheated. And, which is more, his Master himself, a grave man, and
a Widower, is introduc'd taking his Man's counsel, debauching the
Widow first, in hope to marry her afterward. . . . But now it will be
objected that I patronize vice by the authority of former Poets, and
extenuate my own faults by recrimination. I answer that as I defend my
self by their example; so that example I defend by reason, and by the
end of all Dramatique Poesie. In the first place therefore give me leave to
shew you their mistake who have accus'd me. They have not
distinguish'd, as they ought, betwixt the rules of Tragedy and Comedy.
In Tragedy, where the Actions and Persons are great, and the crimes
horrid, the laws of justice are more strictly to be observ'd: and examples
of punishment to be made to deterre mankind from the pursuit of vice.
Faults of this kind have been rare amongst the Ancient Poets: for they
have punished in *Oedipus*, and in his posterity, the sinne which he knew
not he had committed. *Medea* is the only example I remember at
present, who escapes from punishment after murder. Thus Tragedie
fulfils one great part of its institution; which is by example to instruct.
But in Comedy it is not so; for the chief end of it is divertisement and
delight: and that so much, that it is disputed, I think, by *Heinsius*,[2]
before *Horace* his art of Poetry, whether instruction be any part of its
employment. At least I am sure it can be but its secondary end: for the
business of the Poet is to make you laugh: when he writes humour he
makes folly ridiculous; when wit, he moves you, if not always to
laughter, yet to a pleasure that is more noble. And if he works a cure on
folly, and the small imperfections in mankind, by exposing them to
publick view, that cure is not perform'd by an immediate operation. For
it works first on the ill nature of the Audience; they are mov'd to laugh
by the representation of deformity; and the shame of that laughter,
teaches us to amend what is ridiculous in our own manners. This being,
then, establish'd, that the first end of Comedie is delight, and instruction
only the second; it may reasonably be inferr'd that Comedy is not so
much oblig'd to the punishment of the faults which it represents, as

Tragedy. For the persons in Comedy are of a lower quality, the action is little, and the faults and vices are but the sallies of youth, and the frailties of humane nature, and not premeditated crimes: such to which all men are obnoxious,[3] not such, as are attempted only by few, and those abandonn'd to all sense of vertue: such as move pity and commiseration; not detestation and horror; such in short as may be forgiven, not such as must of necessity be punish'd. But, lest any man should think that I write this to make libertinism amiable; or that I car'd not to debase the end and institution of Comedy, so I might thereby maintain my own errors, and those of better Poets; I must farther declare, both for them and for my self, that we make not vicious persons happy, but only as heaven makes sinners so: that is by reclaiming them first from vice. For so 'tis to be suppos'd they are, when they resolve to marry, for then enjoying what they desire in one, they cease to pursue the love of many. So Chærea is made happy by *Terence*, in marrying her whom he had deflower'd: and so are *Wildblood* and the Astrologer in this play.

SOURCE: extract from Preface to *An Evening's Love, or The Mock Astrologer* (1671).

NOTES

1. [Dénouement.]
2. [Daniel Heinsius (1580–1655), a Dutch classical scholar whose edition of Horace (1610) was used by Jonson for his revised translation of the *Ars Poetica*.]
3. [Open, liable.]

Jeremy Collier (1698)

... what a fine time Lewd People have on the *English Stage*. No Censure, no mark of Infamy, no Mortification must touch them. They keep their Honour untarnish'd, and carry off the Advantage of their Character. They are set up for the Standard of Behaviour, and the Masters of Ceremony and Sense. And at last that the Example may work the better, [the playwrights] generally make them rich, and happy, and reward them with their own Desires.

Mr. *Dryden* in the *Preface* to his *Mock-Astrologer*, confesses himself blamed for this Practise. *For making debauch'd Persons his* Protagonists, *or chief Persons of the Drama; And for making them happy in the Conclusion of the Play, against the Law of Comedy, which is to reward Virtue, and punish Vice.* To this Objection He makes a lame Defence. . . . He lets us know that *Ben*

Johnson after whom he may be proud to Err, gives him more than one example of
this Conduct; That in the Alchemist *is* notorious, where neither *Face* nor his
Master are corrected according to their Demerits. But how Proud soever
Mr. *Dryden* may be of an Errour, he has not so much of *Ben Jonson's*
company as he pretends. His Instance of *Face &c.* in the *Alchemist* is
rather *notorious* against his Purpose then for it.

For *Face* did not Council his Master *Lovewit* to debauch the Widdow;
neither is it clear that the Matter went thus far. He might gain her
consent upon Terms of Honour for ought appears to the contrary. 'Tis
true *Face* who was one of the Principal Cheats is Pardon'd and
consider'd. But then his Master confesses himself kind to a fault. He
owns this Indulgence was a Breach of Justice, and unbecoming the
Gravity of an old Man. And then desires the Audience to excuse him
upon the Score of the Temptation. But *Face continued in the Cousenage till*
the last without Repentance. Under favour I conceive this is a Mistake. For
does not *Face* make an Apology before he leaves the *Stage*? Does he not
set himself at the *Bar*, arraign his own *Practise*, and cast the Cause upon
the Clemency of the Company? And are not all these Signs of the Dislike
of what he had done? Thus careful the *Poet* is to prevent the Ill
Impressions of his *Play*! He brings both Man and Master to Confession.
He dismisses them like Malefactours; And moves for their Pardon
before he gives them their Discharge.

SOURCE: extract from *A Short View of the Immorality, and Profaneness*
of the English Stage (1698).

John Upton (1749)

Act i. Scene i.

FACE, SUBTLE, DOL Common.

FACE   Beleev't, I will.
SUBTLE   Thy worst. I fart at thee.
DOL   Ha' you your wits? Why gentlemen! for love – . . .

Our poet could not possibly have chosen a happier incident to open his
play with: instead of opening with a dull narration, you have action;
and such action too, as cannot possibly be supposed to happen at any
other time, than this very present time. Two rogues, and their punk, are
introduced quarrelling, and just so much of their secrets is discovered to
the audience, as is sufficient for the audience at present to know. – The
reader too, perhaps, is to be informed, that our learned comedian does

not deal in vulgar *English* expressions, but in vulgar *Attic* or *Roman* expressions. '– I fart at thee,' πέρδω σύ, *oppedo tibi*. ARISTOPHANES in *Plut[us]* l.618. τῆς πενίας καταπαρδεῖν, *paupertati oppedere*. HORACE, the polite HORACE, did not think himself too delicate for this phrase: '*Vin' tu curtis Judæis oppedere*.' L[iber] 1. S[atirae] l. 70.

SOURCE: extract from *Remarks on Three Plays of Benjamin Jonson* (1749).

Richard Hurd (1757)

The ALCHYMIST, some will think, is exaggerated throughout, and so, at best, belongs to that species of comedy, which we have before called *particular* and *partial*. At least, the extravagant pursuit so strongly exposed in that play, hath now, of a long time been forgotten; so that we find it difficult to enter fully into the humour of this highly wrought character. And, in general, we may remark of such characters,[1] that they are a strong temptation to the writer to exceed the bounds of truth in his draught of them at *first*, and are further liable to an imperfect, and even unfair sentence from the reader *afterwards*. For the welcome reception, which these pictures of prevailing *local* folly meet with on the stage, cannot but induce the poet, almost without design, to inflame the representation: And the want of *archetypes*, in a little time, makes it pass for immoderate, were it originally given with ever so much discretion and justice. So that whether the *Alchymist* be farcical or not, it will *appear*, at least, to have this note of Farce, 'That the principal character is exaggerated.'[2] But then this is all we must affirm. For as to the *Subject* of this Play's being a *local folly*, which seems to bring it directly under the denomination of Farce, it is but just to make a distinction. Had the *end and purpose* of the Play been to expose *Alchymy*, it had been liable to this objection. But this mode of *local folly*, is employed as the *means* only of exposing *another* folly, extensive as our Nature and coeval with it, namely *Avarice*. So that the subject has all the requisites of true *Comedy*. It is just otherwise, we may observe, in the *Devil's an Ass*; which therefore properly falls under our censure. For there, the folly of the time, *Projects and Monopolies*, are brought in to be exposed, as the *end and purpose* of the comedy.

On the whole, The *Alchymist* is a Comedy in just form, but a little *Farcical* in the extension of one of it's characters.

SOURCE: extract from 'A Dissertation Concerning the Provinces of the Several Species of the Drama', appended to Horace's *Ars Poetica*, 3rd edition (1757).

NOTES

1. [Elements, components.]

2. [Farce, Hurd has argued, 'represents the whims, extravagancies, and caprices, which characterize the folly of *particular persons or times*', whereas 'the characters of just comedy are *general*' (pp. 264, 300). Farce is essentially exaggerative: 'the perfection of *comedy* lying in the accuracy and fidelity of universal representation, and *farce* professedly neglecting or rather wantonly transgressing the limits of common nature and just decorum' (p. 303).]

Charles Lamb (1808)

The judgment is perfectly overwhelmed by the torrent of images, words, and book-knowledge with which Mammon confounds and stuns his incredulous hearer. They come pouring out like the successive strokes of Nilus. They 'doubly redouble strokes upon the foe'. Description outstrides proof. We are made to believe effects before we have testimony for their causes: as a lively description of the joys of heaven sometimes passes for an argument to prove the existence of such a place. If there be no one image which rises to the height of the sublime, yet the confluence and assemblage of them all produces an effect equal to the grandest poetry. Zerxes's army that drank up whole rivers from their numbers may stand for single Achilles. – Epicure Mammon is the most determined offspring of the author. It has the whole 'matter and copy of the father, eye, nose, lip, the trick of his frown': It is just such a swaggerer as contemporaries have described old Ben to be. Meercraft, Bobadill, the Host of the New Inn, have all his 'image and super-scription': but Mammon is arrogant pretension personified. Sir Samson Legend, in *Love for Love*, is such another lying overbearing character, but he does not come up to Epicure Mammon. What a 'towring bravery' there is in his sensuality! He affects no pleasure under a Sultan. It is as if 'Egypt with Assyria strove in luxury.'

SOURCE: extract from *Specimens of English Dramatic Poets* (1808).

Samuel Taylor Coleridge (c. 1823)

In Ben Jonson you have an intense and burning art. Some of his plots, that of *The Alchemist*, for example, are perfect. . . . Upon my word, I think the *Œdipus Tyrannus*, *The Alchemist*, and *Tom Jones* the three most perfect plots ever planned.

SOURCE: extracts from *Table Talk* (1835).

Charles Kingsley (1856)

Why does [Jonson] rail at the Puritans for making their complaints [against the stage]? His answer would have been that they railed in their ignorance, not merely at low art, as we call it now, but at high art and all art. Be it so. Here was their fault, if fault it was in those days. For to discriminate between high art and low art they must have seen both. And for Jonson's wrath to be fair and just he must have shewn them both. Let us see what the pure drama is like which he wishes to substitute for the foul drama of his contemporaries, and, to bring the matter nearer home, let us take one of the plays in which he hits deliberately at the Puritans, namely, *The Alchemist*, said to have been first acted in 1610, 'by the king's majesty's servants'. Look, then, at this well-known play, and take Jonson at his word. Allow that Ananias and Tribulation Wholesome (as they very probably are) are fair portraits of a class among the sectaries of the day: but bear in mind, too, that if this be allowed, the other characters shall be held as fair portraits also. Otherwise, all must be held to be caricature; and then the onslaught on the Puritans vanishes into nothing, or worse: in either case, Ananias and Tribulation are the best men in the play. They palter with their consciences, no doubt; but they have consciences, which no one else in the play has, except poor Surly, and he, be it remembered, comes to shame, and is made a laughing-stock, and 'cheats himself', as he complains at last, 'With that same foolish vice of honestie', while in all the rest what have we but every form of human baseness? Lovewit, the master, if he is to be considered a negative character, as doing no wrong, has, at all events, no more recorded of him than the noble act of marrying by deceit a young widow for the sake of her money, the philosopher's stone, by the by, and highest object of most of the seventeenth century dramatists. If most of the rascals meet with due disgrace, none of them is punished; and the greatest rascal of all, who, when escape is impossible, turns traitor, and after deserving the cart and pillory a dozen times for his last and most utter baseness, is rewarded by full pardon, and the honour of addressing the audience at the play's end in the most smug and self-satisfied tone, and of putting himself 'On you, that are my countrey', not doubting, it seems, that there were among them a fair majority who would think him a very smart fellow, worthy of all imitation.

Now, is this play a moral or an immoral one? Should we take our sons and daughters to see it? Of its coarseness we say nothing. We should not endure it, of course, now-a-days; . . . but if we were to endure plain speaking as the only method of properly exposing vice, should we endure the moral which, instead of punishing vice, rewards it?

And, meanwhile, what sort of a general state of society among the Anti-Puritan party does the play sketch? What but a horrible background of profligacy and frivolity?

SOURCE: extract from 'Plays and Puritans', *North British Review* (1856).

L. C. Knights (1937)

In *The Devil is an Ass*, in *Volpone* and *The Alchemist* Jonson is drawing on the anti-acquisitive tradition inherited from the Middle Ages. But this account is too narrow; the tradition included more than a mere distrust of, or hostility towards, riches. Understanding is, perhaps, best reached by studying (with Volpone in mind) the speeches of Sir Epicure Mammon. Each of them, it seems to me, implicitly refers to a traditional conception of 'the Mean'. Mammon, wooing Dol, describes their teeming pleasures:

> and, with these
> Delicate meats, set our selves high for pleasure,
> And take us downe againe, and then renew
> Our youth, and strength, with drinking the *elixir*,
> And so enjoy a perpetuitie
> Of life, and lust. And, thou shalt ha' thy wardrobe,
> Richer then *Natures*, still, to change thy selfe,
> And vary oftener, for thy pride, then shee.

The reference to '*Nature*', which gives the proper angle on 'a perpetuitie of life, and lust', is important. The accepted standard is 'natural', and although exact definition would not be easy we may notice the part played by that standard throughout Jonson's work. An instance from *Volpone* has been quoted [III vii 193–205]. Mammon's folly is that he expects Subtle to 'teach dull nature / What her owne forces are'. Similarly in the masque, *Mercury Vindicated*, the alchemists 'pretend . . . to commit miracles in art, and treason again' nature . . . a matter of

Immortality is nothing'; they 'professe to outworke the *Sunne* in vertue
and contend to the great act of generation, nay, almost creation'. The
obviously expected response is similar to that given to the description of
Mammon's jewels whose light shall 'strike out the stars'. Who wants to
strike out the stars, anyway? . . .

The Alchemist, like *Volpone*, is built on the double theme of lust and
greed, and the whole play is constructed so as to isolate and magnify the
central theme. The extraordinary complications of the plot all centre on
Subtle and Face, and all work to one end. The play is completely self-
consistent; all of the simplified characters are actuated by variations of
the one motive, and no extraneous passions are allowed to enter. To put
it another way, all the interests aroused in the reader point in one
direction, so that effects of exaggeration are possible here as they would
not be in a 'realistic' play or in a play involving more complicated
emotions. In a world of caricature the speeches of Sir Epicure Mammon
do not appear 'unnatural'; they are merely a characteristic heightening
of the effect. . . . Mammon's first speech [II i 1–24] is representative.
There is the typical inflation, containing within itself the destructive
irony, and exploding when the height of ambition and the commonest
sin are linked together in the concluding lines ['You shall start up yong
Vice-royes, / And have your punques, and punquettees, my SURLY'].
. . . The effect is pervasive:

> I will have all my beds, blowne up; not stuft:
> Downe is too hard. And then, mine oval roome,
> Fill'd with such pictures, as TIBERIUS tooke
> From ELEPHANTIS: and dull ARETINE
> But coldly imitated. Then, my glasses,
> Cut in more subtil angles, to disperse,
> And multiply the figures, as I walke
> Naked betweene my *succubae*. . . .
>   Where I spie
> A wealthy citizen, or rich lawyer,
> Have a sublim'd pure wife, unto that fellow
> I'll send a thousand pound, to be my cuckold.
> . . . I'll ha' no bawds,
> But fathers, and mothers. They will doe it best.
> Best of all others. And, my flatterers
> Shall be the pure, and gravest of Divines,
> That I can get for money. My mere fooles,
> Eloquent burgesses.

The exaggeration is of course the very opposite of simple hyperbole.
The astonishing comparisons ('dull ARETINE'), the violent alignment
of characters which convention assumes are natural opposites (flat-

terers: divines; fools: eloquent burgesses), generate an intensely critical activity in the reader, make him aware that he is called on to judge a mode of experience as well as to enjoy the representation.

Mammon's speeches are central; every other scene, although an end in itself, leads up to them, and they in turn reflect on the whole course of the action. There is no need to comment on Drugger, Dapper and Kastril, . . . but the Puritans, Ananias and Tribulation Wholesome, have a special significance. They stand not merely for hypocrisy, but for acquisition with a good conscience. Subtle explains that

> such as are not graced, in a state,
> May, for their ends, be adverse in religion,
> And get a tune, to call the flock together:

and certainly the hypocrisy is there ('Casting of dollers is concluded lawfull'). But there is also a complacence in Tribulation's willingness to ally himself and 'the holy brethren of *Amsterdam*' with riches. [Quotes III i 36–44.] Indeed, 'We may be temporall lords, our selves, I take it.' Neither Ananias nor Tribulation 'represents' Puritanism, but their concern with the stone, their shrewd dealing, and Subtle's ironic catalogue of their offences –

> (You) take the start of bonds, broke but one day,
> And say, *they were forfeited, by providence* –

caricature an absorption in worldly business against which the Protestantism of the new business classes was insufficiently armed.

SOURCE: extracts from *Drama and Society in the Age of Jonson* (1937) pp. 190–1, 207–10.

C. H. Herford and P. and E. Simpson (1950)

Jonson had read alchemical literature sufficiently to talk intelligently about the chemical processes employed by the experts real or supposed. Of course he knew well such literary sources as *The Canon's Yeoman's Tale* of Chaucer and the dialogue 'Alcumista' in the *Colloquies* of Erasmus. And he used the *Disquisitiones Magicae* of Martin Delrio, which he had found useful for the witchcraft of *The Masque of Queens*; the debate of Subtle and Surly in II iii 131–207 is taken wholly from this work. Jonson may also have used the first three volumes of the *Theatrum Chemicum* of Lazarus Zetzner, a collection of alchemical treatises published in 1602; later volumes followed in 1613 and 1622. He quotes Arnold of Villa Nova's *Rosarium Philosophorum*,[1] Geber's *Summa Per-*

fectionis,[2] Paracelsus's *Manuale de Lapide Philosophico*,[3] and Robertus Vallensis's *De Veritate et Antiquitate Artis Chemicae*.[4]

Jonson's satire on the Puritans also can be fully illustrated from their literature, as Hugh Broughton learnt to his cost. Jonson had already said in *Volpone* (ii ii 117–18) that the mountebank's jargon in that play had no parallel 'but *Alchimy*, . . . or BROUGHTONS bookes'.

Margaret of Newcastle in *The Description of a New World, called the Blazing World* (1668) worked out, as she imagined, the personal satire of the play; describing people who conversed with spirits, she ends by saying (p. 66),

> but yet they proved at last but meer Cheats; and were described by one of their own Country-men, a famous Poet, named *Ben. Johnson*, in a Play call'd, *The Alchymist*, where he expressed *Kelly* by Capt. *Face*, and *Dee* by Dr. *Subtle*, and their two Wives by *Doll Common*, and the Widow; by the *Spaniard* in the Play, he meant the *Spanish* Ambassador, and by Sir *Epicure Mammon*, a *Polish* Lord. The Empress remembred that she had seen the Play, and asked the Spirits, whom he meant by the name *Ananias?* Some Zealous Brethren, answered they, in *Holland*, *Germany*, and several other places. Then she asked them, Who was meant by the *Druggist?* Truly, answered the Spirits, We have forgot, it being so long since it was made and acted.

This theory carries its own refutation, but Gifford in a note on IV i 90 was inclined to accept the 'indenture tripartite' of Subtle, Face, and Dol as a presentment of Dee, Kelly, and their confederate Laski, the young Pole. 'Subtle', he says, 'was beyond question meant for Dee', the 'more daring' Face suits Kelly, and Dol is a counterpart of Laski because in their seances he played the part of an angel. 'But enough of such folly', as Gifford himself remarks.

For the fraud practised on Dapper (III v), introducing him to the Queen of the Fairies, C. J. Sisson has found in the archives of the Public Record Office a contemporary parallel.[5] The evidence was given in Chancery in November–February 1609–10 in a suit *Rogers* v. *Rogers* (C 24/341/47; C 24/343). Young Thomas Rogers, of a distinguished Dorset family with their seat at Hinton Martel, brother-in-law to Sir George More, Donne's father-in-law, fell into the hands of Sir Anthony Ashley and his brother Saul, who found means to profit by Rogers's wealth. 'Rogers is described as "a very phantasticall and humerous fellowe by his behaviour", and everything points to an epileptic and degenerate condition which made him an easy prey to the Ashleys.' A tool of theirs, Greene, got into touch with Rogers and promised that he should be introduced to the Queen of the Fairies and that, with Greene's favour, he should marry her. Meanwhile he was to give Greene five or six pounds in gold to be offered 'to the Fayrees' to ensure his welcome. 'Rogers did so, and it is one of the counts, in a complicated suit dealing

mainly with landed property, that this minor fraud was committed.'
Jonson raises the bid a little (i ii 172–3):

> 'Tis but your bestowing
> Some twenty nobles, 'mong her *Graces* servants,

he tells Dapper, and adds ritual touches about clean linen, fasting,
drops of vinegar, and pronouncing the magic words 'hum' and 'buz'.[6]

PLACE AND TIME IN THE PLAY

Jonson's setting of the scene and careful dovetailing of the events of the
plot are exceptionally well thought out, even for him. There is no
change of scene. Everything takes place in a single room of Lovewit's
house or in front of the door that opens on the lane outside. The house
has a window which commands a view of the lane; Dol constantly uses it
(i i 180, iv 6, 7; ii iv 20; iii iii 76, 81, v 50–2; iv vii 107–8). There is a
backway by which Dapper is shown out (i ii 163; iii v 78) and
Mammon got rid of after the collapse (iv v 95). It leads into the garden
(iv i 172, iv 81). There is also a door into the laboratory; Face and
Subtle enter by it (ii ii 1, iii 1). Subtle has a 'chamber of de-
monstrations' (iv ii 63), to which he takes Kastril and Dame Pliant; it is
entered by one of these doors, probably by the former. How were the
three doors managed? At iii v 58 there is a stage-direction, '*He speakes
through the key-hole, the other knocking*'; and Face must do this at v iii 71,
where the speeches on the other side of the door are audible. The doors
were in an interior wall built on the stage, 'for action such as speaking
through the keyhole requires both sides of the door to be practicable'.
The laboratory and inner rooms 'are not discovered, and no use is made
of the upper stage. Jonson here is a clear innovator, so far as the English
public theatre is concerned; no other play of our period reproduces this
type of permanent interior setting.'[7]

    The time-sequence is worked out with exceptional fullness. Morning
is indicated in the opening scene by Dol's oath, 'By the light that shines'
(119). From this point onwards it is possible to construct a time-table.

9 a.m.   Dapper, the first visitor, arrives (i. ii); he is late, has 'lent his watch' (l.
         6). He is ordered to return 'against one a clock' (l. 164).

10 a.m.   Mammon is seen coming 'at far end of the lane' (i iv 7); Subtle
         expected him 'with the sunnes rising' (l. 12). Face tells him that
         projection will take place in three hours (ii ii 4). Subtle hints at his
         covetousness: 'you meet your time / I' the just point: prevent your day,
         at morning' (ii iii 5, 6). Face makes an appointment with Surly 'some
         halfe houre hence' (l. 290), and invites Mammon to return 'within
         two houres' (l. 292), in order to have an interview with Dol.

11 a.m.   Ananias is threatened if he does not return 'quickly', prepared to pay

more money (II v 77); later the time is defined as one hour.
Face may be late for Surly (II vi 94).

12 a.m. Ananias returns just on the stroke of the hour (III ii 1). Face has
waited for Surly and missed him (III iii 1, 2), but has secured a
Spanish count (l. 10) who will not come for an hour (l. 76).

1 p.m. Dapper comes to time (III iii 76: see I ii 164).
Subtle is 'preparing for projection' (IV i 2), within three hours after
II ii 4 and two hours after II iii 292.

2 p.m. The disguised Surly comes a full hour after III iii 76 (IV iii 20).
Projection has been held up 'this halfe houre' (IV v 42–3). The
explosion follows (ll. 56–62).

3 p.m. Lovewit returns home: it is not yet 'deepe i'the after-noone' (v ii 30).
Subtle had intended to get away with Dol and the stolen goods 'soone
at night' (v iv 74).

SOURCE: extracts from *Ben Jonson*, vol. x (1950) pp. 46–8.
49–50.

NOTES

1. II i 39, 40, 65–7; iii 106–14.

2. II v 35–6.

3. II ii 25–8; v 28.

4. II i 101–4.

5. 'A Topical Reference in *The Alchemist*', *Joseph Quincy Adams Memorial Studies* (Washington, 1948) pp. 739–41.

6. [For a full discussion, see Franklin B. Williams Jr, 'Thomas Rogers as Ben Jonson's Dapper', *Yearbook of English Studies*, II (1972) 73–7.]

7. E. K. Chambers, *The Elizabethan Stage*, 4 vols (Oxford, 1923) vol. III, p. 123.

Edward B. Partridge

'THE IMAGERY OF *THE ALCHEMIST*' (1958)

A poet re-enacts the roles of God and Adam: he creates a world and names the animals. The naming of the animals in Jonson's plays is, as anyone can recognize, particularly important. So are the epithets, the names which the animals give each other. Mammon calls Face,

> [Subtle's] fire-drake,
> His lungs, his *Zephyrus*, he that puffes his coales,
> Till he firke nature up, in her owne center. (ii i 26–8)

This immense blower of bellows blows so hard on the coals of the plot that the whole thing explodes in his face. '*Till it* [the stone], *and they, and all in* fume *are gone*.' The explosion of the furnace in the fourth act is an objectification of what happens to the plot. More than one play of Jonson's seems to work on the same principle of an explosion. Jonson's favourite rhetorical device – hyperbole – radiates into all parts of his plays so that the dialogue trembles on the edge of bombast, the situations move close to burlesque or mock-heroic, the characters become grotesques, and the plot explodes. . . .

Indecorum and irony characterize the comic imagery of *The Alchemist*. This imagery brings into the context of the play vehicles[1] which are taken from religion, medicine, sex, commerce, and warfare. In part, these vehicles only extend the implications suggested by the fable of a clever servant, a quack, and a whore engaged in cheating fools. In part, too, they help form the immense scene in which this little war against the world is fought. The imagery does what nothing else in the poet's command can do with equal economy and intensity: it brings in those very values by which one can measure the pretensions and desires of the fakers and fools.

The centre of this complex of religion, medicine, sex, and business is alchemy, which, in one way or another, transmutes all of these diverse elements of life. The first extended mention of alchemy comes during the opening quarrel between Face and Subtle. To impress on Face how much has been done for him, Subtle uses alchemic terms.

> Thou vermine, have I tane thee, out of dung,
> So poore, so wretched, when no living thing
> Would keepe thee companie, but a spider, or worse?
> Rais'd thee from broomes, and dust, and watring pots?
> *Sublim'd* thee, and *exalted* thee, and *fix'd* thee
> I' the *third region*, call'd our *state of grace*?
> Wrought thee to *spirit*, to *quintessence*, with paines
> Would twise have won me the *philosophers worke*?   (i i 64–71)

To use such terms in reference to gold is nonsense – it's alchemy, but it's nonsense. But to use them in reference to man's nature is not merely nonsense, but also impiety. Subtle claims to have alchemized a man. Significantly, the only man that Subtle cannot alchemize is Surly, who says to Mammon, 'Your *stone* / Cannot transmute me' (II i 78–9). Perhaps the sinister significance of the title is in this transmutation of man: Subtle or rather the power of gold can sublime and exalt man. In *Volpone* we found that the final food of man is man; here the final stuff to project on is man. Man himself can be alchemized; money can give a man spirit. In short, the alchemist (Subtle or gold) becomes a parody of the Creator. To sincere alchemists, who were mystical idealists, alchemy was a religion or quasi-religion. To Jonson, a moral idealist and a dogmatic Christian who approached alchemy with no sympathy for the religious impulse in its heart, it seemed only an obscene fraud, and alchemic terms only a parody of the Word.

In order to ridicule alchemy and to show how it seemed to be a caricature of Christianity, Jonson had his knaves use terms which had one meaning for alchemists and another for Christians.[2] The religious references in Subtle's speech are evident enough – '*Sublim'd*', '*exalted*', '*state of grace*', '*spirit*'. . . . Gradually we see that this religion is a parody of Christianity. It has its Creator and its catechism, its prayers and devotions. There is even a body of religious writings, which Surly questions in a long and suspiciously knowing passage. The terms of alchemy seem to him 'like tricks o' the cards'; besides, none of the writers agrees with the others. Subtle's answers to this heresy have been heard before in ecclesiastical disputes. According to him, the alchemic names are used 'to obscure their art': 'Speake not the *Scriptures*, oft, in *parables*?' (II iii 201–7). Subtle proves almost as adept as Mammon in dressing up the nasty fact in a pretty fiction. The same inflation by means of comparisons which was evident in the epithets is at work in Subtle's speech. Alchemic writings are to the Scriptures as Dol is to the Queen of Faery. . . .

Mammon's language is, aside from Face's, the best example of how thoroughly the implications of the imagery relate business, religion, and sex. His name is an example of this. According to the *OED*, Mammon, the Aramaic word for 'riches', was taken by medieval writers as the proper name of the devil of covetousness. Even in the Elizabethan Age Thomas Lodge in *Wits Miserie, or the Worlds Madnesse* (1596) used Mammon as the devil incarnate who tempted man by avarice. After the sixteenth century it was current as a term of opprobrium for wealth regarded as an idol or evil influence. Loosely, 'Epicure' meant 'one who disbelieves in the divine government, and in a future life'. More particularly, it came to mean one who gives himself up to sensual pleasure, especially eating. . . . In short, Epicure carries with it a sense of atheism and materialism, just as Mammon symbolized covetousness, riches, and worldliness. 'Epicure', which comes from Greek, and 'Mammon', which is exclusively a Christian term, unite to form a name which is at once a humanistic and Christian comment on impious wealth and immorality.

The geographical allusions of this immense symbol of worldliness and sensuality reveal him to be a more romantic merchant venturer than Face.

> Now, you set your foot on shore
> In *novo orbe*; Here's the rich *Peru*:
> And there within, sir, are the golden mines,
> Great SALOMON's *Ophir*! He was sayling to't,
> Three yeeres, but we have reach'd it in ten months.
>
> (II i 1–5)

Mammon is not merely the explorer setting his foot on the shore of the New World – not even primarily the explorer – but essentially the merchant venturer. His primary interest is in the 'golden mines' within which shall make him rich. Not the least of many ironies in this scene is that Face has been thinking of Mammon himself as a 'vein' to be mined (I iii 106). This idea of exploiting distant lands is brought even closer home when Mammon declares that he will purchase Devonshire and Cornwall and make them 'perfect *Indies*' (II i 35–6). These counties were noted for tin and copper mines, which Mammon would transmute into 'golden mines'. The commercial note which opens the scene is brought in most emphatically in his lines on Subtle who makes the stone, 'But I buy it. / My venter brings it me' (II ii 100–1). The use of the commercial terms – 'buy' and 'venter' – in reference to the stone shows how intimate is the connection between religion and business in Mammon's world. Mammon can buy his god, the elixir. Divinity and immortality can be bargained for. There is a certain justice, as Mammon himself admits, in the fate to which this business venture in religion comes. The sensual dreams which had drawn him on and his pursuit of Dol are said by Subtle to be the cause of the bursting of the glass and the failure of all his hopes. He cries, 'O my voluptuous mind! I am justly punish'd' (IV v 74). It is characteristic of Mammon that he should consider the loss of the power of making gold a just punishment for a voluptuous mind.

Mammon's psychic sensuality is its own best criticism. As L. C. Knights says, each of his speeches 'implicitly refers to a traditional conception of "the Mean" '.[3] The images he uses more than once betray the essential meanness of his vision. Not simply their constant extravagance – though that is one way of indicating hollowness – but also the action within the image itself shows this. For instance:

> My mists
> I'le have of perfume, vapor'd 'bout the roome,
> To loose our selves in; and my baths, like pits
> To fall into: . . .   (II ii 48–51)

Other associations with losing one's self or falling into pits suddenly betray such lines, suggesting that Mammon may have lost himself already and calling up memories of an Inferno where sinners have fallen into pits of fire. Or the dramatic irony implicit in the imagery he uses may reveal him. Thus he explains to Surly that, once his friends are rich, they shall not have to deal with 'the hollow die' or 'the fraile card', nor keep a 'livery-punke', nor worship 'the golden calfe', nor 'Commit idolatrie with wine, and trumpets' (II i 9 ff.). But we know, from the previous act, that the dice are loaded, that Dol is a punk, that Mammon is worshipping a golden calf and committing idolatry with words if not wine. Or when Mammon, to convince Surly of the authenticity of the elixir, alludes to a classical myth, the myth itself betrays him.

> SISIPHUS was damn'd
> To roule the ceaslesse stone, onely, because
> He would have made ours common.[4]   (II iii 208–10)

Sisyphus was punished for his fraud and avarice. Mammon, who is avaricious, if not fraudulent, suddenly turns into Sisyphus, rolling the ceaseless stone of alchemy. . . .

The denouement of the play has troubled more than one observer. Subtle and Dol escape over the back wall without their 'purchase', but also without punishment. Face cuts off his beard, changes his clothes, talks Lovewit into going along with the hoax, and becomes that 'very honest fellow', Jeremy, again. Lovewit, 'with some small straine / Of his owne candor', accepts a rich wife and a cellar full of Mammon's goods. Where, one might ask, is the justice in such an end? Elisabeth

Woodbridge Morris, who held that Jonson's comedy is 'judicial' but not
always 'moral' (a distinction that, in a work of art, escapes me), said
that 'the moral of *The Alchemist* . . . would be hard to find'.[5] . . . The
answer to such criticism is that Face and Lovewit are convicted by their
own words and actions. . . . Lovewit is drawn into intimate association
with the fraud by Face who begs for a chance to advance his own
fortune:

> I'll helpe you to a widdow,
> In recompence, that you shall gi' me thankes for,
> Will make you seven yeeres yonger, and a rich one.
> 'Tis but your putting on a *Spanish* cloake. (v iii 84–7)

There are several remarkable things about this passage. One of them is
that Lovewit is invited to take the place of Face, who previously had
said, concerning Drugger, 'He is gone to borrow me a *Spanish* habite, /
Ile be the *Count*, now' (IV vii 99–100). Lovewit, then, takes Face's place,
both as the husband of Dame Pliant and as the manipulator of the fools
whom he gets rid of in a manner worthy of Face. The other remarkable
implication of Face's words concerns Dame Pliant's effect on Lovewit: it
resembles the supposed effect of the elixir. Like that infallible medicine,
she will make him younger and richer. Lovewit's final lines carry on this
same implication.

> if I have out-stript
> An old mans gravitie, or strict canon, thinke
> What a yong wife, and a good braine may doe:
> Stretch ages truth sometimes, and crack it too.
>   (v v 153–6)

Lovewit has found what Mammon sought – the elixir of life which will
stretch, perhaps even crack, the truth of old age – found it in a rich
young wife and in his 'good braine', Jeremy. He does not claim that he
has found the fountain of perpetual youth, as Mammon did, but he
clearly hopes that the quick-silver of Dame Pliant and the sulphur of
Face may alchemize away old age for the time being. By such
implications as well as by his actions Lovewit is drawn into the orbit of
Face and Mammon, both of whose places he takes in one way or
another. Use of the same language in a play is one way of striking up
similarities between characters. Thus Lovewit's use of martial images
like Face's or of alchemic allusions like Mammon's suggests that he is
not much different from them.

 Face, too, is accused by the words he uses. His final address to the
audience reveals him to be the same Face that he was when 'Captaine'.

> My part a little fell in this last *Scene*,
> Yet 'twas *decorum*. And though I am cleane
> Got off, from SUBTLE, SURLY, MAMMON, DOL,
> Hot ANANIAS, DAPPER, DRUGGER, all
> With whom I traded; yet I put my selfe
> On you, that are my countrey: and this pelfe,
> Which I have got, if you doe quit me, rests
> To feast you often, and invite new ghests.

To the very end he remains the business man, giving the monthly report of the companies with whom he has 'traded', and keeping a sharp eye on those with whom he will trade in the future. His plea that he is putting himself on the audience, which is his 'countrey' has a sinister note. 'Countrey', which he is ostensibly using in its legal sense of 'jury', has a more normal sense of 'land' or 'nation'. The audience may be there to judge his case, but it is also a nation to be exploited. The bait is a 'feast', but when we remember that Epicure's vision of a golden age was largely one of eating and that various things from gold to Dol and Dame Pliant had been proposed as a meal, we discover that Face is suggesting that we become Epicures in our turn. Furthermore, by using the legal phrase, 'putting himself on his country', he is making the insulting suggestion that he and the audience are, after all, fellow citizens of the same native land, since such a jury was summoned from one's own peers in the neighbourhood. . . .

The imagery of *The Alchemist* is perfectly functional in several ways. First, it develops, as alchemy develops, beginning with base metals, such as a whore, a pander, and a quack, which it tries grandiloquently to transmute into finer beings – a Faery Queen, a precious king of present wits, and a divine instructor – finally ending, as the dream of the philosopher's stone ends, in a return to the state of base metals. The various vehicles which alchemize the base situation – the inflated epithets, the erotic allusions, the religious and commercial terms – ultimately show how thoroughly mean the situation is by bringing into the context the very standards by which it could be measured: the Christian and humanistic civilization of rational men. Against that immense background the three impostors and their commonwealth of fools play out their mock-heroic life, their violent little actions contrasting sharply with the permanent values suggested by the imagery. When Subtle is compared to a priest, the comparison itself shows how much he disappoints the ideal. When Dol calls herself Queen of Faeries, we see how far she really is from the Faery Queen.

The imagery is functional in another way. The images work on the same principle that the play as a whole and usually each scene work.

They are extravagant, inflated, and ludicrous, because the tenors (gold, Dol, Mammon) are related to great vehicles (god, Queen, Jove). The monstrous gap that opens between the tenor that we know to be mean and the vehicle that we assume to be great, and the demand that we find some similarities between them to bridge that gap, outrages our sense of decency and decorum. That outrage, within the imagery, produces part of the comic tone of the play.

A third function of the imagery is to extend and develop the multiple references that alchemy had in actual life – especially the religious, medical, and commercial references. The alchemic process in this play has religious implications because the desire for gold is thought of as a religion; it has medical implications because the elixir is thought of as a sovereign remedy; it has sexual implications because the elixir is thought to have a sexual power; it has commercial implications because business terms are used in reference to the whole fraudulent practice. When gold or the power of producing gold is spoken of as one normally speaks of a deity, we are expected to question whether this has any connections with reality. Do some people make gold their god? What is the sense in saying that man's nature can be alchemized? Is money in any sense the great healing power of the world? Does the great god, gold, have a sexual power? What is the relation of business to this religion of gold? Is sex to some people a business? Is religion? And so on. In other words, the imagery suggests that, in the Alchemist's world, the acquisition of gold is a religion, a cure-all, a sexual experience, and a commercial enterprise. The world that opens before us, once we understand these multiple references of alchemy, is outrageously obscene, crude in metaphysic and vulgar in emotion. Since this world is, in part, a caricature of the real world, one can make numerous connections between its crudity and obscenity and the crudity and obscenity latent in human experience. But as a universe of discourse, it exists in its own right, comic because it is a caricature, solid and substantial because it has a religion, an ethic, a government, and a flourishing business.

The imagery also suggests that the various peoples whose lives are dedicated to the acquisition of gold – whether they be in secular or religious life, in prostitution or other kinds of business – bear some relation to the alchemists of old. Dol Common is metaphorically an alchemist because she, too, is trying to turn base metals into gold. Mammon's cook is an alchemist in the same way; the reward of all his cooking is the accolade – 'there's gold, / Goe forth, and be a knight'. Perhaps the true philosopher's stone is not the stone itself, but simply business – that is, selling the public the things it wants. Face's threatening of Subtle is pertinent:

> I will have
> A booke, but barely reckoning thy impostures,
> Shall prove a true *philosophers stone*, to printers.
>
> (I i 100–2)

The Golden Age comes when you find that you have what someone else
wants – a sensational book or a new medicine, a shiny gadget or an old
fraud. The true alchemist may be Face, that 'parcell-broker, and
whole-bawd' who always has something someone wants and who
perpetually finds the elixir of life in Drugger, Mammon, Dame Pliant,
Subtle, Dol, and finally Lovewit. Face may be the face of the future, the
prophetic vision of the super-salesman who can sell anything to anyone.
All that he needs to work on is man – man who, himself another Face,
will sell even things he needs in order to buy things he wants. With
naked impudence he expresses his philosophy early in the game.

> You [Subtle] must have stuffe, brought home to you, to worke on?
> And, yet, you thinke, I am at no expence,
> In searching out these veines, then following 'hem,
> Then trying 'hem out. 'Fore god, my intelligence
> Costs me more money, then my share oft comes too,
> In these rare workes.   (I iii 104–9)

That little world, man, contains the base metals on which an alchemist
can work. The seams or lodes may lie deep, but they can be searched out
and followed. The 'golden mines' of Mammon, his '*novo orbe*' and 'rich
Peru' are only new names for this old world of man – new names,
ironically, for Sir Epicure Mammon. Though alchemy itself is a fraud,
Subtle, Dol, and Face are successful alchemists in that they have found
this golden secret. All who discover this secret – all whores like Dol, all
quacks like Subtle, all shrewd rascals like Face, all unscrupulous
opportunists like Lovewit – these are the true alchemists.

   This conviction that in man's nature lie the base metals of alchemy
appears in a different form in an image that Face uses in speaking of his
futile search for Surly.

> 'Slight would you have me stalke like a mill-jade,
> All day, for one, that will not yeeld us graines?
>
> (III iii 5–6)

Man could be harvested as well as transmuted. Once ground down in
the mill, he could yield 'graines'. This kind of gain was the 'common
way' which Volpone avoided: '[I] have no mills for yron, / Oyle, corne,
or men, to grinde 'hem into poulder' (I i 35–6). But the final source of
money for Face is the final source of food for Volpone – man.

SOURCE: extracts from *The Broken Compass*: *A Study of the Major*

Comedies of Ben Jonson (1958) pp. 114, 126–7, 129–30, 149–52, 153–5, 156–60.

NOTES

1. [In discussing metaphoric language Partridge makes use of I. A. Richards's terms *tenor* and *vehicle*. He gives the following illustration: 'In a simple metaphor such as "This fell sergeant, Death, / Is strict in his arrest", the tenor is "Death", and the vehicle is "This fell sergeant [who] Is strict in his arrest"' (p. 29).]

2. Edgar H. Duncan has shown the relation of *The Alchemist* to the writings on alchemy in 'Jonson's *Alchemist* and the Literature of Alchemy', *PMLA*, LXI (1946) 699–710. Note particularly his interesting analysis of the passage under consideration.

3. [See above, Part Three, section 1: Knights's sense is 'normative standard'; Partridge seems to take it to be 'ignoble, penurious'.]

4. The stage direction may be important here: '*Dol is seene*', exactly on the word 'common'. Is this another way to suggest an equation between the stone and Dol Common? [In his note on this line in the Revels edition F. H. Mares describes this cueing of Dol as 'a neat theatrical joke' – Ed.]

5. *Studies in Jonson's Comedy* (New York, 1898) p. 29.

Alvin B. Kernan

'BASE METAL INTO GOLD' (1959)

The materials out of which the mountebank compounds his medicinal oil and the materials out of which Jonson the satiric poet constructs *Volpone* are one and the same:

> All his ingredients
> Are a sheepes gall, a rosted bitches marrow,
> Some few sod earewigs, pounded caterpillers,
> A little capons grease, and fasting spittle.   (II vi 17–20)

These chunks of matter constitute the underlay, the basic substance of all of Jonson's satiric plays. These are the basic elements, the primal stuff, on which all the swirling life of the plays rests, and the base material which Jonson's alchemists – and all of his characters are in their many vanities alchemists – attempt to transmute into gold.

> . . . *materialls,*
> Of pisse, and egge-shells, womens termes, mans bloud,
> Haire o' the head, burnt clouts, chalke, merds, and clay,
> Poulder of bones, scalings of iron, glasse,
> And worlds of other strange *ingredients,*
> Would burst a man to name.   (*The Alchemist,* II iii 193–8)

This dense substratum is created in the plays not only by catalogues
such as these but by an enormous amount of incidental reference to a
world of unregenerate, roiling biological substance and mere chemical
process. Never in Jonson's plays are we very far above this world of
sodden ale, pellitory of the wall, fat ram-mutton lying heavy on the
stomach, torsion of the small gut, the scotomy, golden lard, cramps,
convulsions, paralyses, the stranguary, hernia ventosa, a spoonful of
dead wine with flies in it, hot blood, scalded gums, gobs of phlegm, the
swelling unctuous paps of a fat pregnant sow. This world of chemical
process and layers of organisms exists along side another equally dense
stratum of inanimate things: plate, gold, carbuncles, diamonds,
gingerbread, tobacco, feathers, wax, and clay.

No amount of quotation can convey the incredible density of *things*
which Jonson rams into his plays, but perhaps a few examples of
concentrated references will suggest the quality he achieves. Here is
Captain Otter, in *The Silent Woman,* describing his wife: 'A most vile
face! and yet shee spends me fortie pound a yeere in *mercury,* and hogs-
bones. All her teeth were made i' the Blacke-*Friers*: both her eye-browes
i' the *Strand,* and her haire in *Silver-street.* . . . She takes her selfe asunder
still when she goes to bed, into some twentie boxes; and about next day
noone is put together againe, like a great *Germane* clocke' (IV ii 91–9).
Or here is another instance of density but in this case on a more 'heroic'
level:

> We will be brave, *Puffe,* now we ha' the *med'cine.*
> My meat, shall all come in, in *Indian* shells,
> Dishes of agate, set in gold, and studded,
> With emeralds, saphyres, hiacynths, and rubies.
> The tongues of carpes, dormise, and camels heeles,
> Boil'd i' the spirit of SOL and dissolv'd pearle,
> (APICIUS diet, 'gainst the *epilepsie*)
> And I will eate these broaths, with spoones of amber,
> Headed with diamant, and carbuncle.
> My foot-boy shall eate phesants, calvered salmons,
> Knots, godwits, lamprey's: I my selfe will have
> The beards of barbels, serv'd, in stead of sallades;
> Oild mushromes; and the swelling unctuous paps
> Of a fat pregnant sow, newly cut off,

Drest with an exquisite, and poynant sauce;
For which, Ile say unto my cooke, there's gold,
Goe forth, and be a knight. . . .
                    My shirts
I'll have of taffeta-sarsnet, soft, and light
As cob-webs; and for all my other rayment
It shall be such, as might provoke the *Persian*;
Were he to teach the world riot, a new.
My gloves of fishes, and birds-skins, perfum'd
With gummes of *paradise*, and easterne aire. . . .

                                        (II ii 71–94)

Out of materials such as these, organic and inorganic, Jonson creates in
his satiric plays a dense layer of primal stuff, what Subtle calls 'remote
matter', or '*maleria liquida*', existing anterior to any human meaning or
purpose. It is important to note, however, that this remote matter is not
treated as inherently hideous and repulsive. It is raw life full of
potential, and as such is exciting. The phrases and passages in which
Jonson describes it, even when it is being misused by a Volpone or Sir
Epicure, are never merely grotesque, but pulsing, vital, and thoroughly
exciting.

Just above this layer in Jonson's plays, but still existing only in the
form of metaphor and incidental reference, appear the first forms of
complex life, the animal world. On this level the vulture, the raven, the
crow, and the flesh-fly hover over the body of the dying, decaying fox,
while to one side the parrot (Sir Pol) chatters away, miming those
whom he takes for his betters and his models. Here the parrot and
monkey parade 'with all the little long-coats about him, male and
female' (*Bartholomew Fair*, I iv 115–16). The 'wel-educated Ape' jumps
'over the chaine, for the *King* of *England* and backe againe for the *Prince*',
but sits 'still on his arse for the *Pope*, and the *King* of *Spaine*!'
(*Bartholomew Fair*, Induction, ll. 17–20). The sub-devil Pug lames a
cow, or enters into a sow 'to make her cast her farrow' (*The Devil is an
Ass*, I i 9). This is the world of the pig led forth squealing to slaughter, the
flea and the dog-leech sucking blood, the bear or horse at the stake
striking out frantically at the savage, snarling dogs, the rat daintily
picking its way into the garbage. References to animals are everywhere,
the calf, the brach, the horse leech, the boar, the stallion, the cat, the
turtle, the mouse, the monkey, the swallow. Only slightly above these
animals appear such malformations of humanity as Volpone's dwarf,
eunuch, and hermaphrodite. Paralleling the crude arrangements of
organic matter into animal forms, we have the equally crude arrangement by man of inorganic matter into compounds, forms, and
machines: drums, hobbyhorses, cosmetics, alembics, perpetual motion
devices, windmills, elaborate foods, rich clothes, coaches, puppets,

weapons, stills, clocks, palaces, money. Human artifacts in these plays are as numerous and most often as devoid of practical purpose or expression of ethical values as the raw materials out of which mankind has ingeniously constructed them to satisfy his animal desires for material display and for conquest of his fellows.

At this point we emerge from the subhuman into the human world, but we are still not at the level of plot and dramatis personae, for at this level we encounter, by means again of indirect reference and metaphor, the vast, busy, noisy world of humankind. The sprawling metropolis of London with its countless numbers of men going about their varied activities is ever present in Jonson's plays. The cooks sweating over their ovens, the glass blowers at their smoky trade, the bell founders casting metal; fishwives, orange-women, broom-men, costard-mongers crying out their wares in the streets; the braziers, armorers, pewterers and other 'hammer men' pounding metal on the anvil; here are the sword-and-buckler man, the tooth-drawer, the juggler, the hobbyhorseman, the horse-courser, the tapster. At one place the Puritan drones a grace 'as long as thy tablecloth', while elsewhere the parasite, he who has 'your bare town-arte', fawns, fleers, and licks 'away a moath' in his nervous efforts to please; the 'sonnes of *sword*, and *hazzard*', longing for satin cloaks lined with velvet, swagger into Madam Augusta's in their rude homespun and 'fall before / The golden calfe, and on their knees, whole nights, / Commit idolatrie with wine, and trumpets'. While the young dandy gathers his 'learned counsell' 'your *french* taylor, barber, linener' about him in the morning and the lady of fashion excitedly plans to take coach for '*Bed'lem* . . . the *China* houses, and . . . the *Exchange*', the young punk at the fair is being stood on her head 'with her Sterne upward' to be 'sous'd by my wity young masters o' the *Innes o' Court*'.

The various details on the preceding pages have been drawn from all of Jonson's later satiric plays, but the quality of scenic density which they illustrate is present to an almost incredible extent in each individual play. This dense mass of life, composed of successive layers of being rising gradually from primal matter into the animal kingdom and then into the town, is the basic scene of Jonson's plays and the background for the plot. It is also, of course, an excellent example of the typical satiric scene, for here is raw life and being, surging, noisy, dense, gross, weighty, and chaotic – the great fair of the world, the field full of folk. Jonson's unparalleled ability to manufacture this hubbub of creation accounts for half of the greatness of his plays; the other half results from his rock-hard, unrelenting moral grasp of this material, his ability to marshal it into significant forms and subject it constantly to the play of ironic wit.

The chemical life, the inert matter, the animals, the men have, in my illustrations, been arranged into a hierarchy of being extending from the lowest and simplest forms of matter and process to the highest and most complex. What I have done, in short, is to take the 'stuff' of Jonson's plays and fit it very roughly into its proper place in that all-inclusive and familiar scheme, the great chain of being. But in the actual plays these things and processes are jumbled together in a fantastic mixture, and no one layer ever stands out distinctly from those above and below it. Life in Jonson's plays is not still and at rest at any one point on the great chain, but moves ceaselessly up and down it in an unending cycle of aspiration and fall. We can perhaps best see this by employing one of Jonson's own central metaphors, that of alchemy, as an organizing principle of discussion. In dealing with this movement up and down the ladder of existence we shall necessarily come forward from the scene, which is built up primarily by incidental reference and metaphor, into the world of dramatis personae and plot, the more obvious elements used by the playwright in constructing his dramatic image of the world.

In a very real sense, life in all of Jonson's plays is viewed as a process of alchemy, the transmutation of base matter into gold; and each of the characters is an alchemist attempting to transform himself by means of his particular 'philosopher's stone' into some form higher up on the scale of being than the point at which he began. The lady who paints, the young man who dresses himself in silks and feathers, the pedant who pretends to vast amounts of learning, the fool who seems to know all the great men of the world, the amorous fop who sighs after his lady and writes her sugared sonnets, all these are alchemists trying by various means to transmute their base metal into the gold of beauty, learning, sophistication, love. And while their particular 'stones' or 'elixirs' – cosmetics, books, a grave demeanor – may vary, in the final analysis the ultimate 'stone' of all the fools is language. Jonson must have had the most sensitive ear in the kingdom for colloquial speech rhythms, tricks of phrasing, misuse of metaphor, and other verbal peculiarities. His plays are one vast din, a true Babel, where the magniloquent, Messianic tones of a Sir Epicure Mammon and a Volpone, announcing the dawn of a world of unlimited sensuality and joy, mingle with the pious apocalyptic mouthings of Zeal-of-the-Land Busy, the chatter of the Collegiate Ladies discussing books, fashions, and lovers, Subtle's mishmash of alchemical terms, the soaring phrases of business and finance rolled out endlessly by the projector Meercraft, the lists of Latin authors proudly recited by Sir John Daw. Every character seems to be talking endlessly, seeking – as is actually the case in *The Silent Woman* – to empty the world of all sounds but that of his own voice and create a silence of sameness. This vast flow of language, for all the different tones employed, has, however, a common denominator, for in every case – from the chattering sound of Sir Politic Would-be's discussion of political plots to the soothing, oily tones of Mosca duping some fool with praises – the intent of the language is an alchemical transformation of the foolish and vicious into something 'rich and strange', or of a vulgar, unlawful act into decent and honorable conduct.

A particularly striking instance of this kind of transformation occurs in *The Alchemist* where Subtle finds it necessary to encourage the Puritans, Tribulation Wholesome and Ananias, who are waiting impatiently for 'projection' to occur. He offers to counterfeit some Dutch 'dollers' for them which will 'bide the third examination'. Greedy but cautious, Tribulation asks, 'This act of coyning, is it lawfull?' (III ii 149). Subtle replies, 'It is no coyning, sir. It is but casting.' Miraculously, language has transformed an unlawful act into honest labor! and Tribulation can now exclaim joyfully, 'you distinguish well. Casting of money may be lawfull.' Ananias and Tribulation – and all of Jonson's Puritans – are particularly skilled in this kind of linguistic alchemy, and their stone is always a greasy piety expressed in Old Testament language. These two brethren are in actuality 'fences' dealing in stolen goods, and they are particularly anxious to acquire a basement full of metal which Face and Subtle have persuaded Sir Epicure Mammon to send them to be turned into gold. This shady deal is neatly turned into a beneficent and worthy act by verbally transforming the stolen articles into 'widows and orphans goods', and so careful is Ananias that before he will pay for the goods he insists on knowing that the orphan's parents were 'sincere professors'. In the course of *The Alchemist* Jonson carries us beyond these particular bits of Puritan alchemy and depicts the entire Puritan movement as an attempt to transform the base human motives of greed and desire for political power into piety and religious zeal. The stones used to create the transmutation are a 'holy vizard' and such

> scrupulous bones,
> As whether a *Christian* may hawke, or hunt;
> Or whether, *Matrons, of the holy assembly*,
> May lay their haire out, or weare doublets:
> Or have that idoll *Starch*, about their linnen.
>
> (III ii 78–82)

Libelling prelates, long graces, railing against plays, lying with 'zealous rage', and the use of such names as 'Tribulation, Persecution, Restraint, Long-patience' round out the list of stones used by those 'as are not graced in a state' to gather a flock and gain power. For the Puritan, of course, these are all but 'wayes . . . invented for propagation of the *glorious cause*'.

What the Puritans achieve in their own way, every character in
Jonson's plays attempts in some manner, and we might look briefly at
the efforts of 'projection' in *The Alchemist*. Abel Drugger, 'A miserable
rogue, and lives with cheese, / And has the wormes' (ii vi 81–2), wants
to be changed into a rich merchant, a man of importance and
substance. Since he lacks the imagination to effect the change himself,
he turns to Face and Subtle, and the pseudo-alchemists oblige, and
construct for him a sign suggesting profound meanings in him:

> He first shall have a bell, that's ABEL;
> And, by it, standing one, whose name is DEE,
> In a rugg gowne; there's *D*. and *Rug*, that's DRUG:
> And, right anenst him, a Dog snarling *Er*;
> There's DRUGGER, ABEL DRUGGER. That's his signe.
> And here's now *mysterie*, and *hieroglyphick*!   (ii vi 19–24)

The rustic gentleman Kastril is essentially no more than,

> a gentleman, newly warme in'his land, sir,
> Scarse cold in'his one and twentie; that do's governe
> His sister, here: and is a man himselfe
> Of some three thousand a yeere, and is come up
> To learne to quarrell, and to live by his wits,
> And will goe downe againe, and dye i' the countrey.
>   (ii vi 57–62)

This fortunate booby, however, wants to be translated into a fashionable swaggerer and a dangerous duelist:

> I have heard some speech
> Of the angrie Boyes, and seene 'hem take *tabacco*;
> And in his shop: and I can take it too.
> And I would faine be one of 'hem and goe downe
> And practise i'the countrey.   (iii iv 21–5)

The simple-minded clerk Dapper wants to become a successful
gambler; Dame Pliant, the country widow, wants to be a lady of
fashion; and Sir Epicure Mammon, who is ordinarily 'a grave sir, a rich,
that has no need, / A wise sir, too' (ii iii 279–80), desires to be the new
messiah of wealth and joy, the man who pronounces to the world '*be
rich*', who will 'firke nature up, in her owne center', who will confer
'honour, love, respect, long life' on man, and 'make an old man, of
fourescore, a childe'.

All of the gulls are momentarily transformed by the rogues who prey
on them: Face, Subtle, and Dol Common. These creatures, in turn, do
seem in fact to have the true stone for changing base metal into gold in
an almost literal sense, for they manage to convert all of the fools and

their foolishness into pure gold. The cellar of their house is filled with the money, jewels, and valuable merchandise of which the fools have been bilked. The stone which Face, Subtle, and Dol possess is knowledge of man's greed, egoism, and gullibility, and they turn this knowledge into profit. But the rogues, enormously successful though they are, are finally themselves imposters whose magnificent command of language and supreme ability to shift from disguise to disguise, making themselves in each case just what the gulls desire them to be, are only covers and overlays on their unregenerate animal natures. Dol Common may pretend to be Queen of the Fairies and the mad sister of a great nobleman – and significantly enough she may be taken for such by the gulls – but she remains always no more than a 'smock rampant'. Subtle may appear most reverent, grave, wise, and stuffed with erudition and arcane knowledge, but he remains no more than the poor creature described by Face:

> at *pie-corner*,
> Taking your meale of steeme in, from cookes stalls,
> Where, like the father of hunger, you did walke
> Piteously costive, with your pinch'd-horne-nose,
> And your complexion, of the *romane* wash,
> Stuck full of black, and melancholique wormes,
> Like poulder-cornes, shot, at th' *artillerie-yard*.   (1 i 25–31)

And Face, though the most cunning of the lot, for all of his masks of the gorgeous and magniloquent Captain, or the humble Lungs, the alchemist's assistant, is still no more than Jeremy the butler with his petty schemes for getting a few pounds by selling 'the dole-beere to *aqua-vitae* men', and 'letting out of counters' (1 i 51–6).

The characters of Jonson's other plays are also involved in similar attempts to raise themselves from the poor things which they essentially are into something magnificent and important. Each desires to be 'the sole sir of the world' – Cleopatra's description of Octavius – and the limits of aspiration are set only by the limits of the imagination of each character. . . .

Jonson's characters are all satiric portraits of Renaissance aspiration, of the belief that man can make anything he will of himself and of his world, that he can storm heaven and become one with the gods, or make of earth a new paradise. Human nature and 'remote matter' are considered by Jonson's characters – as they are by the characters of Elizabethan tragedy – as endlessly plastic and therefore subject to the alchemical process. Their dream of life is as spacious and as free of any limiting concept of reality as that of a modern Madison Avenue advertising copywriter who with a flash of the pen and a few colors changes toilet paper into mink, an internal combustion engine into the winged horse Pegasus, a rubber girdle into beauty, and a deodorant into popularity. But in Jonson's plays these dreams are never allowed to float entirely free of earth; they remain always solidly anchored to reality. And the reality is that dense substratum of primal matter, the materia liquida, which is everywhere present in the plays and constantly provides an ironic comment on these men who would soar out of their humanity. This is not to say, of course, that Jonson shows man as potentially no more than beast, or suggests that he must always remain no more than a collection of 'haire o' the head, burnt clouts, chalke, merds, and clay'. Alchemy remains a possibility, but a possibility with very definite limits. The trick lies in getting hold of the right stone, the true elixir.

In *The Alchemist* there are several references to the ancient tradition that the stone can only be discovered by the truly moral man,

> *homo frugi*,
> A pious, holy, and religious man,
> One free from mortall sinne, a very virgin.   (II ii 97–9)

The stone itself is described, in accordance with the traditional lore of alchemy, as,

> The art of *Angels*, Natures miracle,
> The *divine secret*, that doth flye in clouds,
> From *east* to *west*: and whose tradition
> Is not from men, but spirits.   (III ii 103–6)

These lines are Subtle's, and he is, of course, simply pouring out alchemical jargon, but the lines have a significance of which he is totally unaware. They point to a different conception of alchemy and the nature of the stone than that held by the characters of the play. The stone is immanent in the world 'from *east* to *west*', it is resident in 'nature', and it is insubstantial for it belongs to angels, flies in the clouds, and comes from spirits. All of this suggests that the true stone is moral and spiritual, and that man can only be made from beast by the exercise of his moral nature. But the fools with whom Jonson has stuffed his scene are all gross materialists tied so closely to the world of solid substantial things that they can conceive of nothing that is not either a thing or a sensation. This heavy realism finds brilliant expression from time to time in such expressions as Volpone's satisfied remark after drinking a cup of wine, 'This heate is life', or Sir Epicure's invitation to Dol Common to 'enjoy a perpetuitie of life, and lust'.

The determined literalism and single-minded sensuality of Jonson's characters is the source of an ever widening series of ironies which provides both the humor of the plays and ultimately the moral comment on the characters and their activities. On the simplest level it is, of course, the willingness of the various characters to accept the apparent for the real that makes them immediately ridiculous. Just as they believe that the stone will 'really' turn iron to gold, so they will accept Subtle as a genuine alchemist, Dol Common as Queen of the Fairies, the parasite Mosca as a true friend, or the Bible-quoting Zeal-of-the-Land Busy as a genuine saint. What the fools will do for others they will, of course, do for themselves, and so the young fop believes that he only has to dress in the latest styles to become a gentleman of fashion, the lady that she only has to be seen in the right company and at the right places to be distinguished and honorable, the pedant that he only has to spout enough inkhorn terms and drop the names of enough Latin authors to be learned.

This ready acceptance of what seems for what is leads inevitably to a fantastic mangling of language, and the fools usually reveal most tellingly the inadequacy of their views of reality by their insensitivity to words. . . . For example, the opening speech of *Volpone* is a mock aubade in which Volpone greets not the day but his 'sacred gold' and praises it in this manner:

> Well did wise Poets, by thy glorious name,
> Title that age, which they would have the best.

The reference is, of course, to the Golden Age, but Volpone in his literal-mindedness has completely missed the fact that 'Golden' has a metaphorical and spiritual value, not a literal one. The Golden Age was, in fact, so titled because, in this primitive Eden existence, men had no gold or precious metals. In each of his plays, Jonson uses this technique of revealing the limitations of his characters' views of reality through the limitations of their literal and purely denotative use of language. By and large his fools, both great and small, are men who cannot understand metaphor.

This verbal literalness from which much of the plays' humor derives ultimately provides an implicit evaluation of all the frantic human activity in them. If the characteristic action of Jonson's characters is 'to become a god', or 'to transmit base metal into gold', then the fundamental irony is that each of the characters in striving to be more than man always reduces himself to less than man. Because he can conceive of alchemy – i.e. 'progress' – in no other than literal terms, because he can measure value only by gold and by physical sensation, a Volpone, a Sir Epicure, or a Fitzdottrel always by his very efforts to rise above himself drives himself down the scale of being and back into the world of process, mere organism, and mechanics. . . . In Sir Epicure Mammon's description of the jewels with which he will surround himself, the fantastic and exotic animals he will consume, the rich stuff

and skins in which he will be clothed, we see a man slipping back into the
same 'remote matter' out of which he thinks he is hoisting himself. Every
mask or disguise, whether of language or vizard, becomes in this way a
revelation of true character, and the commenting function of the satirist
in formal verse satire is performed by the language of the fools
themselves. Where he describes them as animals and machines they
now, unawares, present themselves as such.

  Just as the moral commentary is provided in Jonson's plays by this
indirect method, so the 'ideal' is stated in the same manner. There are a
few instances of virtue in Jonson's plays, a few characters who seem to
represent something approaching a humane ideal, standing isolated in
the middle of the satiric scene. But each of these characters is suspect in
some way. . . . Characters such as Bonario form a pleasant contrast to
the depraved world in which they find themselves, and occasionally a
line like Celia's heartbroken exclamation at the villainy she has seen, 'I
would I could forget, I were a creature' (IV v 102) rings true; but on the
whole these examples of virtue are too placid and lifeless to save
themselves or make us very concerned about whether they are saved.
Their virtue is as mechanical as the villainy and foolishness of the
corrupt characters. Jonson often presents another and more effective
type of virtue, the 'Truewit', and while it is clear that these witty and
intelligent characters who are not too depraved often serve as 'heroes' in
the plays, it is equally clear that wit alone is not held up as a moral ideal
and the hope of the world. Lovewit in *The Alchemist*, Dauphine and
Clerimont in *The Silent Woman*, Quarlous in *Bartholomew Fair*, and
Wittipol in *The Devil is an Ass* are all attractive and far preferable to
either the complete fools or the clever schemers around them. Life might
at least continue if the world were made up of these Truewits – as it
would not if the world were given over to the monsters and fools – but it
would never achieve the status of a civilization.

  The absence of any truly reputable hero combining both wit and
moral virtue in Jonson's plays suggests that while the alchemical
miracle of transforming man into saint might be accomplished by *homo
frugi*, the man 'free from mortal sin', such men do not exist. At his best,
Jonson's man, like Shakespeare's, gets 'a little soil'd in th'working'. But
if man in himself and by his own virtue lacks the stone in these satirical
comedies, he does not entirely lack the means to raise himself above the
level of mere thing. The ideal, the true stone available to man, is – as in
Shakespeare's comedies – compliance with the dictates of Nature as
they are manifested in society with its customs, institutions, and
traditions. The plays, of course, present us with a spectacle of the
breakdown of society and a near return to primitive chaos. . . . Jonson,
like all great satirists, concentrates on the sensitive areas of social life,
both public and private, and shows the distortion and infection

produced in each place and relationship by the desire to be the 'sole sir of the world'. . . .

The restoration of these values, the return to reality from illusion, is the business of the plot, and it is in his management of the plot that Jonson reveals his leanings toward comedy. The satiric elements in Jonson's comical satires – and those of Middleton, Marston, and other authors of this type of play – are concentrated in the portraits of the fools and the scenes in which they display their various brands of idiocy and vice. But for all their numbers as they pour down on London at Michaelmas Term, swirl about at Bartholomew Fair, or congregate to discuss some grandiose scheme such as draining the English Fens or turning all the base metal of the world into gold, the foolish and vicious never prevent the continuation of civilized life. They do, of course, by their greed, their lust, their waste, their intolerant zeal, and their sheer stupidity interfere with the operation of those virtues and social forms which are both the subject matter and the ideals of comedy and satire: marriage, procreation, education of the young, tolerance of others, and provision of the necessaries of life for all. But in these comical satires social health and the balance of nature are always restored, not by the heroic activities of a scourging satirist, but by a natural process. Just as there are always enough redheaded woodpeckers who have a taste for downy caterpillars, so there are always just enough sharpers to prey on the fools and render them harmless; and the fools because they are fools attract their natural enemies and feed them fat. In turn these sharpers can be counted on to eat up one another, for in the comic world every Volpone has his Mosca and every Subtle his Face.

But while it is true that Jonson's plots tend toward the comic, it is equally true that in some cases at least there is a lingering suggestion of the satiric in them, as if Jonson were unwilling to provide his material with a fully triumphant comic conclusion. Northrop Frye describes the basic comic plot in this way:

In the first place, the movement of comedy is usually a movement from one kind of society to another. At the beginning of the play the obstructing characters are in charge of the play's society, and the audience recognizes that they are usurpers. At the end of the play the device in the plot that brings hero and heroine together causes a new society to crystallize around the hero, and the moment when this crystallization occurs is the point of resolution in the action, the comic discovery, *anagnorisis* or *cognitio*.[1]

A large number of Jonson's plays lack the romantic hero and heroine referred to in this passage, but I take it that comedy may employ as an image of its values other types of plots than the ultimate reunion of two lovers who have been separated by some unnatural force in the form of either an individual or social custom. Thus, in *The Silent Woman* comic values find expression in the failure of old Morose in his related attempts to prevent his young nephew Dauphine from inheriting his money and to silence all the noise of a busy world. It would seem that the basic comic ideals of growth, development, change, and vitality can be stated in a wide variety of terms in the comic plot and that the romantic love affair is only one of these terms, though certainly the most common one in English comedy.

Once we recognize that comedy employs a large number of plot situations, we can make use of Frye's description of the standard comic plot to test the degree of the comic in Jonson's plays. The essential point of Frye's theory is that comedy moves inevitably toward the elimination of the unhealthy, the disabling, the sterile elements in society, and that this movement culminates in the creation of a new and healthier society serving the realistic needs of its people. Elsewhere Frye adds that 'the tendency of comedy is to include as many people as possible in its final society: the blocking characters are more often reconciled or converted than simply repudiated'.[2] This sounds very much like Jonson's own early comic formula, Every Man Out of His Humour, and a large number of Jonson's plays have plots of this kind. In The Silent Woman, for example, Morose, with his antisocial passion for absolute quiet and his equally antisocial refusal to allow his nephew to have any money, is so badgered and tricked that by the end of the play he is driven out of his humor – along with the other fools – and a new society forms around Dauphine. Here, and in Bartholomew Fair and the plays following it there is something approaching a tone of reconciliation at the end, though the various fools are always scourged and cursed in a harsh manner more reminiscent of satire than comedy.

But in Volpone and The Alchemist, though the plot moves toward the purging of society, and the usual satiric stasis is not allowed to prevail, there is no final reconciliation. In Volpone the disturbing or sick characters, rather than being incorporated in the new society, are either driven out or imprisoned. . . . Viciousness and idiocy, the play states through its plot, are incorrigible and can only be chained up, for, once loose, such is their energy that they will soon control the city again. The Alchemist moves toward a similar conclusion, for, in the end, while fool after fool is tricked and shamed and sent away with a verbal whipping, there is no sense of a better and more stable society having evolved. The master trickster, Face, has simply combined with his equally tricky master, Lovewit, to outwit the greedy idiots and carry off the spoils; and one of the spoils is the vapid Dame Pliant, the wealthy widow who, ironically enough, fills the part of the comic heroine.

Neither Volpone nor The Alchemist contains that savage despair and sense of utter frustration expressed in the plots of the blackest kinds of satire, for willy-nilly Jonson's world does right itself each time, not through any virtue immanent in man, not by the clever activity and opportunism of a single hero, not through the intervention of a beneficent, supernatural Nature,[3] not through the effectiveness of society and its laws – the usual restorative forces in comedy – but merely by a defect inherent in vice and folly which leads them to overreach themselves. If the plots of these plays do not fit the satiric formula of an endless round of purpose and passion, neither do they quite fit the comic formula of an irresistible and joyous triumph of vitality and reality over death and illusion in which the perverted elements of society are salvaged and included in the brave new world. In *The Alchemist* and *Volpone* Jonson came very close to creating pure satire of the Menippean kind,[4] and, once again, it is perhaps not very profitable to try to decide whether these plays are either satire or comedy in an absolute and exclusive sense.

SOURCE: extracts from *The Cankered Muse: Satire of the English Renaissance* (1959) pp. 168–78, 180–4, 185–6, 186, 187–9, 190–1.

NOTES

1. Northrop Frye, *Anatomy of Criticism* (Princeton, N. J., 1957) p. 163.
2. Ibid., p. 165.
3. The nature referred to here is that mystical healing power which so often operates in the comic world, not the nature of physical law and mechanical operation. The Nature which moves through Shakespeare's *The Winter's Tale* is a good example of the first meaning of the word, while the concluding moral of *Volpone*, spoken by one of the corrupt judges, expresses very clearly the second meaning:

Mischiefes feed
Like beasts, till they be fat, and then they bleed.

Both of these 'natures' are present in Jonson's plays, but the first Nature never interferes with the acts of men. It is present in man and the world to be utilized and realized, but it remains a potentiality for men to strive for. For an interesting dramatic treatment of this idea see *The Alchemist*, II iii 121 ff., where Surly and Subtle debate whether alchemy is natural.
4. [Kernan defines as Menippean 'any satiric work obviously written in the third person or, to put it another way, where the attack is managed under cover of a fable' (p. 13). The figure of the satirical commentator is absent, for satire of this type, 'stressing the scene rather than the satirist', achieves 'the satiric end of scourging the fools . . . by allowing them to reveal their fundamental ridiculousness in their own speeches and actions' (pp. 164, 242). Cf. Clement's comment on Matthew and his kind in *Every Man in* (v v 44–5): 'They cannot expect reprehension, or reproch. They have it with the fact.']

F. H. Mares

'THE STRUCTURE AND VERSE OF THE ALCHEMIST' (1967)

All through the play there is a disparity between what people are and what they say they are. The servant, the quack, and the prostitute are the Captain, the Doctor, and the Lord's sister, or a priest and the Queen of Fairy. These high titles are counterpointed with abusive ones. In trying to stop the quarrel of Face and Subtle in the opening scene Dol calls them 'gentlemen', 'Soveraigne', 'Generall', and in return is called a bitch: 'Away this brach.' When she in turn gets angry they become an 'abominable paire of stinkards', 'snarling dog-bolts', and 'perpetuall curres'. As the quarrel is smoothed over, the men become 'good babounes' and she is elevated to 'Royall DOL'. It is not only the partners in the 'venter *tripartite*' who suffer this transmutation. The lawyer's clerk is made a nephew of the Queen of the Fairies, and is to become the envy of all the men about town. Drugger, 'A miserable rogue, and lives with cheese, / And has the wormes' (II vi 81–2), is to 'be of the clothing of his companie: / And, next spring, call'd to the scarlet'. Mammon swings from being King of Bantam, and his dreams of unlimited food and unending sexual intercourse, to mounting a 'turnep-cart', to 'preach / The end o' the world, within these two months'. The Anabaptists are obliged by Subtle to confess their own hypocrisy. In the theatre this illusionism is given its visual counterpart in the rapid assumption of different rôles – the alchemist presents a different personality to each of his customers – or in frequent changes of costume: Face becomes 'Lungs', the mad lady becomes the Queen of the Fairies. Surly disguises himself as a Spaniard, and this costume is proposed in turn for Drugger and Face, and finally assumed by Lovewit. Costume itself is an important ingredient in Mammon's fantasies. He promises Dol:

> thou shalt ha' thy wardrobe,
> Richer then *Natures*, still, to change thyselfe,
> And vary oftener, for thy pride, then shee:
> Or *Art*, her wise, and almost-equall servant.
>
> (IV i 166–9)[1]

In this general shifting of appearances even the Neighbours who crowd

on to the stage at the beginning of the last act become 'changelings' in
scene ii and accept with apparent equanimity the opposite of what they
have just been vehemently asserting:

> NEIGHBOUR 2   He'has had the keyes:
>   And the dore has beene shut these three weekes.
> NEIGHBOUR 3   Like enough.   (v ii 42–3)

At the end of the play, when Lovewit and Face come forward to speak
their last words directly to the audience, the dramatic illusion itself is
questioned; and not there only: there are the numerous references to the
action of the play taking place in the Blackfriars, where the theatre in
which it was performed was situated, as was Jonson's own house, and
there is the joke about Drugger:

> FACE   . . . Hast thou no credit with the players?
> DRUGGER   Yes, sir, did you never see me play the foole?
>   (IV vii 68–9)

Drugger, almost certainly, was played by Robert Armin, the 'fool' of
the King's Men. Jonson often uses framing or bridging devices – the
chorus characters of *Every Man out*, the complex prologue and the
puppet-play within the play of *Bartholomew Fair*, the bogus spectators
who chatter between the acts of *The Staple of News* – but commonly they
are more overt and more emphatic. In *The Alchemist* we are not obliged
to hold the play at a greater distance from us by having some characters
come between us and it: we are invited to come closer, to identify
ourselves with it. Lovewit and Face address the audience directly – Face
even offers a comment on the dramaturgy:

> My part a little fell in this last *Scene*,
> Yet 'twas *decorum*   (v v 158–9)

– but they do so without coming out of the characters they have
supported in the play. Lovewit, the good-humoured opportunist,
invites us to consider, if we think he has behaved in an unseemly way for
a responsible citizen and an elderly man, what he has got out of it: cash
in hand, fire-irons in the cellar, and an eminently beddable (and
biddable) young wife with a good dowry. Would we not have been
tempted to do the same? Face admits his guilt, but calmly invites our
complicity and sets out to bribe the jury:

> I put my selfe
> On you, that are my countrey: and this pelfe,
> Which I have got, if you doe quit me, rests
> To feast you often, and invite new ghests.   (v v 162–5)

The argument is clever, for much of our pleasure in the play does depend on complicity: on a kind of comic dramatic irony, as we watch the fools of the play walk into the traps we have seen prepared for them. Face's appeal to his 'countrey' is to a jury of his peers: *hypocrite lecteur! – mon semblable, – mon frère!* We are all rogues and hypocrites, though some of us are bigger fools than others; and this being the case, Face suggests, isn't it better to be on the side of the clever rogues and not cultivate either the delusion that our wishes will all suddenly come true or 'that same foolish vice of honestie' (v v 84) as Surly does? The play is the world and the world is the play: what goes on in the 'house, here, in the *friers*' (I i 17) is going on, on this day, in this place, for exactly the time that the spectators are watching it. This is not to make Jonson a seventeenth-century Pirandello, trapped in the insoluble problem of distinguishing illusion from reality, or a Genet, asserting at once man's inevitable need for illusion and the illusory nature of all conventional moral authorities. It is not King Lear's 'change places; and, handy-dandy, which is the justice, which is the thief?' (IV vi 156–8). Jonson does not doubt for a moment that truth can be distinguished from illusion, that right and wrong are absolute and not relative terms. For him vice and folly can be known because the moral law can be known. To complain that *The Alchemist* lacks moral point because the fools lose their property, the rogues escape unpunished, and Face and Lovewit keep the loot, is to expect a crude moralism that Jonson would have despised. Partridge claims that 'all endure the most comic of all punishments: they remain themselves – a deadly retribution if one is a fool like Mammon or a rascal like Face'.[2] Even this is only part of the truth: the realism of Jonson's illusion is forced on us so strongly because we must see ourselves in his knaves and fools. We must admit that it is all too likely that like Lovewit we should prefer self-interest to propriety, that we should turn a blind eye on Face's tricks as long as there was something in it for us. We must feel in a degree that the foolish and vicious fantasies of the dupes are our own fantasies. The speeches of Sir Epicure, with their grandiose imagery and their powerful, almost Marlovian, verse movement, can serve for a paradigm of the effect of the whole play. We are momentarily carried away, the bogus grandeur takes us in, and then with a shock we discover that we are condoning grotesque excesses of gluttony or sensuality: poets

> that writ so subtly of the *fart*,
> Whom I will entertaine, still, for that subject.
>
> (II ii 63–4)

Jonson is a genial moralist in *The Alchemist*; he provides no punishments for villainy and offers no overt condemnation, but he obliges us to recognize, in the mirror of his play, how strong is our own potentiality for vice and folly.

> They are so naturall follies, but so showne,
> As even the doers may see, and yet not owne.
>
> (Prologue, ll. 23–4)

That is, even while we enjoy this brilliant play, we shall recognize that
the follies it ridicules are our own follies; but we are not obliged to make
this recognition public.

JONSON'S VERSE

The *Poet* is the neerest Borderer upon the Orator, and expresseth all his vertues,
though he be tyed more to numbers; is his equall in ornament, and above him in
his strengths. And, (of the kind) the *Comicke* comes neerest: Because, in moving
the minds of men, and stirring of affections (in which Oratory shewes, and
especially approves her eminence), hee chiefly excells.

> (*Discoveries*, ll. 2528–34)

Jonson's dramatic verse is functional: it is the rhetorical means to the
ends of his art. *The Alchemist* is in blank verse except for Surly's phrases
of Spanish and a few lines in the two scenes where Dapper is prepared
for and then meets the Fairy Queen. Here the mock-ritual is
emphasized by the addition of rhyme. The use of the one form of verse
for all the varieties of idiom, mood, and social status in the play insists on
its essential unity, but within this common form Jonson is capable of
very varied effects. He can range from the coarse insults of the opening
quarrel to the grandiose fantasies of Mammon. The language and the
forms of syntax it takes are always appropriate to character and
situation and the blank verse has great variety and rhythmic vitality.

> I am a yong beginner, and am building
> Of a new shop, and't like your worship; just,
> At corner of a street: (Here's the plot on't.)
> And I would know, by art, sir, of your worship,
> Which way I should make my dore, by *necromancie*.
> And, where my shelves. And, which should be for boxes.
> And, which for pots. I would be glad to thrive, sir.
> And, I was wish'd to your worship, by a gentleman,
> One Captaine, F A C E, that say's you know mens *planets*,
> And their good *angels*, and their bad.   (i iii 7–16)

In this passage Drugger's stammering nervousness, his clumsy re-
petitions, and his low and monosyllabic vocabulary dislocate the verse
until it scarcely exists. Only two of the lines above have ten syllables:
they are consecutive, and linked by a violent enjambement which
virtually imposes a different division on the speaker: 'just, / At corner of
a street'.

Tribulation, the practised preacher, has by contrast an unctuous fluency:

> The children of perdition are, oft-times,
> Made instruments even of the greatest workes.
> Beside, we should give somewhat to mans nature,
> The place he lives in, still about the fire,
> And fume of mettalls, that intoxicate
> The braine of man, and make him prone to passion.
> Where have you greater *Atheists*, then your Cookes?
> Or more prophane, or cholerick then your Glasse-men?
> More *Antichristian*, then your Bell-founders?   (III i 15 – 23)

This is much more regular and the units of syntax tend to coincide with the divisions of the verse. While he can carry a sentence over two or three lines of verse Tribulation never goes far before coming firmly to rest on a metrical and syntactic pause. The repeated rhetorical questions (a line apiece) indicate the pulpit orator as clearly as phrases like 'children of perdition', 'instruments . . . of the greatest workes', or 'more prophane'. Mammon's syntax, like his range of allusion, is much more adventurous. His clauses spring from one another and proliferate in apposition as his fantasy moves (by association) to wilder visions:

> I'am pleas'd, the glorie of her sexe should know,
> This nooke, here, of the *Friers*, is no climate,
> For her, to live obscurely in, to learne
> Physick, and surgery, for the Constables wife
> Of some odde Hundred in *Essex*; but come forth,
> And tast the aire of palaces; eate, drinke
> The toyles of *Emp'ricks*, and their boasted practice;
> Tincture of pearle, and corrall, gold, and amber;
> Be seene at feasts, and triumphs; have it ask'd,
> What miracle shee is? set all the eyes
> Of court a-fire, like a burning glasse,
> And worke 'hem into cinders; when the jewells
> Of twentie states adorne thee; and the light
> Strikes out the starres; that, when thy name is mention'd,
> Queenes may looke pale: and, we but shewing our love,
> NERO'S POPPÆA may be lost in storie!   (IV i 130–45)

The natural rhythm of the voice speaking these lines does not destroy the pattern of recurrence in the metre, as so nearly happens in Drugger's lines. Nor, as with Tribulation, does it reinforce it, offering only crude and simple variations. Rather it counterpoints and harmonizes to produce a rich and exciting rhythmic texture. The sixteen lines are all one sentence and can scarcely be divided: the energy of Mammon's vision carries through and unifies the almost Miltonically relaxed syntax. The syntax itself is like a dream or vision, where things shift into each other and change their form.

The syntax of Subtle's exposition of alchemy (II iii 142 ff.) is, like the verse, regular, logical, and orderly. As with Tribulation's speech, the verse- and sense-units tend to coincide, but here the linguistic structures are those of reasoned argument, not emotional exhortation. What Subtle is saying is grand and terrible non-sense, for the language of alchemy defines itself, and has no reference, for all its sonority and glamour, to the real world. But the forms the language takes are those of ordered rational discourse, of logical, learned, unimpassioned disputation. This tone is emphasized by the regular but not over-emphatic forward march of the verse. Here in the verse-form and the syntax is a parallel to the concern with disguise and the playing of parts noticed above. Subtle disguises his language in the forms of learning and reason, and therein demonstrates his subtlety. Surly cannot dispute with him on these terms, for to do so would be to move into Subtle's self-defining world and argue upon his premises. Accordingly he launches into a catalogue, a violent piling-up of terms (ll. 182–98) that 'Would burst a man to name' and almost burst the actor in speaking. The continued appearance of sweet reason in Subtle's response to this irascible and (in form) irrational outburst leaves Surly no reply. In the scene which follows, where Subtle has to deal with the much less sophisticated Ananias, his tone is more authoritative, his rhythm much more staccato. It is, as he says, 'In a new tune, new gesture, but old language' (II iv 27).

The pattern of the verse is maintained not only in the longer set speeches. It persists in the most rapid exchanges of dialogue:

SUBTLE		Cheater.
FACE	Bawd.	
SUBTLE	Cow-herd.	
FACE		Conjurer.
SUBTLE		Cut-purse.
FACE		Witch.
DOL		O me!
We are ruin'd! lost!		(I i 106–8)

Jonson admirably manages effects of interruption and rapid changes of gear:

SUBTLE   The *divine secret*, that doth flye in clouds,
     From *east* to *west*: and whose tradition
     Is not from men, but spirits.
ANANIAS   I hate *Traditions*:

    I do not trust them –
TRIBULATION   Peace.
ANANIAS   They are *Popish*, all.
    I will not peace. I will not –
TRIBULATION   ANANIAS.
ANANIAS   Please the prophane, to grieve the godly: I may not.
SUBTLE   Well, ANANIAS, thou shalt over-come.

                                     (III ii 104–10)

Tribulation's 'Peace' fits into the caesura of Ananias's line. His 'Ananias' cuts a line short and completes it, but Ananias's next line is long and he need hardly pause in his delivery (which must be rapid) for Tribulation's interruption. Subtle's much slower line would come after a marked pause, leaving 'I may not' hanging in an embarrassing silence. Mammon (and on occasion other characters) interrupts himself:

                       my baths, like pits
    To fall into: from whence, we will come forth,
    And rowle us drie in gossamour, and roses.
    (Is it arriv'd at *ruby*?) – Where I spie
    A wealthy citizen. . . .   (II ii 50–4)

The most ingenious verse effect is the passage at IV v 25–32, where, against the background of Dol's incantatory ravings 'Out of BROUGHTON', Face and Mammon have an agitated colloquy about what is to be done.

    Jonson's dramatic verse is less easily quotable than Shakespeare's. Set pieces do not detach themselves so readily from context. (Of course many a much-quoted passage is radically changed by detachment from its context: Iago's 'Who steals my purse, steals trash . . .', for example.) It is exactly Jonson's 'art', in his sense of the term, the art that he said Shakespeare wanted, that makes this so. His dramatic verse has great range and energy but it is always ordered and controlled by a considered dramatic context, and this is both its strength and its limitation.

      SOURCE: extract from Introduction to *The Alchemist* (1967) pp. liv–lxii.

NOTES

    1. This is a preoccupation of Jonson's: *Volpone* has more specific designs for Celia; when Stuffe, the tailor in *The New Inn*, makes a fine dress, before he delivers it to the customer he takes his wife out in it, pretending she is a countess and he her footman:

A fine *species*,
Of fornicating with a mans own wife.   (IV iii 76–7)

Cf. also Epigram XXV, 'On Sir Voluptuous Beast'.
  2. [See Edward Partridge's essay extracted above.]

J. B. Steane

'CRIME AND PUNISHMENT IN *THE ALCHEMIST*' (1967)

... this much, a comedy directed against false values, folly and trickery, covers, I think, only a part of the attitude to life which *The Alchemist* expresses. This much is readily acceptable as sound morality, and when it is enforced by all the arts of the poetic dramatist, as here, the effect is great. But the play's 'morality' is more complicated than this, less orthodox and more interesting.

In an essay called 'Crime and Punishment in Ben Jonson',[1] D. J. Enright wrote of *The Alchemist* that it 'has not the fine unity' of *Volpone*. He continues:

The end, when Lovewit comes along and quite irresponsibly snaps up Dame Pliant from under Surly's nose (Surly is a very half-hearted character altogether) and even more irresponsibly turns a blind eye to Face's misbehaviour, is not far above the level of *Bartholomew Fair* [described earlier as 'a frivolous play']. It will not bear comparison with the end of *Volpone*.

'Crime and punishment' is a useful heading, and it is certainly interesting to see how the theme is treated in the three comedies just mentioned. In *Volpone* the criminals are punished severely: Mosca goes to the galleys, Volpone to prison, and various humiliating penalties are inflicted upon the gulls themselves. In a last speech the lesson is sent home:

            Now, you begin,
When crimes are done, and past, and to be punish'd,
To thinke what your crimes are: away with them.
Let all, ·that see these vices thus rewarded
Take heart, and love to study 'hem! Mischiefes feed
Like beasts, till they be fat, and then they bleed.

The judgment is authoritative, and the last image neatly summarises the plot, reminding us, incidentally, of the 'Argument' poem preceding *The Alchemist*. The mischief-makers here go about their business till with trick piled on trick there comes an explosion, '*and they, and all in* fume *are gone*'. But when they (Subtle, Face and Dol) 'are gone', it is not with the harsh judgment of these lines in *Volpone* ringing in our ears. On the contrary, their offences are palliated: Subtle and Dol lose their loot but escape the law, and Face not only retains his position but has his master Lovewit connive at the trickery for which orthodox morality would say he deserved punishment.

In his explicit statements, Jonson was a sternly sincere, orthodox moralist. In such plays as *Volpone*, *Sejanus* and *Catiline* evil is fully exhibited, given its scope and judged. *The Alchemist*, which seems to Mr Enright less satisfying partly for the reason that the crime is virtually left unpunished, seems to me rather more interesting, and ultimately stronger, partly for the very reason that the morality is less bluntly unambiguous, and in fact less orthodox.

Of course Subtle, Face and Dol are tricksters, and of course we see them as anti-social, irresponsible, unprincipled even among themselves, and so forth. There is no sentimental creation of the 'lovable rogue' or the 'whore with a heart of gold'. These people yelp and snarl at each other in the opening scene, and remain predatory creatures, less than civilised, less than fully human, throughout. On the other hand, they are infinitely resourceful and entertaining; the energy, thought, wit and action seem inexhaustible. Moreover, in all their confrontations with the rest of the world we are placed on *their* side rather than on the other: the fun of their schemes and the folly of their victims make us turn a much more tolerant eye on their doings than orthodox morality soberly permits. And in this we are being worked upon in the spirit of the master, Lovewit, who, when he sees these enormities, is more amused than outraged.

Lovewit does not appear in the play until the last act, but his position is crucial. D. J. Enright, in the passage quoted, says that Lovewit behaves irresponsibly, and so by the standards of *Volpone* he does. But Lovewit is what his name proclaims him to be. 'I love a teeming wit, as I love my nourishment', he says, and consequently he places a high value upon his butler Face, and surveys the whole social scene with a relish that has little or nothing of the moralist about it. Lovewit's arrival in the play is like that of the *deus ex machina*. We have heard of him long ago in Act I:

> O, feare not him. While there dyes one, a weeke,
> O' the plague, hee's safe, from thinking toward *London*.
> Beside, hee's busy at his hop-yards, now:

> I had a letter from him. If he doe,
> Hee'll send such word, for ayring o' the house
> As you shall have sufficient time, to quit it.

Very faintly, the religious overtone makes itself felt: 'watch ye therefore: for ye know not when the master of the house cometh . . .'. Meanwhile like naughty children in the absence of their parents, the trio of rogues use the house left in Face's care; they dress up, have people in, play game after game till they nearly come to blows, and then scurry about frantically to put the place straight before the master can find out about them. Inevitably there is some suggestion of a parable about such a plot. But however subdued the suggestion, and however comic the context, it still places Lovewit in this very important position: that of the master whose power is formidable and whose judgment may come like the wrath of God unexpectedly from on high. So by his status in the plot, Lovewit's judgment should be the one which we as audience are called on to respect.

Mr Enright found Lovewit's judgment unsatisfactory and the ending flawed therefore. Another writer, Edward Partridge in *The Broken Compass*, argues that Lovewit is intentionally presented in a bad light and that the author is judging him too.[2] I do not believe it; for it is not only Lovewit's position in the plot that confers this authority upon him. It is also the prevailing spirit of fun which makes *The Alchemist* something different from the moral play that both these critics want it to be.

Supporting this is the odd treatment of the sceptic, Surly. Surly is Lovewit's opposite number. He condemns what Lovewit condones and scowls where Lovewit smiles. Yet their dramatic function is alike in this, that both are judges. Surly is intelligent and strong enough to be proof against Subtle; he is even able for a while to gull the gullers. But the working of the drama accords him very little respect. When he appears in his Spanish disguise we laugh at him more than with him, even though we know that he is for the time outwitting Face and Subtle. He cuts a ridiculous figure and they are amusing at his expense. Then finally his plans come to nothing and in the end he stands glumly, a butt for Lovewit's gibes, having lost the game because he was not quick-witted enough to keep pace. There is right-mindedness in his scowls, an admirably rational scepticism in his determination not to be gulled; but the final impression is that he too, like Lovewit, is defined by his name. And whereas Lovewit has life in his name and nature, Surly is heavy and has no touch of that zest and relish which in the judgment of Lovewit (and, I think, the play) go far to redeem the rogues.

The rogues themselves ought, in an orthodox morality, to be merely ruthless and despicable. Instead, we find ourselves laughing with them too often. Moreover, if we laugh it is in appreciation of a kind of mind. For example, Face in the first scene attacks Subtle, reminding him of what he was when he (Face) met him:

> at *pie-corner*,
> Taking your meal of steeme in, from cookes stalls,
> Where, like the father of hunger, you did walke
> Piteously costive, with your pinch'd-horne-nose,
> And your complexion, of the *romane* wash,
> Stuck full of black, and melancholique wormes,
> Like poulder-cornes, shot, at the *artillerie-yard* . . .
> When you went pirrn'd up, in the severall rags,
> Yo'had rak'd, and pick'd from dung-hills, before day,
> Your feet in mouldie slippers, for your kibes,
> A felt of rugg, and a thin thredden cloake,
> That scarce would cover your no-buttocks . . . .

The mind that can depict with this kind of vividness is at any rate wonderfully alive. He draws a caricature of Subtle ('your com- plexion . . . like poulder-cornes, shot, at the *artillerie-yard*') with a Dickensian attack and sureness. The language takes its substance from the world around: a mind evidently open-eyed and keenly receptive to the sights of the city. Each of the little pictures has its own vigour: the picture, for instance, of the wretched man searching through the 'dung- hills, before day' is given pictorial life by the verb 'rak'd', strong and specific. One idea generates another; so that we see 'Your feet in mouldie slippers', which is external and part of the general caricature, and then look underneath them to the chilblains ('for your kibes') chafing miserably in their rawness.

This vitality of speech is inseparable from the character of the speaker: Face is not just a 'bad character' who happens to be given lively lines. We, as audience, warm to the liveliness, and therefore to the character; and so it is throughout the play, for Face's vitality never flags. The same is true of Subtle and Dol. After Face's denunciation just quoted, Subtle replies, painting a brilliant picture of the butler-on-the- make. The wit is quick and fertile, the images are specific and the lines packed. Characters whose speech can dazzle in this way, keeping an audience on its mettle, must command a kind of respect. We see them also as artists. Subtle, Pygmalionlike, has created Face, he claims:

> Have I tane thee, out of dung . . .
> Rais'd thee from broomes, and dust, and watring pots?
> *Sublim'd* thee, and *exalted* thee, and *fix'd* thee
> I' the *third region*, call'd our *state of grace*?
> Wrought thee to *spirit*, to *quintessence*, with paines

> Would twise have won me the *philosophers worke?*
> Put thee in words, and fashion? made thee fit
> For more then ordinarie fellowships?

Partridge notes that these are alchemic terms, and comments: 'Subtle claims to have alchemized a man.' He sees this as 'impiety', with Subtle as 'a parody of the Creator' and the jargon as 'a parody of the Word'.[3] Possibly so; but I cannot believe that the 'impiety' was ever taken very seriously by any audience – there is too much amusement. And as the scene proceeds there is every inducement for the audience to identify themselves with the rogues. It is Dol who has the last word in the argument. She harangues formidably, a low-life Queen Bess, and proposes a programme full of promise for their entertainment and ours:

> Shall we goe make
> A sort of sober, scirvy, precise neighbours,
> (That scarse have smil'd twise, sin' the king came in)
> A feast of laughter, at our follies?

The 'feast of laughter' is to be our own too, and of course we relish the prospect and warm to these quick-witted providers of the feast. Partridge speaks of their 'impiety' and 'pretentiousness of language', seeing them as 'animals which live on a lower plane than men', and he remarks that Face 'is really [only] the clothes he has on'.[4] But there are far more powerful forces working to counteract this heavily moralistic reaction: and chief among these is laughter. We laugh *with* the trickers: they are the entertainers, and every speech that is put into their mouths expresses energy, humour and life. They pipe, and the foolish human race jigs to their tune. Mammon, Kastril, Ananias, Drugger are all entertaining characters, but they are put in motion, made to dance in their ludicrous way for us, by the ingenuities of the three. They are the hosts at this 'feast of laughter' and by the fifth act they have so conditioned us to the appreciation of 'a teeming wit' that we are quite prepared, dramatically, to accept Lovewit's 'irresponsible' judgment when he makes it.

This does not mean that Jonson is an irresponsible moralist here, or that *The Alchemist* is 'mere' entertainment. It is a very highly organised, sharply pointed moral comedy, but its sting is directed not so much at the exploiters as at the society which by its greed and folly is so open to exploitation. And, of course, the rogues themselves are quite firmly 'placed'. However great their vitality, we are left in no doubt about the limitations of their humanity. There is no depth and no loyalty about them. Their horizon is narrow and their values are often flashy and

vulgar. In the speech quoted above, Subtle claims to have created Face
('tane thee, out of dung') and made him 'fit / For more then ordinarie
fellowships':

> Giv'n thee thy othes, thy quarrelling dimensions?
> Thy rules, to cheat at horse-race, cock-pit, cardes,
> Dice, or what ever gallant tincture, else?

This, to them, is the crown of creation; this is what life is for – cutting a
dash among the sporting lads and cheating better than they can. Jonson
is perfectly realistic and truthful about these people: their native wit and
vitality are remarkable, but social and economic conditions (and we are
made strongly aware of them) have constricted and contorted them so
that their lives are confined within the narrow limits of petty crime.

It would be all too easy, however, for the professedly respectable,
virtuous folk in Jonson's audiences to spend their condemnation on this
small game, and to miss the broader and more unsettling social criticism
that the play presents.

The gulls are so varied as to show in cross-section a society led by
greed and lust to folly and loss. The nobleman, the countryman, the
little clerk, the churchman, the small shopkeeper: Jonson's net is cast
widely enough over society to take in all these. Morally the scope is
equally wide. Their faults include: greed and lust, excess, triviality;
coarseness, thickheadedness; false ambition, credulity and feeble
submissiveness; hypocrisy, double-think and extortion; mere silliness.
The frailties of the race are on show. But what might have been a parade
of assorted vices gains unity and purpose from the motive that is
common to all of them: an obsessive desire for easy money. In this way
the play does more than offer a rich collection of satirical portraits; it
depicts a whole society, ruthlessly individualistic and acquisitive, and
ultimately deluded and impoverished by its own false values. . . .

The Alchemist is that remarkable thing, a work of art classically
controlled yet striking one at all points as enjoying the freedoms of a
spontaneous, fresh liveliness. So much of the rarity of Ben Jonson lies
there. He was a scholar, who knew the dramatic laws and respected
them. He applies them in this play; the action takes place in twenty-four
hours and in, or just outside, a single house. He constructs his plot with
formal perfection, each episode neatly dovetailed into the next, and he
keeps the various plots going with the virtuosity of a juggler. But this is
all at one with a sense of fun that has nothing dully academic about it,
and a verbal energy that is entirely of its own period.

Finally there is the satisfaction of an entertainment that, in a much
more serious way than, say, the comedies of Sheridan and Goldsmith, is
directed by a mature moral and social consciousness. The hard,
grasping energy of the age, the life that springs out of the dunghills of

London's poverty, the outrage of a luxurious, cavalier self-indulgence among silly courtiers, and of a pale-faced power-seeking puritanism at the other extreme; all these are caught and condemned. This is one side of the play's morality. The other is more positive, less explicit and probably less expected. That is the joy in wit that the play expresses. Wit in the trio of rogues is a creative force. They create for Sir Mammon the *novo orbe*, the Eldorado of his hopes: this cobwebby London house has become for him a fantasy place of glamour and promise. The spell over his mind is the creation of this wit. They create too the characters of 'the cunning man', of 'Captain' Face and of 'Lungs', the alchemist's assistant. Dol creates the mathematical lady mad from overmuch study of Broughton's works. They are artists. As against this, Surly with his heavy scepticism and his passive, rather absurd impersonation of the Spanish Don has no real life to offer. Jonson's own creative joy is with his entertainers, and that is no doubt why he lets them off lightly at the end. Perhaps this is 'irresponsible' and inferior to the stern judgment at the end of *Volpone*. Yet in that play too there is a sense of a creative liveliness in Mosca and Volpone that comes near to redeeming them. Volpone joys not so much in 'the glad possession' as in 'the cunning purchase', and Mosca could skip out of his skin with the spring in his blood. In *The Alchemist* it is this confrontation that is finally brought to focus; a creative vitality that is precious even in criminals, against a heavy, delusive folly that is deadly even in the law-abiding and respectable. The zest and challenge of the play are in that.

SOURCE: extracts from Introduction to *The Alchemist* (1967) pp. 10–15, 22.

NOTES

1. *Scrutiny*, IX (1940–1) 231–48.
2. [See Partridge's essay in Part Three, section 2 above.]
3. [See Partridge's essay above.]
4. ['The impostors are compared to mongrels, scarabs, vermin, curs. These, in their several ways, suggest animals which live on a lower plane than men, or insects which prey on other beings. The dog imagery occurs most often. Dol is a bitch, and Face and Subtle are mastiffs. In short, we are among the snarling animals that live on other beings or each other' (Partridge, *The Broken Compass*, p. 115).]

William Empson

'THE ALCHEMIST AND THE CRITICS' (1970)

Probably it is a delusion caused by ignorance, but my impression is that, in the case of this one play, I stand alone like Abdiel against the forces of night. A number of critics have written quite sensibly about *Volpone*, but in *The Alchemist* (I suspect they feel) the crude formula becomes too hard to resist. There seems no way of jolting its adherents, making them willing to recognise the actual merits of the play. Hence it is unusual to deny that Jonson hates and despises all the characters in *The Alchemist*, either for being fools or for being knaves, because he is so moral. And yet the two plays are very alike, in their general tone as well as their electrically geared-up construction – they are the most frequently revived of Jonson's plays, and I agree that they are much the best. The producer of either play, it will be found, never tries to implement our established critical theory about it (not even making it like non-Euclidean geometry), because the audience is sure to reject that. The case is thus rather odd, and might throw some light on the presumptions of Eng. Lit. in general.

The reason for the difference, I think, is that teachers feel *The Alchemist* to be hiding something worse than *Volpone*, needing more urgently to be kept from the students. The romantic appeal of *Volpone* is felt as a tender indulgence even while it is being ignored by an effort of hypocrisy, but somehow *The Alchemist* is felt to have harshly unwelcome 'values' lurking within; this makes it even more urgent for the critic to insist that Jonson has no 'values', in that he despises all the characters he describes. The term 'values', it seems as well to point out, has the serious function of helping us to recognise the variety of the world. The chief use of reading imaginative literature is to make you grasp that different people act on different ethical beliefs, whereas the chief use of critical jargon is to obscure this basic fact, making you feel at home where you are not. Jonson in this play has a splendid range of characters with wildly different values, and the effect is very funny, but if you think he despises them all you are taken aback when he begins to express his own. However, to let him be morally active does not make him a scold; indeed, *Bartholomew Fair* strikes me as rather too permissive, too like the comic Dickens – the audience is expected to love the eccentrics so much that it merely wants them to troop back onto the stage, each repeating his fixed gimmick. It is not the sterner morality but the clockwork plots of the two great farces that haul them up into the cold exhilarating air of the mountains.

Even so, one cannot get on with *The Alchemist* without accepting its moral. This might seem easy to grasp; the play sets out to dissuade its audiences from superstitious belief. But nowadays the rivetting home of the chains of superstition upon captive children is regarded as the prime duty of an educator; so naturally this activity of Jonson, though the critics are always trying to invent ways to tell us how moral he is, cannot be recognised as moral at all. 'Do you imagine he was like H. G. Wells?' I shall be asked with exasperated astonishment. Only like Wells on a few plain-man issues, I grant, because he was also prone to the seductive role of the working-class reactionary. But in this play we find him solidly and consciously backing a progressive cause; and I do not see why he should not be respected more for it than Shakespeare in *Macbeth*, lavishing his art upon an encouragement for James to torment old women. I do not, indeed, think we need be so solemn as is now usual over the repeated claims of Jonson to be an improving author. The theatre was under Puritan attack, and to provide a defence for himself and his fellows was one of the uses of his learning. He would expound the classical defence whenever convenient; it should apply, of course, to all good playwrights. Evidently he believed in it, but it would not actually deflect his mind while he was being inspired to create a farce. On the other hand, when the structure of a play required a moral, the doctrine enabled him to present one with vigour; and that is what we find going on here.

Both *Volpone* and *The Alchemist* depend for their intended effect upon rogue-sentiment, upon making the audience half-sympathise with the tricksters. I think this was helped in *Volpone* by the jealousy of London at the maritime trade of Venice, but anyway jealousy at rich business-men would excuse quite a lot. In the more homely setting of *The Alchemist*, the audience are to feel: 'People oughtn't to be such mugs. If a man can be cheated by obvious rogues like this, he deserves it. They may be doing him a kindness by teaching him a bit more sense.' The fun was permissible as in a good cause; and this at least explains why the rogues don't have to be punished at the end.[1] The sentiment comes out strongly in the poetry at III iii, the right place for a high boast before the fall. Dol on returning to the house says to the exultant Face:

> Lord *Generall*, how fares our campe?
> FACE   As, with the few, that had entrench'd themselves
> Safe, by their discipline, against a world, DOL;
> And laugh'd, within those trenches, and grew fat

> With thinking on the booties, DOL, brought in
> Daily, by their small parties.

We ought to share in the sense of glory here. But the two rogues are
pretty flat and straightforward; Jonson feels that Dol is too good for
them, but she cannot make much difference, and the main interest has
to arise from their dupes.

The play begins, like *Volpone*, with a prologue telling the audience
they are supposed to laugh. As always, Jonson intends to better them,
but here nobody need be offended, because nobody need admit that he
is one of the people laughed at. Jonson is no longer writing about an
imaginary Italy:

> Our *Scene* is *London*, 'cause we would make knowne,
>   No countries mirth is better than our owne.
> No clime breeds better matter; for your whore,
>   Bawd, squire, impostor, many persons more,
> Whose manners, now call'd humors, feed the stage. . . .

The sentence goes on *and which*, so *for* has to mean 'as providing' not
'because' – it does not introduce a clause explaining why England is
good for comedy. The confusing grammar perhaps helps to imply a
joke, that the English are good comic material for bad reasons (as when
Hamlet's madness is said not to matter in England, where all the men
are as mad as he), but even so this would be a cosy bit of disguised self-
praise. The audience is being put in a good humour at the start; and for
that matter Jonson had just returned to the Anglican Church, so he was
rather inclined to draw attention to his patriotism. He had no need to
tell the major reason, known to all, why England might be expected to
produce amusing eccentrics – because it was a uniquely free country
(even if they had little reason to believe so). It is thus very absurd to
make this passage mean that Jonson the Morose despised his own
countrymen even more than the rest of mankind.

The first two dupes presented to us, Dapper the clerk and Drugger
the shopkeeper, are silly chaps who take up little time, though they
should be acted as earnestly and patiently deluded. Drugger needs a
little magic to make his shop pay, and he is let off lightly; Dapper has the
worst time, because his object in wanting magic to win bets is to be
admired by men friends of better class. It is a democratic or Dickensian
moral; if Dapper had only wanted to make money, Jonson would never
have driven him into such fierce shame. For the Puritans he feels real
enmity; they wanted to close the theatres and interfere with his private
life, and he is trying to make mischief, though not lying, when he
presents them as inherently traitors intriguing against the King. One
does not much hate them, because they are so funny, but they are

allowed no spark of decent feeling. On the other hand Sir Epicure Mammon is genuinely admired for being so advanced and public-spirited; he is a patron of the new sciences, which already excited great hopes, and such a man deserved respect not only for his generosity but for his readiness to make a fool of himself – plainly, if he met with any success, it could only be by luck. He enters at the start of Act II, and Act I closes with a fanfare of glowing praise for him by Subtle, too good as poetry to be meant as spiteful or jeering:

> He will make
> Nature asham'd, of her long sleepe; when art,
> Who's but a step-dame, shall doe more, then shee,
> In her best love to man-kind, ever could.
> If his dreame last, hee'll turne the age, to gold.

Mammon himself is always generous-minded, and speaks much the best poetry throughout the play. His most absurd scene has nothing to do with science; it is when he proposes marriage to Dol, accepting her as an aristocrat who studies philosophy in retirement:

> DOL   Bloud we boast none, sir, a poore Baron's daughter.
> MAMMON   Poore! and gat you? Prophane not. Had your father
>   Slept all the happy remnant of his life
>   After the act, lyen but there still, and panted,
>   H' had done inough, to make himselfe, his issue,
>   And his posteritie noble.

It is of course very absurd, but to think him contemptible for it would be mean-minded; and Jonson had no such temptation, as he considered that Dol really had got high courage and the power of command – not admiring Dol, but admiring ladies, was what he found absurd in the man's delusion, and a part of the artisan audience would agree.[2]

Mammon of course expects luxury, as well as world power, from the chemical operation; and here I meet a grave obstacle. Nowadays everybody seems to take for granted that Jonson loathed and despised luxury, and indeed only mentioned it here to express his hatred and contempt for science, which was already known to be irreligious and materialistic. The critics do not, I think, offer evidence for this interpretation, because they find it obvious from the 'whole tone' of Jonson as they read him. And they read him so, no doubt, because they are sure that all other seventeenth-century poets hated and belittled such achievements of science as had yet occurred. It is a pleasure to be able to report that all this is false, and that the small-mindedness which it imputes needs only to be sponged away. (In fact, it is rather hard to see why the poets felt that so much had already happened.) And then, if you read what Drummond of Hawthornden reports about Jonson, or

Isaac Walton, for instance, it is surely hard to remain confident that he
had a holy contempt for bodily pleasure; and their gossip does not seem
malignant, though they probably exaggerate for fun. One should
remember,too, that the Golden Age of Latin literature, the time when
the authors lived whom Jonson genuinely did revere and never ceased
to emulate, was notorious for its impudent luxury, which had chiefly
meant a display of power; obviously, to win it back would mean a final
recovery from the Dark Age. To see this play as when new, I have come
to feel, one needs to unwind layer behind layer of false assumptions,
rucked and rotting together about a foot deep, as Fenollosa unwound
them from the Yumedono Kwannon, the most beautiful statue in the
world. Of course, none of this is meant to deny that Mammon is a
shockingly silly man, who ought to have been able to see through
Subtle, and ought anyway to have attended to what his friend Surly told
him.

Anyhow, an audience commonly feels at home with Mammon,
whereas poor Kastril really does need a bit more appreciation. He has
recently inherited three thousand a year from land, a great deal then,
and he feels that the position brings with it obligations; he must become
terrifically sporting, an expert in the technicalities of duelling and any
other line that may be required. The obligations indeed have become so
heavy that they might drag him loose from the position; he at least
listens without protest when Face insinuates that he had better sell the
estate and use the capital to set himself up as a leading London trickster
(III iv 49). It is useless to scold Kastril as irresponsible and sybaritic; he
is hag-ridden by his imaginary duties, accepting an early death but
terrified that he may fail to die in proper style. This is a case in which
the'values' of the modern literary critic, for reasons which are about two
centuries old and quite creditable to him, make him blankly unable to
read the text. He has never met a young man like that; well, nor have I,
or Ben Jonson either I should fancy, because they cropped up mainly
under the Regency; but Jonson is grasping the first stage of a historical
development there.

In the play, what matters is his affection for the character; it decides
the structure. Jonson takes for granted that poor Kastril has been badly
educated – his impulses have been almost fatally misdirected – but that
the impulses themselves are splendidly good; he deserves, if ever man
deserved, to escape from the suicide into which he is driving himself
with frank cries of pain and fear. This gives the play its happy ending;
Kastril is saved at the last moment by a quite unexpected twist of his
psychology. He finds that the middle-aged business-man is what he
really admires, so now he need not be a gangster leader, only another
business-man; he and Lovewit can play tricks together for ever after. It
is very like the deep thankfulness with which Fielding, acting as a family

lawyer, allots good luck at the end to Tom Jones, which Tom fully deserved though he was so very unlikely to have stumbled across it in real life. A modern audience, I should think, would accept this if it were firmly enough presented to them. It does not involve any intellectual sell-out to the ethical claims of the business-men (that is, a good production need not). Surely the discovery of Kastril, that they are quite criminal enough for an aristocrat to admire them, ends the play to the satisfaction of all concerned.

A few years ago I was asked to address a large audience of young people who were just going to take an 'A level' exam in this play, which would partly decide whether they went to a university; and the vocal ones were sure the play simply tells us that Kastril was a coward. It made me realise the strength of the opposition. I suppose they felt that a man who wants lessons in how to be a bully was necessarily a coward (and duelling can no longer be recognised as a sport). But if a man frequently tells you that he is afraid of doing something, and then invariably does it, you are mistaken to think him a coward; and if Kastril had not told the audience that he realised his plan to be next door to suicide they would only have thought him a fool. But probably the effect of the final scene, at the time, turned on a social detail now forgotten. Kastril enters dragging and beating his sister, angry because she has married Lovewit and has thus not even become a 'lady' (as by marrying a knight); Lovewit advances upon him:

LOVE-WIT Come, will you quarrell? I will feize you, sirrah.
  Why doe you not buckle to your tooles?
KASTRIL   Gods light!
  This is a fine old Boy, as ere I saw.
LOVE-WIT What, doe you change your copy, now? Proceed,
  Here stands my dove: stoupe at her, if you dare.
KASTRIL 'Slight I must love him! I cannot choose, i-faith!
  An I should be hang'd for't. Suster, I protest,
  I honor thee, for this match.
LOVE-WIT   O, doe you so, sir?
KASTRIL Yes, and thou canst take *tabacco*, and drinke, old Boy,
  I'll give her five hundred pound more, to her marriage,
  Then her owne state.
LOVE-WIT   Fill a pipe-full, JEREMIE.

Lessons in fencing have been the most important part of Kastril's education, and we have often seen him stumbling over the sword he wears. But a business-man, not being expected to defend his honour, did not carry a sword, any more than he carried 'tooles', like an artisan. He advances upon the young gentleman unarmed, in the mere confidence that he is the new ruling class. Or perhaps that is dragging in more social significance than we need here; the bare fact of his coolness is what leaves Kastril, who has always been much impressed by these tools, morally disarmed. Also his sister has run and sheltered from him behind Lovewit, who threatens him to defend her; this is hard for him to resist. Of course you may still think Kastril a great booby, but if you act him as a coward you have to leave out nearly all the points of this concentrated little scene.

The poet Yeats has pluckily recorded, in the preface to *On the Boiler*, that he was bowled over by business-men in very much this style (though on a different plane), as soon as he had reached enough political eminence to encounter them. 'When I was first a member of the Irish Senate', he is recalling, some of the members had been nominated, not elected:

in its early days some old banker or lawyer would dominate the House, leaning upon the back of the chair in front, always speaking with undisturbed self-possession as if at some table in a board-room. My imagination sets up against this some typical elected man, emotional as a youthful chimpanzee, hot and vague, always disturbed, always hating something or other.

The spontaneous admiration, indeed, was what got him into very odd political company, where he never felt at home. One might say that the play is a prophecy; Kastril regularly has been bowled over by Lovewit ever since, and it has been rather a bad thing. But one need not, I think, go on to say that Jonson analysed the first stirrings of capitalism.

Another point where Kastril is like Yeats, making him very unlike the stock cowardly swashbuckler, is his desire to build up all his new acquaintance into legends, so that he feels surrounded by the kind of life he admires. This point of character is firmly established at his first appearance, as soon as he has finished mentioning his income:

FACE   Is your name KASTRIL sir?
KASTRIL   I, and the best of the KASTRILS, I'lld be sorry else,
    By fifteene hundred, a yeere. Where is this Doctor?
    My mad *tabacco*-Boy, here, tells me of one,
    That can doe things. Has he any skill?

We in the audience have just been hearing the modest hopes of Drugger for his shop, and feeling that they hardly deserve the help of a magician; so it comes as a shock to find him considered reckless and romantic. The note of loony aspiration or highmindedness is habitual to Kastril, so that he does not seem feeble even when he says, childishly, 'doe you thinke, Doctor, I e'er shall quarrell well?' (IV iv 93–4). He quarrels well enough later on – to be sure, Surly refuses to fight out of contempt, and Ananias helps him unwittingly; but then, Surly is tough and has a fortune at stake and is keen to expose the rogues. One cannot think Kastril merely ineffective after he has driven out Surly.

Some critics have argued from the name that the character is meant to be despised. A kestrel is a small kind of hawk, which was not trained like the large ones for aristocratic sport, and as it did damage could be regarded as vermin. The term *coistrel* for a low trouble-maker was derived from it, and no doubt *Kastril* was simply a local pronunciation. The young man is a notably unaristocratic squire, meant to be absurd; but no hawk is really contemptible. The kestrel is the windhover. Kastril knows he is not very big or strong; it is only his unquenchable desire for glory that makes him hurl himself into trouble, with his feathers all scuffed up. Ordinary men take a rather different view of him in each generation, and it chiefly turns on how much we need him to fight in our defence. Jonson had himself killed a man in a duel, and was partial to brave young cocks; he would think it very odd of us not to be glad when Kastril is saved.

Much more puzzle arises over Surly. As the name implies, he is an honest man of the sort Jonson liked; not only intelligent enough to see through the cheats, he also labours to expose them in the public interest, or at least to help his friend Mammon. The author is attacking popular superstition exactly as Surly does; but he makes Surly look a fool for it. Surly in order to overhear the cheats dresses himself as a Spanish nobleman (who knows no English), and does so well that they try to marry him to Kastril's sister – Kastril wants this, knowing that the Spaniards are far ahead of the English at the game of aristocracy. Left alone with her, he scolds her and tells her that any other man would have raped her (apparently this would secure her money, because she could only recover her reputation by marrying him):

SURLY   For yo'are a handsome woman: would yo' were wise, too.
    I am a gentleman, come here disguis'd,
    Onely to find the knaveries of this *Citadell*,
    And where I might have wrong'd your honor, and have not,
    I claime some interest in your love. You are,
    They say, a widdow, rich: and I am a batcheler,
    Worth naught: Your fortunes may make me a man,
    As I ha' preserv'd you a woman. Thinke upon it,
    And whether, I have deserv'd you, or no.
DAME PLIANT   I will, sir.

The moral atmosphere being so firmly like Dickens, one expects this good deed to be rewarded with an ample competence. But Lovewit on his return takes the lady and her fortune for himself; he then 'rallies' Surly, apparently literally for not having raped her when he got the

chance. Kastril has stumped off to search the house for his sister, and
Lovewit explains that she

> should ha' marryed a *Spanish Count*, but he,
> When he came to't, neglected her so grosly,
> That I, a widdower, am gone through with her.
> SURLY How! Have I lost her then?
> LOVE-WIT   Were you the *Don*, sir?
> Good faith, now, shee do's blame yo'extremely, and sayes
> You swore, and told her, you had ta'en the pains
> To dye your beard, and umbre o'er your face,
> Borrowed a sute, and ruffe, all for her love;
> And then did nothing. What an over-sight
> And want of putting forward, sir, was this!

The plot is winding up rapidly, but Surly snatches a moment to say

> Must I needs cheat my selfe,
> With that same foolish vice of honestie!

before he goes out to search for Face, saying he will beat him if he
catches him. The reconditioned Face opens the door and bows him out,
saying

> in troth, they were strangers
> To me, I thought 'hem as honest as my selfe, sir.

So we are forced to join in laughing at Surly, who is not even allowed to
stick to saying he behaved like a gentleman.

    C. G. Thayer is the only critic I happened to come across who
recognised this problem (most of them just assume we are meant to
despise the whole cast); he says:

in Mammon and Surly, then, we have the willing victim and the jealous rival.
Surly is dishonest, but is outraged that Face and Subtle should be dishonest too,
and this feeling of outrage leads him to his attempt to unmask them, with
disastrous results for himself. This is a fairly complicated matter; Surly is one of
those ironic commentators who would be effective if he were not immoral.[3]

A wild flight of fancy, and yet, come to think of it, there very likely was a
Victorian melodrama which plugged home this tiring platitude. How
totally unlike *The Alchemist* it must have been. To make Mr. Thayer's
point, the other characters must have been ready to believe Surly, so
that he would have succeeded in exposing the cheats, had they not
already known him to be smirched; from practically the first scene, we
must observe the ladies as they pass him in silence labouring not to
touch him with their crinolines. But nobody even hints at this idea, and
no character however unsmirched could get heard against the hulla-

baloo of Kastril and Ananias combined (IV vii). Also Surly cannot be
trying to cheat Mammon, as a 'rival' to Subtle, because Mammon knows
all about him, or at least gives us the only insinuations against him. I
would even deny that Surly meets 'disastrous results'; he only escapes a
marriage which would have been painful to him – the type of woman he
wants would have responded to the approach he made. Admittedly, this
refined thought is not insisted upon by the play, but it is less remote from
the play than the refined thought of my opponent.

Mammon tells Surly, when they first appear, that he is going to make
all his friends rich, and he rather spreads himself on the disagreeable
things, very unsuited to poor Surly's character one would think, that
Surly will never have to do again. He begins with the really splendid
phrase

> You shall no more deale with the hollow die,
> Or the fraile card

and seems next to envisage his pimping for rich young men. On the
stage, Surly had I suppose better spit and look round defiantly; he is not
going to confess to it, whatever it was. Mammon himself is fairly well off
and quite respectable; his friends are assumed to be of the same class,
though some of them get driven to unfortunate shifts. In fact, this is
meant to be the world of *Vanity Fair*, though Jonson is no good at
marking fine shades of gentility. Most of the ways of earning money
which are now considered honest are not open to Surly, as they would
cost him his status as a gentleman; cadging is about all he can do. He
can also gamble, and may well have to 'deal with' people who cheat at
it; the words do not have to mean that he is a cheat too. At what point
giving manly advice to a young friend brought one within danger of the
shameful word 'Pimp' was extremely moot. In short, Jonson is trying to
present Surly not as a petty criminal but as a shabby gentleman, and
Surly tells Dame Pliant he is a gentleman in his first words to her.

One part of this was very familiar to the Elizabethan mind. If a man
is educated above his status, especially by being sent to a university, and
does not afterwards get the white-collar job which he regards as his due,
then he is sure to make trouble, probably as a revolting politician. For
example, the doctrine is used to explain Bosola, at the start of *The
Duchess of Malfi* (when I was young, it was always being said about
Indians). Such a man is the Malcontent, who makes the severe
epigrams or wisecracks; Jaques was in part a parody of him but shows
the character in the round. However, most playwrights insinuate that
their malcontent isn't *really* a gentleman; to assume that the cadging life
was quite normal for a gentleman down on his luck (for Rawdon
Crawley before he had landed his Governorship) would, I should think,

make many people in the first audiences feel rather dubious, like ourselves.

We may now recognise that Dame Pliant is not necessarily an imbecile; she is merely a satire on ladies. Having been brought up to marry for wealth and status, she will accept any man who treats her with cool authority. The theatre was always against the Arranged Marriage (which may have made the operation of the custom less severe, though it went firmly on) and showed this by sympathy for girls in revolt; but to mock the type of girl who accepted it was very unusual. Jonson, it seems clear, had got on better at Court with the men; they were impressed by his learning, his fighting sense of honour, and his conviviality, but the ladies found him coarse. The decisive comment on ladies here is entrusted to Dol Common, who expresses confidence when told to imitate a lady for the plot:

> I'll not forget my race, I warrant you.
> I'll keepe my distance, laugh, and talke aloud;
> Have all the tricks of a proud scirvy ladie,
> And be as rude'as her woman.

The last clause may seem off the point, but Jonson and Dol assume that any professional who has learned the tricks will be better at them than an amateur.

It will now be plain what the 'values' are which establishment critics are so unwilling to recognise. Jonson is militantly anti-Puritan, but also anti-Cavalier from a working-class point of view; you might say he is just spiteful about ladies and gentlemen. I am not at home with this tone myself, and I think he is unfair to Surly; but one cannot be surprised if the Globe audiences found it a treat, and no doubt some of the people in our modern audiences like it better than dons do.

To make an audience accept a successful business-man as a good character is always hard, and no wonder Lovewit has to ingratiate himself at the end by jeering at Surly in a coarse manner. A critic however argues that Lovewit has 'taken the wrong turning and joined the fools' when he marries the fortune at the end, and that Jonson 'indicates' this by Subtle Irony. We are not even told where the irony comes. The duty of toeing the critical line is no doubt much eased by this rule that you can impute subtle irony wherever you like, but one would like to hear how it could be put across in production amid the uproar of the happy ending of the farce. In its quiet way, this is perhaps the most deadly interpretation of all.

Various critics have tried to show that Jonson had a deep understanding of the rise of capitalism in his time; and I agree at least that, after Volpone, the apotheosis of Lovewit needs a bit of comment. Jonson's own attitude to money, there is plenty of evidence to show, was the traditional one of the artist. An artist should flatter a King till he tosses him a bag of gold (for example, by telling James in a Court masque that he is chaste because he does not keep mistresses); and when he has drunk up all that gold, in the course of his devoted labours, he should go back and flatter the King again. Many good artists have lived like this, and the procedure takes endurance as well as nerve; but it can't be a model for the rest of us, and is unlikely to give much insight into mass economic changes. Jonson understands his business-man well enough, and does not inflate him; but I think the major insights of the play, or bits of moral advice if you prefer, concern matters of vanity or social advantage, which readily distract the characters from their none the less oppressive duty of monetary gain. There is a wonderful lot of truth in it.

SOURCE: 'The Alchemist', The Hudson Review, XXII (1969–70) 595–608.

NOTES

1. A student objected that Face must needs be presented morally, because he repents:

> They'll tell all.
> (How shall I beate them off? What shall I doe?)
> Nothing's more wretched, then a guiltie conscience.
>
> (v ii 45–7)

Face is afraid of losing his confidential relation with his master, and snatches every occasion to beg the sympathy of the audience, with comic despair, from here to the end of the scene, rather over a hundred lines, when he invents the plan of marrying his master to the fortune. No one denies that the characters use moral language; I only say that this is not an impressive repentance. It may have served the purpose of coaxing the audience to forgive Face. [Cf. Ezekiel Edgworth's 'Guilt's a terrible thing!' in Bartholomew Fair, IV ii 12, a similar instance of 'comic despair'.]

2. I used to think there is a Bitter Irony when he says:

> This lip, that chin! Me thinks you doe resemble
> One o' the Austriack princes

– because the Hapsburg jaw came to be the standard example of the degeneration caused by dynastic inbreeding. But Jonson wrote before the sinister change had occurred; the prominence of the jaw might still be taken to mark decisiveness and firm will, with which we know Dol to be endowed.

3. [C. G. Thayer, Ben Jonson: Studies in the Plays (Norman, Okla., 1963) p. 93.]

J. B. Bamborough

'QUICK-CHANGE ARTISTRY' (1970)

[Jonson's] greatest fault is that he often carries his love of detail to the point of gross over-writing. He is particularly given to over-indulgence in technical jargon – *The Alchemist* is the obvious example of this – and one sometimes feels that he is so proud of having 'got up' the appropriate technical language that he cannot bear to leave any of it out (this is not unusual with writers who pride themselves on reproducing the language of specialists; Kipling is another writer who indulges himself in this way). All Jonson's comedies need cutting if they are to be comfortable for the actors and acceptable to the audience, and we may hope that we are justified in this by the evidence which suggests that the plays as he printed them are longer than the versions that were acted in his own day. Critics have occasionally seen something unbalanced, even neurotic, in Jonson's tendency to provide excess of material,[1] but there seems no need to attribute it to more than a natural delight in language, together with a normal Renaissance belief in the virtue of *copia*, or abundance of matter. Perhaps we might object, in terms which he would have understood, that he tended to write with a fullness of style more suitable to an encyclopedic work such as *The Anatomy of Melancholy* (he is sometimes quite close to Burton stylistically) than to the Decorum of drama, but this was integral to his whole conception of comedy. In the long run it has not helped his reputation. His technique of accumulation, of heaping one absurdity or humorous clause on another until the audience is almost battered into laughter, works well in the theatre, but is difficult to demonstrate in a lecture-room, and because even his shorter comic passages depend so much for their effect on the context in which they occur they cannot easily be detached by the critic. We do not swap quotations from Jonson as we do from Shakespeare or Wilde, and this perhaps may have contributed to the belief that he is a slow and ponderous writer.

A visit to a production of *The Alchemist* should prove an adequate corrective to this belief. It is the most energetic and fast-moving of all Jonson's robust and vigorous comedies, a non-stop display of ingenuity and invention, centering flawlessly in the quick-change artistry of Face, Subtle, and Dol Common. The basic comic situation is the same as that of the first part of *Volpone*, with the dupes visiting the place where they are to be mulcted, but the tricksters have more roles to play than Volpone has, and a more assorted clientele, so that both the variety and the tension are greater; there is more interaction, too, between the gulls. The greatest use is made for comic effect of argument and dispute. Kastril, who has come to town to learn to quarrel, has come to the right place, for quarrelling is the dominant form of social relationship in Lovewit's house. The play begins with a violent row between Face and Subtle, which degenerates into a straightforward slanging match –

SUBTLE	Cheater.
FACE Bawd.	
SUBTLE	Cow-herd.
FACE	Conjurer.
SUBTLE	Cut-purse.
FACE	Witch. (i i 106–7)

We can trace this back if we wish to the Italian comic debates or *contrasti*, or to the 'flytings' of medieval poetry, but its ancestry might just as well have been the 'and you're another' exchange of the Westminster school-yard. The argument is also a first-rate piece of explication for the benefit of the audience, and by the time Dol Common has joined in with her threat to leave the gang if the others will not 'cossen kindly', the spectators have been most effectively and quickly told all they need to know of its operations. From this scene onwards *The Alchemist* progresses largely by a series of quarrels. In the second scene Face, in disguise, argues with Subtle on Dapper's behalf; in the first scene of Act II Surly and Mammon dispute about Alchemy, and in the third scene of this act Surly and Subtle argue the question out. Ananias then enters the fray: he has a short brush with Subtle in II v, a discussion with Tribulation Wholesome in III i as to whether the coining of money is lawful, and in the following scene rumbles mutinously the whole time as Tribulation tries to smooth Subtle down again ('I hate *Traditions*: I do not trust them. . . . They are *Popish*, all. I will not peace. I will not . . .'). In IV ii Kastril begins his lessons from Subtle in the art of managing a quarrel, and in IV iv he sets about his sister because she is reluctant to marry the alleged Spanish Count; meanwhile, in the previous scene, Face and Subtle have started their argument about which of them shall have Dame Pliant. In IV v Mammon, who was previously warned that Dol, in her disguise as the Lord's sister, must hear no word of controversy, follows her in as she raves about the interpretation of prophetic history, is scolded by Subtle, and told that her brother is at the door 'as furious, as [she] is mad' – a threatened quarrel that never materialises. The great set-piece occurs in scenes vi and vii of this Act, when Surly reveals himself and attacks Face and Subtle. Subtle loses his nerve, but Face sets Kastril on to 'quarrell

[Surly] out o'the house', and in quick succession Drugger and Ananias
are brought into the argument. There is no better example than this
scene of Jonson's extraordinary gift for quickly turning the action of a
play. The audience has just seen Surly apparently about to destroy the
whole basis on which Face and Subtle work, and then with magnificent
speed this threat to the fabric of the comedy is not only averted but
turned to new comic effect. Ananias enters with his Puritan greeting,
'Peace to the household' – a magnificent line to deliver into the middle
of the violent altercation which is at this moment in full swing on the
stage. Subtle tells him that the cause of the quarrel is Kastril's 'zeale'
against Surly's Spanish clothes, and he is immediately launched into
one of his diatribes:

>   That ruffe of pride,
>   About thy neck, betrayes thee: and is the same
>   With that, which the uncleane birds, in *seventy-seven*,
>   Were seene to pranke it with, on divers coasts.
>   Thou look'st like *Antichrist*, in that leud hat. . . .
>   (IV vii 51–5)

Jonson beautifully catches here the way in which a stupidly irascible
fanatic will give rein to his own prejudices in any situation of conflict,
just as earlier, in the dispute between Ananias and Subtle, he illustrates
how two specialists, each speaking the jargon of his own trade, can have
an argument in which neither understands a word said by the other.
The out-facing of Surly in these scenes in Act IV might be regarded as
Face and Subtle's finest hour because it is all improvised, whereas the
discomfiture of Mammon is something they have planned long before.
Effectively, as the audience actually experiences the play, both scenes
contribute to the feeling that *The Alchemist* is being made up by Face
and Subtle as it goes along. The whole of the last Act, after the return of
Lovewit, consists of frustrated attempts by the gulls to argue him into
returning their goods, and at the very end he silences Kastril, the 'angrie
Child' who is berating his sister:

>   Come, will you quarrell? I will feize you, sirrah.
>   Why doe you not buckle to your tooles?   (V v 131–2)

Confronted with this unexpected determination on the part of his new
brother-in-law Kastril compounds the final quarrel of the play.
    All this gives a great sense of excitement and movement to *The
Alchemist*, and like all Jonson's comedy it demands to be played quickly
and without pause. It has also, as *Volpone* has, a strong atmosphere of
high spirits and enjoyment. Subtle, Face and Dol take great pleasure
and pride in their trickery, and, like Volpone and Mosca, they form a
little mutual-admiration society. Their language about their 'venter

tripartite' is inflated and euphoric: Subtle is 'Soveraigne' and Face
'*Generall*' of their 'campe'; Dol is their 'republic', their prized possession,
'our Castle, our *cinque*-Port, / Our *Dover* pire'; their camp fares

> As, with the few, that had entrench'd themselves
> Safe, by their discipline, against a world, Dol:
> And laugh'd, within those trenches, and grew fat
> With thinking on the booties, Dol, brought in
> Daily, by their small parties. . . .   (III iii 34–8)

Their professions of loyalty to their little commonwealth are of course
quite fraudulent, since each is always ready to betray the others in his
own interest; there is dispute between Face and Subtle at the beginning
of the play, the arrival of Dame Pliant brings out again their distrust of
each other, and once Lovewit arrives it is a question of *sauve qui peut*.
Nevertheless their way of speaking about themselves casts an ambience
of eagerness and jollity about their activities which is not tainted, as in
Volpone, by cruelty or violence. Delusions of grandeur, stimulated by the
promises of Face and Subtle, affect everyone in the play: Mammon is
the supreme example, with his visions of impossible luxury and
grotesque voluptuousness, but in their humbler way Dapper and
Drugger have their own rich fantasies – Dapper with the aid of his
familiar will win their money from all the gamblers of the town, and
Drugger will have a magnet under his shop-door to draw in all the
gallants by their spurs, and will shortly be 'call'd to the scarlet' of his
company. Although we know that all these hopes are absurd, and will
be utterly destroyed before the play is over, we become infected by a
kind of giddy excitement in which we feel that perhaps such things are
possible, and are not wholly wrong.

The Alchemist, indeed, lends a good deal of colour to the charge that
Jonson seems at times to approve more of his rogues than his fools. If we
bring a strict moral judgment to bear, no one in the play is blameless.
We might expect Surly, the one person who sees through Face and
Subtle, to represent honesty and virtue, but in fact he is himself a man
who lives by his wits (he is described as 'a gamester'), and he is very
quick to try and take advantage of the opportunity of marrying Dame
Pliant when it arises: what motivates him in his attempts to expose the
cheats is not love of truth, but, as he says, his objection to being gulled.
As for Lovewit, Jonson makes him acknowledge that he may have acted
in a way unbecoming 'an old mans gravitie' and the 'strict canon' – that
is, the rules both of morality and artistic decorum – but he offers no
excuse beyond 'what a yong wife, and a good braine may doe'. He must
be played, in fact, as the sort of whimsical, humorous man – a '*Jovy*
Boy*', as Kastril calls him – who would admire Face's roguery and think
it served Mammon and the rest right if he refuses to give back their

goods. His return ends the transformation of his house to a palace of illusion, reduces Face to his proper station in life and despoils Dol and Subtle of their ill-gotten gains, but what he brings with him is more an air of good-humoured commonsense than the pure, keen wind of moral rectitude. It is inevitable that the audience throughout the play will take its greatest pleasure in the activities of the tricksters, and it is Mammon, with his insane visions of limitless wealth and insatiable lechery, and to a lesser extent Tribulation Wholesome, the religious fanatic, who seem the real villains. It almost begins to look as if in his portrayal of 'naturall follies', as he calls them in the preface to *The Alchemist*, Jonson has begun to lose sight of his sterner moral purpose.

SOURCE: extract from *Ben Jonson* (1970) pp. 96–101.

NOTE

1. See Edmund Wilson, 'Morose Ben Jonson', in *The Triple Thinkers*, revised edition (New York, 1948). Mr Wilson regards Jonson's combination of sulkiness and outpourings of words as a sublimation of infantile anal eroticism.

Ian Donaldson

LANGUAGE, NOISE, AND NONSENSE (1971)

Comedy conventionally ends with a celebration of things won: feasts and dances signal the arrival of a legacy or a once-lost relative, the imminence of a marriage or the conclusion of a quarrel. Ben Jonson's comedy, on the other hand, rarely ends on this note of happy achievement; the expected prizes tend instead to disappear or to prove worthless. A silent wife turns out to be no wife, a legacy turns out to be no legacy, an elixir fails to materialize, a project comes to nothing, a bride deserts her husband on their wedding day. The comic action is insistently negative. Such prizes as are won – Sir Dauphine's legacy in *Epicoene*, for example, or Celia's trebled dowry in *Volpone* – seem finally less conspicuous than these major, central losses.

What the characters in Jonson's plays are left with at the end of the

fifth act is often worthless trash. In *The Devil is an Ass*, Meercraft tells
Fitzdottrel of the ease with which money may be made:

> I'le never want her! Coyne her out of cobwebs,
> Dust, but I'll have her! Raise wooll upon egge-shells,
> Sir, and make grasse grow out o' marro-bones,
> To make her come.   (II i 7–10)

Needless to say, money does not come, and all that remains (so to speak)
is small and random items of rubbish: cobwebs and dust, eggshells and
marrow bones, quite untransmuted and worthless. Images such as these
recur throughout Jonson's dramatic and nondramatic work. The world
itself is described in one of Jonson's poems as 'a shop / Of toyes, and
trifles',[1] an image that returns in a familiar passage of his *Discoveries* (ll.
1437–44):

What petty things they are, wee wonder at? like children, that esteeme every
trifle; and preferre a *Fairing* before their Fathers: what difference is betweene us,
and them? but that we are dearer Fooles, Cockscombes, at a higher rate? They
are pleas'd with Cockleshels, Whistles, Hobby-horses, and such like: wee with
Statues, marble Pillars, Pictures, guilded Roofes, where under-neath is Lath,
and Lyme; perhaps Lome.

'Trifles' such as these form the lure in *Bartholomew Fair* to draw the
curious to Smithfield: puppets and pears and gingerbread – 'trash', like
its vendor's name. Could one but explore the inside of Bartholomew
Cokes's head, remarks his tutor Humphrey Wasp, doubtless one would
find the same worthless trifles there as in the fairground itself:
'cockleshels, pebbles, fine wheat-strawes, and here and there a chicken's
feather, and a cob-web' (I v 95–7).

In Jonson's world people are drawn magnetically to a 'Center
attractive'[2] – a fairground, a house, a 'fountain of self-love' – not so
much out of any feelings of real concord as out of common folly and
greed. Fundamentally such people are divided and alone: 'the great
heard, the multitude; that in all other things are divided; in this alone
conspire, and agree: To love money' (*Discoveries*, ll. 1450–2). The
separateness of person from person is suggested by another (and closely
related) kind of imagery in Jonson's work, which may be called the
imagery of division. It takes many forms, one of which may be seen in
this description by Crites in *Cynthia's Revels* (III iv 75–80) of the way in
which a new gallant's appearance is appraised at court:

> you shall heare one talke of this mans eye;
> Another, of his lip; a third, his nose;
> A fourth commend his legge; a fift his foot;

> A sixt his hand; and every one a limme:
> That you would thinke the poore distorted gallant
> Must there expire.

Such piecemeal and minute opinions seem positively to rend the new courtier limb from limb; the cumulative effect of the passage is to suggest the larger fragmentation of the whole society of the court. Similar imagery of dismemberment, as Christopher Ricks has shown,[3] is also to be found extensively in *Sejanus*, where the final destruction of the protagonist and the disintegration of the body politic are each hinted at by the constant mention throughout the play of distinct parts of the body: eyes, tongues, hands, knees, arms, ears. In *Epicoene*, too, the constant casually humorous talk of physical mutilation and collapse helps create a similar sense of social fragmentation: Captain Otter reveals that his wife 'takes her selfe asunder still when she goes to bed, into some twentie boxes; and about next day noone is put together againe, like a great *Germane* clocke' (IV ii 97–9); Truewit threatens to lop a leg or an arm, a thumb or a finger from Sir John Daw (IV v 122–39), and Morose despairingly wishes he might redeem his rash act of marriage 'with the losse of an eye (nephew) a hand, or any other member' (IV iv 8–9). The play ends, not, as many comedies do, with a marriage, a symbolic act of union, but with a divorce, a symbolic division.[4]

Imagery of this kind is of quite a different order from the imagery of a play like (let us say) *The Merchant of Venice*, where images of bonds and rings and musical harmony suggest at once the cohesiveness of the social group and the value of the objects that most of its members pursue. Jonson's imagery, like the larger action of his plays, tends instead to suggest the vanity of human wishes and the fragmentation of the social group, picturing a world in which 'Things fall apart; the centre cannot hold.'

In some obvious ways the action of *The Alchemist* is not so self-defeating as that of, say, *Volpone* or *The Devil is an Ass*. Lovewit, after all, gets his rich widow, and Face is allowed to keep his loot; the play ends with master and servant united in a pact that is somewhat firmer than the original pact among Subtle, Face, and Dol. Yet for the majority of characters in the play, action proves circular and frustrating in much the way I have described above; riches exist only in the imagination, nothing is finally won. 'Action', indeed, does not seem quite the word to describe what these characters do; most of them, frankly, do very little. Even Surly, apparently one of the more vigorous visitors to the house, gets bogged in the execution of his counterplot and is finally dismissed by Lovewit as one who, having had the opportunity to act, 'did nothing' (v v 54). Characters such as Sir Epicure Mammon and Tribulation Wholesome similarly do virtually nothing – nothing, that is, except talk. *The Alchemist* is often praised for the vigor of its action, yet it is also the most verbal of plays, a play in which talking becomes a substitute for doing and achieving.

In *Discoveries* (ll. 1881–3) Jonson traditionally describes speech as 'the only benefit man hath to expresse his excellencie of mind above other creatures', adding that speech 'is the Instrument of *Society*'. The word 'instrument' is carefully chosen: speech puts society in tune and joins man to his fellows as other creatures may not be joined.[5] It is a natural corollary of Jonson's lofty view of language that he should also consider corruptions of language as evidence of an untuning of the individual mind and of a wider disturbance in society as a whole:

> Neither can his mind be thought to be in tune, whose words doe jarre; nor his reason in frame, whose sentence is preposterous; nor his Elocution cleare and perfect, whose utterance breakes it selfe into fragments and uncertainties.
>
> (*Discoveries*, ll. 2142–6)

> Wheresoever, manners, and fashions are corrupted, Language is. It imitates the publicke riot. The excesse of Feasts, and apparell, are the notes of a sick State; and the wantonnesse of language, of a sick mind.
>
> (*Discoveries*, ll. 954–8)

For all Jonson's obvious delight in chronicling the exact notations of linguistic extravagance, he views language soberly as an index of moral and intellectual health: '*Language* most shewes a man: speake that I may see thee' (*Discoveries*, ll. 2031–2).[6] One of the recurring figures in Jonson's plays is the interminable and inconsequential talker whose discourse seems to consist of nothing more than noise or wind. Crispinus in *Poetaster*, Lady Would-be in *Volpone*, and the Collegiate Ladies in *Epicoene* all talk powerfully, unceasingly, and often nonsensically, using language as an instrument not of reason or of concord but of crude aggression. Moria in *Cynthia's Revels* is described as a 'lady made all of voice, and aire, talkes any thing of any thing' (II iv 14–15), and Saviolina in *Every Man out of his Humour* as one whose talk is 'nothing but sound, sound, a meere *eccho*; shee speakes as shee goes tir'd, in cob-web lawne, light, thin: good enough to catch flies withall' (II iii 208–10). 'Air', 'flies', 'cob-web lawne': such delicate and insubstantial images as these – like Humphrey Wasp's straws and feathers and cobwebs in *Bartholomew Fair* – perfectly convey the vapidity of the characters to which they refer.

Similar images are also found in *The Alchemist*, a play in which language is constantly modulating into parody, rant, and cant, into mock-heroic, foreign, and nonsensical speech, and finally into mere noise; in which language, instead of drawing people to one another,

splits them asunder. The play opens in the midst of a violent quarrel:
'FACE   Beleev't, I will. SUBTLE   Thy worst. I fart at thee.' Language, from the start, is equated with mere wind and noise; Subtle's first
action at once belies his name (later in the play Mammon is to express
an interest in a poet 'that writ so subtly of the *fart*' – II ii 63):

> FACE   You might talke softlier, raskall.
> SUBTLE   No, you *scarabe*,
>   I'll thunder you, in peeces. I will teach you
>   How to beware, to tempt a *furie*'againe
>   That carries tempest in his hand, and voice.
>   (I i 59–62)

The images are again worth noticing; for Subtle, language is like
thunder and tempest, a windy and destructive force. (Later, as Lovewit
knocks at the door, Face ironically observes to Subtle, 'Harke you,
thunder' – V iv 137). Jonson has Ovid use the same phrase while fooling
in the banquet scene in *Poetaster* ('We tell thee, thou anger'st us, cot-
queane; and we will thunder thee in peeces, for thy cot-queanitie' – IV v
124–5; Ovid is playing Jupiter), and in *Volpone* Mosca speaks in similar
terms while counseling Voltore how to destroy their opponents with his
rhetoric:

> MERCURY sit upon your thundring tongue,
> Or the *French* HERCULES, and make your language
> As conquering as his club, to beate along,
> (As with a tempest) flat, our adversaries.   (IV iv 21–4)

Language is pictured as a weapon more than once in *The Alchemist*;
Mammon warns Surly that Subtle will 'Pound him to dust' and 'bray
you in a morter' with his arguments (II iii 142, 178), and later Lovewit
speaks to Kastril about quarreling as one might speak about dueling:

> Come, will you quarrell? I will feize you, sirrah.
> Why doe you not buckle to your tooles?   (V v 131–2)

Conversely, Lovewit speaks to Ananias of weapons as one might speak
of a rhetorical argument: 'I shall confute you with a cudgell' (V v 108).
Language is used several times like grapeshot; in IV vii, for instance,
Surly is actually forced out of the room by the strong blasts of Kastril's
and Ananias's talk. Like any other weapon, language can also injure the
user; it would 'burst a man', says Surly, to try to repeat the alchemical
language used by Subtle (II iii 198).

The notion of 'bursting' is of major interest in the play, and to
understand it, it is helpful to return to one of the topics raised in the
quarrel that opens the play, namely the question of identity:

> FACE   Why! who
> Am I, my mungrill? Who am I?   (I i 12–13)

The question remains poised throughout the play: Who, indeed, is
Face? He slips quickly from one role to another, and Lovewit's final
words to him, 'Speake for thy selfe, knave', do not resolve the problem.
Is the speaker of the epilogue Face, or Jeremy, or the actor playing the
role of Face – Jeremy? In the opening exchange of the play Subtle
claims that Face simply did not exist before Subtle met him:

> Slave, thou hadst had no name – . . .
> Never beene knowne, past *equi clibanum*,
> The heat of horse-dung, under ground, in cellars,
> Or an ale-house, darker than deafe-JOHN's: beene lost
> To all mankind, but laundresses, and tapsters,
> Had not I beene.   (I i 81, 83–7)

Subtle is doing no less than claim responsibility for having created Face
as a character; Face, however, claims that things may be the other way
about:

> Why, I pray you, have I
> Beene countenanc'd by you? or you, by me?
>   (I i 21–2)

Throughout the play there is talk of characters being 'made': 'Come, I
was borne to make thee, my good weasell', says Mammon to Face (II iii
328), and Surly later announces to Dame Pliant that 'Your fortunes
may make me a man' (IV vi 13). The sustained metaphor – and on this
matter Edward Partridge is perceptive[7] – is that of an alchemical
experiment that brings a new being into existence. Continually,
however, the opposite is threatened, the explosion or dispersal of
personal identity: 'Doe you flie out, i' the *projection*?' (I i 79). Later in the
play Mammon ponders the possibility of having his mirrors cut in subtle
angles 'to disperse, / And multiply the figures', and of having mists of
perfume 'vapor'd 'bout the roome, / To loose our selves in' (II ii 46–7,
49–50). Such images as these, like those of dismemberment noted
above, further suggest the potential fragmentation and dissolution of
personal identity.

The image of vapor has other cognates in the play. Adapting a
passage from Martial (I xcii 7–10), Jonson describes how Face first saw
Subtle at Pie Corner, 'Taking your meale of steeme in, from cookes
stalls' (I i 26). A 'meale of steeme' is, indeed, all that Subtle, along with
most of the characters of the play, is finally to get. In any production of
the play smoke drifts out across the stage from Subtle's laboratory fire, a
suitable visual symbol both of the insubstantiality of the hoaxers'

promises and of the densely obfuscating nature of their language, a 'sweet smoke of rhetoric' made literally manifest. Jonson was later to use the same visual symbol in *Bartholomew Fair*, where quarrelsome vapors are accompanied by clouds of steam and tobacco smoke.[8] (The idea is foreshadowed, perhaps, in the tobacco-taking scene of *Every Man in his Humour*, III ii, and in the 'Mist made of delicate perfumes' from which Truth and Opinion emerge to argue their cases in the Barriers of *Hymenaei*, ll. 681 ff.) Other, verbal images of insubstantiality are freely used in *The Alchemist*: the 'drum' with which Dol will keep the Spanish don awake (III iii 44–5), the hollow bouncing balls to which Subtle and Face liken themselves (IV v 98–9), the 'puck-fist' (puffball) to which Face compares Subtle (I ii 63). Mammon's fantasies are likewise gossamer-light: he dreams of shirts 'of taffata-sarsnet, soft, and light / As cob-webs', and eunuchs to

> fan me with ten estrich tailes
> A piece, made in a plume, to gather wind.
> We will be brave, *Puffe*, now we ha' the *med'cine*.
>
> (II ii 89–90, 69–71)

Wind, plume, puff, perfume, mist, vapor, steam, smoke, fume, fart – such words return throughout *The Alchemist*, hinting at the imminent vaporization of wealth, language, and personality itself.

Language is a subject of compelling interest to most of the characters in the play. Mammon vows he has a treatise penned by Adam 'O' the *Philosophers stone*, and in high-*Dutch*. . . . Which proves it was the primitive tongue' (II ii 84–6). Ananias champions Hebrew against all other languages of the world; and on this point, as Jonson's editors have remarked, he resembles many Puritans of the day who believed Hebrew (as well as 'high-*Dutch*', apparently) to be the original language spoken by Adam, and handed down to the Jews after the confusion of Babel. While Mammon and Ananias, in their contrary ways, are occupied with speculations about the language spoken in paradise, the languages spoken in the play are more likely to remind one of Babel itself. High Dutch and Hebrew are not the only languages of which we hear. Dapper speaks words of Turkish, and Face, snatches of Dutch; Subtle speaks in Latin and in the deeply obscure language of alchemy; Surly, dressed as the Spanish don, speaks (somewhat inaccurately) in Spanish, a language that Kastril takes to be French; Kastril himself has come up to London to learn the difficult '*Grammar*, and *Logick*, / And *Rhetorick* of quarrelling' (IV ii 64–5) as practised by the roaring boys. All these people use language to impress and bewilder others. Language does not unite them; it divides them. It is a vehicle not so much of sense as of nonsense.

The more eccentric a man's linguistic habits, the easier (in this play)

it proves to gull him. When Surly as the Spanish don arrives, he looks a
pushover, and Face confidently instructs Dol how to treat him:

> Firke, like a flounder; kisse, like a scallop, close:
> And tickle him with thy mother-tongue. His great
> VERDUGO-ship has not a jot of language:
> So much the easier to be cossin'd, my DOLLY.

> (III iii 69–72)

As Edward Partridge points out, 'mother-tongue' is an obscene pun: sex
is the common language, a language that is nonrational and nonverbal.
Mammon, too, wants Dol to 'talk' with him, 'to give a man a tast of
her——wit—— / Or so' (II iii 259–60). Talk, for Mammon, becomes
confused both with the sexual act and with his imagined Midas touch:

> Now, EPICURE,
> Heighten thy selfe, talke to her, all in gold; . . .
> She shall feele gold, tast gold, heare gold, sleepe gold:
> Nay, we will *concumbere* gold. I will be puissant,
> And mightie in my talke to her!   (IV i 24–5, 29–31)

Such a confusion of activities finally devalues them all: speech, 'the only
benefit man hath to express his excellencie of mind above other
creatures', is reduced to sex, an activity man shares with the beasts; yet
Mammon is so concerned with making pompous speeches to Dol that he
never actually achieves the physical contact of which he dreams. Sex
becomes a substitute for language; language becomes a substitute for
sex.

The 'Queen of the Fairies' scene with the blindfolded Dapper at the
end of the third act continues a similar process of linguistic reduction.
Speech is broken down into nonsensical fragments of sound: '*Ti, ti do ti,
ti ti do, ti da.*' The gibberish spoken to Dapper proves merely the first
stage of a descent to more profound depths of linguistic obscurity. The
fourth act begins with Sir Epicure Mammon's 'talk' with Dol and
proceeds to the interview in broken Spanish between Subtle, Face, and
the disguised Surly; then, as Subtle takes Kastril off to practise his
violent quarreling at the end of the scene, language undergoes an even
more violent fragmentation: the fifth scene of Act IV presents Dol '*In her
fit of talking.*'

The subject of Dol's dislocated and nonsensical speech is, approp-
riately, the history of language since the beginning of the world; like
Mammon and like Ananias, Dol professes a concern for 'the primitive
tongue'. Jonson is borrowing freely from the Puritan Hugh Broughton's
turgid work, *A Concent of Scripture* (1590):

DOL   *For, as he sayes, except*
  We call the Rabbines, and the heathen Greekes –
MAMMON   Deare lady.
DOL   *To come from Salem, and from Athens,*
  And teach the people of great Britaine –
FACE   What's the matter, sir?
DOL   *To speake the tongue of* EBER, *and* JAVAN –
MAMMON   O,
  Sh'is in her fit.
DOL   *We shall know nothing –*
FACE   Death, sir,
  We are un-done.
DOL   *Where, then, a learned Linguist*
  Shall see the antient us'd communion
  Of vowells, and consonants –
FACE   My master will heare!
DOL *A wisedome, which* PYTHAGORAS *held most high –*
MAMMON   Sweet honorable lady.
DOL   *To comprise*
  All sounds of voyces, in few markes of letters.   (IV V 12–23)

'All sounds of voyces': as the speech reaches its climax, the side-note reads, '*They speake together*'; Dol, Face, and Mammon all talk wildly and at once, while offstage the voice of Subtle – interrupted in the middle of the lesson in quarreling he is giving to Kastril – is also heard. Jonson is fond of such moments as these, when language becomes a mere tangle of sound: there is a similar moment at the end of the second act of *Bartholomew Fair* ('*They speake all together* . . . '), and another in the courtroom scene at the end of *The Devil is an Ass*, where Fitzdottrel speaks rapidly in several different languages, and still another in the fifth act of *The Alchemist* when all the neighbors speak to Lovewit simultaneously ('Fewer at once, I pray you' – v v 21).

Dol's wild harangue on the ways of achieving universal linguistic understanding runs as a lunatic counterpoint to this noise and nonsense; 'the instrument of *Society*' has become untuned, and in a moment, as a final climax, comes '*A great crack and noise within*'. The scene may be viewed as a parody of the Pentecostal miracle when the apostles 'began to speak with other tongues, as the Spirit gave them utterance' (Acts 2: 4). But instead of universal comprehension, there is here universal obscurity; instead of union, there is division; instead of the 'sound from heaven as of a rushing mighty wind' (Acts 2: 2) there is merely the (artificially manufactured) blast from the laboratory. The New Testament account of the Whitsun gift of tongues was often considered to be the typological counterpart of the Old Testament account of the destruction of the Tower of Babel and the consequent fragmentation of languages. Hugh Broughton, in the work from which Dol Common quotes in this scene, had written of the Pentecostal happenings in these terms: 'In this Citie they received power in a strong wind, in fiery cloven tongues, were filled with the holy Ghost, and could speake to every one his owne language. So the *Jerusalem* from above was to be buylt, that all nations might woorke in it, as contrariwyse by tongues not understood, the worke was but *Babylon* a confusion.'[9] *The Alchemist* seems to reenact the Babel story, showing people violently split among themselves, driven further from a common language and from common sense as they attempt to fulfill their private fantasies.

The explosion itself comes as a fitting culmination to the earlier talk of bursting and of vaporization. Its symbolic suggestiveness is comparable to that of the explosion that occurs in Newgate in the last act of *The Devil is an Ass* at the disappearance of Pug to hell, and to the description of the dissolution of the staple in *The Staple of News*:

> THOMAS   Our *Staple* is all to pieces, quite dissolv'd! . . .
> Shiver'd, as in an earth-quake! heard you not
> The cracke and ruines? we are all blown up!
> Soon as they heard th' *Infanta* was got from them,
> Whom they had so devoured i' their hopes,
> To be their *Patronesse*, and sojourne with 'hem;
> Our *Emissaries, Register, Examiner,*
> Flew into vapor . . . .   (v i 39–46)

The explosion in *The Alchemist* prefigures a similar disappearance of both rogues and fools:

> FACE   O sir, we are defeated! all the *workes*
> Are flowne *in fumo*: every glasse is burst.
> Fornace, and all rent downe! as if a bolt
> Of thunder had beene driven through the house.
> *Retorts, Receivers, Pellicanes, Bolt-heads,*
> All strooke in shivers! . . .
> MAMMON   Is no *projection* left?
> FACE   All flowne, or stinks, sir.
>
>   (IV v 57–62, 89)

'All flowne': soon Mammon is to discover that not only the projection but the projectors themselves have dispersed: 'The whole nest are fled!' (v v 58); '*it, and they, and all in* fume *are gone*' (Argument, l. 12). The fume in which Face is said to work (II ii 21; III i 19), the fume of which Dapper complains in Lovewit's privy (v iv 5), seems finally to blow the house apart and its occupants with it. What is finally left in the house is eloquently noted by Lovewit on his return:

> Here, I find
> The emptie walls, worse then I left 'hem, smok'd,
> A few crack'd pots, and glasses, and a fornace,
> The seeling fill'd with *poesies* of the candle:
> And MADAME, with a *Dildo*, writ o' the walls.
>
> (v v 38–42)

Shards, smoke, obscene graffiti – it is to such valueless fragments and trifles that the play finally returns us. Nothing has been created. The rubbish mentioned throughout the play – cobwebs, hollow coal, feces, ashes, dust, scrapings, horse dung, 'pisse, and egge-shells, womens termes, mans bloud, / Haire o' the head, burnt clouts, chalke, merds, and clay' (II iii 194–5) – remains untransmuted still. . . .

I have described *The Alchemist* as a highly verbal play, and it might be asked whether the play, for all its deft theatricality, does not in the last estimate seem to live too exclusively in the realm of words: 'Words are Man's province, Words we teach alone.' In ridiculing those who make matters of language their obsession, a writer runs the risk of appearing a little obsessed with matters of language himself. Shakespeare successfully avoids this risk, even in so linguistically self-conscious a play as *Love's Labour's Lost*, for there the action of the comedy is largely a process of discovery; fantasticated words are simply beside the point when one is faced with the bare facts of love, or sickness, or death. Shakespeare has the great power to make silence eloquent of happiness or comprehension of something gained: the silence of Leontes surveying the statue of Hermione, or (a lighter moment) the silence Benedick enforces upon Beatrice with a kiss: 'Peace! I will stop your mouth.' Although Jonson leaves us in no doubt as to his attitude to wanton talk ('*How* much better is it, to bee silent; or at least, to speake sparingly!' – *Discoveries*, ll. 1602–3), the garrulous characters in his plays tend to have silence forced upon them as a harsh and often violent punishment: Crispinus in *Poetaster* is given an emetic; Carlo Buffone in *Every Man out of his Humour* has his lips forcibly sealed up; the prattling Sir Politic Would-be is subjected to a practical joke, and takes silent refuge in his tortoiseshell; Zeal-of-the-Land Busy (like many other Jonsonian characters) is shamed into final silence. The typical antithesis – talkativeness versus enforced silence – is starkly presented, in a way that (despite the comic context) could be felt to be inhumane. 'Sense is wrought out of experience, the knowledge of humane life, and actions, or of the liberall Arts' (*Discoveries*, ll. 1886–9): this statement is not often enacted in the comedies themselves. *The Alchemist*, so centrally concerned, as it is, with questions of language, is particularly susceptible to an objection of this kind; superbly organized the action is, yet the range of 'humane life' it presents is also arguably rather thin. The arrival of Mercade at the end of *Love's Labour's Lost* radically alters the tone of that comedy in a way that the arrival of Lovewit does not radically alter the tone of *The Alchemist*; victory in the latter play goes to those with 'wit', a word that denotes, in the main, a dexterity with language. Right to the end the play retains its slight sense of having been a complex rhetorical tournament or flyting. Yet when all the reservations have been made, *The Alchemist* remains one of the great comedies of the world.

SOURCE: essay in *Seventeenth-Century Imagery: Essays on Uses of Figurative Language from Donne to Farquhar*, ed. Earl Miner (1971)pp. 69-82.

NOTES

1. 'To the World', ll. 17-18.

2. Induction to *The Magnetic Lady*, ll. 108-9.

3. Christopher Ricks, '*Sejanus* and Dismemberment', *Modern Language Notes*, LXXVI (1961) 301-8.

4. The association of dismemberment and divorce is found in Matthew 5: 27-32. For a further discussion of this play as a 'comedy of disunity' see my essay, '"A Martyrs Resolution": Jonson's *Epicoene*', *Review of English Studies*, XVIII (1967) 1-15.

5. This passage in *Discoveries* is taken almost entire from Juan Luis Vives, *De Ratione Dicendi*, i; in *Opera* (1555) vol. I, p. 85 (see Herford and Simpson, vol. XI, p. 265). Vives's *instrumentum* does not permit of a musical sense, but the context of Jonson's passage suggests he may be thinking of the 'instrument' (either the caduceus or the flute) of Mercury, the god of music as well as of eloquence. In *Cynthia's Revels*, V V 10-17, 'HERMES wand' is seen as having power to charm follies that are 'like a sort of jarring instrument, / All out of tune'. Cf. also *Discoveries*, ll. 1753-4: 'For as in an Instrument, so in style, there must be a Harmonie, and concent of parts.'

6. Such a proposition is ably explored in relation to Jonson's prose comedies by Jonas A. Barish in *Ben Jonson and the Language of Prose Comedy* (Cambridge, Mass., 1960).

7. Edward Partridge, *The Broken Compass: A Study of the Major Comedies of Ben Jonson* (London, 1958) ch. 6. I am indebted to this admirable account of the play.

8. See James E. Robinson, '*Bartholomew Fair*: Comedy of Vapors', *Studies in English Literature 1500-1900*, I (1962) 65-80.

9. Hugh Broughton, *A Concent of Scripture* (London, 1590) sig. H4.

3. REVIEWS OF PRODUCTIONS
1743–1970

Anonymous

'DAVID GARRICK AS DRUGGER' (1743)

On the 21st March [1743], he displayed one of the most finished studies of low humour, that the world ever saw, by acting *Abel Drugger* in Ben Jonson's Alchymist. There is a great deal of neatness in the following contemporary criticism. The writer thus describes Mr. Garrick.

'Abel Drugger's first appearance would disconcert the muscular economy of the wisest. His attitude, his dread of offending the doctor, his saying nothing, his gradual stealing in farther and farther, his impatience to be introduced, his joy to his friend Face, are imitable by none. Mr. Garrick has taken that walk to himself, and is the *ridiculous* above all conception. When he first opens his mouth, the features of his face seem, as it were, to drop upon his tongue; it is all caution; it is timorous, stammering, and inexpressible. When he stands under the conjuror to have his features examined, his teeth, his beard, his little finger, his awkward simplicity, and his concern, mixed with hope and fear, and joy and avarice, and good-nature, are above painting.'

When we look at the skeleton text, which the genius of the actor has invested with such comic life and action, it must increase the very profession in our esteem.

The critic next notices the eager *running up* to inform Subtle, that he himself *sells* the tobacco which the philosopher commended; the struggle to make his intended present *two* pound.[1] His *breaking the bottle* in the Doctor's absence, while curiously examining the implements around him. His *beating off* Surley, disarming him, and throwing away the sword with contempt.[2] He does not know friend from foe in his triumphant perambulation, and is going even to strike his favourite Captain Face. Garrick seemed to say, to the very side scenes, 'Will *you* fight me?'

SOURCE: extract from 'Biographical Memoir' prefixed to *The Private Correspondence of David Garrick* (1831).

1. [In Garrick's version – J. Bell (ed.), *Bell's British Theatre*, 18 vols (London, 1776–8) vol. XVII, pp. 42–3. Cf. II vi 77–9.]
2. [See Introduction for a discussion of these theatrical additions to the part of Drugger.]

Anonymous

A BOISTEROUS MODERN FARCE (1935)

Transfer to the broader stage and auditorium of the Princes Theatre has naturally not added subtlety to the Embassy production of *The Alchemist*, which remains very definitely not a version for scholars. It is presented as a boisterous modern farce, and holds the stage as such. Avarice is not one of the mortal sins of which we have lost sight since the seventeenth century, and most of the incarnations of it that Jonson imagined are true enough to modern life. Those historically minded persons who are aware of the place of the Puritan divine in the pedigree of the Economic Man might have wished for a different treatment of Ananias and Wholesome; since we no longer pull a clerical leg quite so savagely or quite in this direction, it is scarcely possible to appreciate these characters except as persons of their own age.

There is justification, however, for reducing them to mere music-hall comedians with white faces instead of red noses: for to represent them in their true colours would require the rest of the group that surrounds them to be restrained within the confines of the reign of James I. Miss Olga Katzin has preferred to let those who can step out of that reign into the England of George V; and very much at home they prove to be. The petty tradesman and the ambitious clerk, the young gentleman who is determined to be a dog, and the old one who creates a fool's paradise of infinite self-indulgence, in fact the whole company of the dupes and the self-deceived can still be found flocking to the doors of any occultist charlatan or vendor of tickets in the Irish Sweep.

As to the deceivers, they are a fascinating trio. They are not so funny as the comic rogues of Shakespeare, for the laughter never touches the

fringe of tears, and therefore, though it has the sparkle that belongs to
the superficial, it has also the monotony. There is a moment near the
end when Jonson seems about to expose with more mordant irony the
honour that is said to prevail among thieves. But that is brushed aside,
and we are left with only the memory of Miss Iris Hoey's [Dol] rippling
fun in the manner of Maria but at the expense of all more trivial fools
than Malvolio, of Mr. Hugh Miller [Subtle], who can frown and frown
and be a sage while all smile who know he is a villain, and of Mr. Austin
Trevor [Face], a newcomer to the cast, whose infinite versatility as the
handy-man of the swindling firm enables him to rival Autolycus as a
snapper-up of unconsidered trifles. Of the dupes Mr. Bruce Winston
[Mammon] gets most out of his part, and reminds the audience of what
they might otherwise forget – that the play is written in verse; but even
he only achieves this effect in the moments when the poetry burgeons
into a luscious parody of itself. Of the intricate quips and verbal
subtleties of Jonson many are omitted, and from the rest this production
gallops rollicking away.

SOURCE: article in *The Times*, 2 April 1935.

Peter Fleming

HARLEQUINADE: *THE ALCHEMIST*
AT THE NEW THEATRE (1947)

In the theatre as well as outside it an imposture only becomes really
interesting when it is threatened with exposure. In this comedy a threat
is exerted at an early stage to the security of Subtle's chicanery; and it is
wholly typical of the author's outlook and technique that Surly, who,
smelling a rat, comes *ex officio* to represent the forces of light, wearing as
it were the Sheriff's badge is described as a 'gamester'. It is a revealing
touch. The other characters comprise a Charlatan, a Rogue, a Bawd,
an Ass, a Creature, a Dreamer, a Sceptic, a Religious Maniac, a
Wealthy Bumpkin and so on; almost any other dramatist would have
welcomed the chance to let in a little wholesome fresh air, almost any
other dramatist would have flashed the Sheriff's blameless badge and
put down Surly as an Honest Fellow or a Plain Dealer. But not Ben

Jonson, whose mood here is that no amount of black presupposes the existence of any white at all; if the black has to be relieved – as for the purposes of drama it has – let it be relieved by a dubious shade of grey. So a Gamester is the nearest we get to Galahad.

Disenchantment, rather than righteous indignation, underlies and animates this merciless exposure of the early seventeenth-century underworld. The author's attack on folly and vice is sustained and vigorous, but it has little or nothing about it of the crusade; his technique may suggest Hogarth but his motives approximate to those of the Candid Cameraman. He no more condemns the quacks than he pities their gulls. With the tough, skilful, disillusioned relish of a barker calling our attention to the peculiarities of a Bearded Lady or Siamese Twins, Ben Jonson analyses, with a nice blend of precision and extravagance, a recurrent campaign in the long, one-sided war between knaves and fools.

There must be many like myself who, put off by memories of 'Jonson's learnéd sock' or by dialogue which, in the study, seems indigestibly rich in contemporary cant and allusion, have never expected *The Alchemist* to be good entertainment. I can only say that I know of none better in London. Mr. John Burrell's production attacks this harsh, murky, potentially atrabilious comedy with light-hearted gusto, and the Old Vic company seize with alacrity its numerous and great acting opportunities. The result is a kind of harlequinade, swift but full of lasting verities, seamy and sardonic but essentially gay. Mr. Ralph Richardson's Face is smooth and bold and full of resource, and he gives a fine performance; but I thought he was almost too sure of himself, that as an imposter he was less interesting than he might have been if he had seemed less insensible to the risks of exposure which he courted so readily. Mr. George Relph, as the Alchemist, exuded mumbo-jumbo with glib and compelling authority; Mr. Alec Guinness gave a curious, elfin importance to Abel Drugger; Mr. Nicholas Hannen's superb portrait of Sir Epicure Mammon found (it seemed to me), the one weak spot in Jonson's armour of toughness, for it is to this worthless and ludicrous old lecher that Jonson characteristically entrusts a hint of the poet's immortal longings. Miss Joyce Redman, though not perhaps ideally cast, was a spirited Dol Common, and Mr. Frank Duncan [Dapper], Mr. Michael Warre [Surly], Mr. Peter Copley [Ananias], Mr. George Rose [Kastril], and Miss Margaret Leighton [Dame Pliant] rose splendidly to their diverse opportunities.

I left the theatre with the unexpected conviction that, if the object of comedy is to amuse the audience, Ben Jonson must be a much better comic dramatist than Shakespeare.

SOURCE: article in the *Spectator*, 24 January 1947.

Kenneth Tynan

'A SLAMMING OF DOORS' (1950)

It is hard to over-praise this play. It mingles together sweet dirt, smart gulling and coxcombry into a wonderful theatrical confection. It thrives on malice and savagery and makes them palatable. This is the heart of our native humour, a vein of bitter, harsh venom: Jonson's angry caricatures take a central place in our comic literature, and project themselves by homespun craft into the work of all our indigenous satiric artists, blazing up furiously in Swift and Hogarth, and finally rekindling in Dickens, whom, in their last weak days, they strengthened.

And there is such a thing as a good episodic play: *The Alchemist* is such a thing. Like bead after bead, the episodes click together upon the connecting string, which is chicanery and chiselry. Singly or in pairs, the gulls are drawn to the chisellers to be snared and trimmed. What is piquant, they like it: humble and gladdened, they depart penniless, sometimes upon a servile errand for their cheaters. They have come in search of panaceas, of the Philosopher's Stone, and they are beguiled by three glorious impostors: the exuberant Janus, Face, the shadow-conjuror, Subtle, and the female spiv, Dol. So far you laugh sporadically; soon you can hardly stop, for by Jonson's art the hoaxes start to react on each other, wires cross, gull is involved with gull, and there is a buzz of entrance and exit, accompanied by a fine slamming and reslamming of doors. The peak of the hubbub comes, I suppose, with the belated release of Dapper, locked blindfold in a privy, and freed after a whole act in smoking darkness.

The Old Vic production missed none of this. Morris Kestelman's agreeable Augustan set abounded in doors and queer coigns, and nothing seals a scene as tellingly as a slammed door. I query Mr. Burrell's wisdom in shifting the setting to the eighteenth century; a move which made nonsense of Dame Pliant's line about the Armada having sailed three years before her birth.

George Relph plays Subtle: heavy lids, bright eyes, sagging bulbous face and somehow a sagging bulbous voice. I remember vividly the slow, jovial smile of anticipated triumph which greets the news of some new arrival to the cozenage; his eyes pop with avidity. Mr. Relph plays gallantly down to allow Ralph Richardson, as Face, to climb on to his back and then hoist the play squarely on to his own shoulders. Sir

Ralph's Face is a performance of great versatility, but (I thought) considerable professional dishonesty. He is opportunism itself, shuffling and grimacing most impertinently, pushing in his lines swiftly and selfishly, as if each were a last straw at which the play might clutch. Sir Ralph acts as if he were an eager, benevolent but tired scoutmaster, diverting himself by watching a rabble of tenderfeet practising first-aid. At first he condescends to simulate equality with them, and partakes of their ingenuousness; but this is bogus, and you know that he will soon have to show them himself how it is really done. With no real hope: for, worst of all, he makes you sense that this has been going on for months, to his increasing bewilderment and boredom. He patronizes his fellows roguishly and provokingly, and needless to say, every minute of his performance is a sheer delight to watch.

Joyce Redman . . . gave Dol Common the right abandon, though I got no sense of *rapport* with the other cony-catchers. Of the gulls: there are the rich who come out of greed, and the poor who come out of a need for illusions. Nicholas Hannen made a Balzacian figure of Sir Epicure Mammon, and even pulled pathos out of the sauces in his golden cauldron of a belly: I know of no better voluptuous writing than this part. Peter Copley's Ananias, tatty and outraged, swaying like a black eel and gesticulating, is the best thing he has yet done. I was less happy about Margaret Leighton's Dame Pliant. This is an attempt to coax a certain facile kind of phrase out of a certain facile kind of critic – 'a brilliant little study, delicately etched in' – 'makes a character out of a few lines'. There *is* a character to be made out of the widow, but so far Miss Leighton has not found it. A similar but successful experiment is Alec Guinness's Abel Drugger. He, you remember, is the puny tobacconist who becomes Face's creature, and brings his paltry gifts to Subtle as to a shrine. Mr. Guinness manages to get to the heart of all good, hopeful young men who can enjoy without envy the society of wits. I was overjoyed to watch his wistful, happy eyes moving, in dumb wonder, from Face to Subtle: a solid little fellow, you felt, and how eager to help! At last he puts in a tolerable contribution to the conversation. *O altitudo!* His face creases ruddily into modest delight, and he stamps his thin feet in glee. In a later scene, Mr. Guinness demonstrates a very rare gift, that of suggesting the change that comes over a man when he is alone. Drugger is commissioned by Face to bring him a Spanish costume as disguise. He trots away, and returns shyly, clad in its showy cloak and hat. Waiting for Face to answer the door, he begins to execute timid dance-steps under the porch. He treads a rapt, self-absorbed measure with himself, consumed with joy. Then Face appears: the pretence is over, he recognizes his intellectual master, and, not regretfully or pathetically, but smartly and prosaically, he sheds his costume and hands it over. It is most touchingly done.

Mr. Guinness, in spite of Sir Ralph's exertions, carried off every scene in which he appears, and one or two in which he ought not to appear at all. Drugger used to be Garrick's part, but, Mr. Guinness having now appropriated it, I name him the best living English character-actor.

SOURCE: extract from *He That Plays the King* (1950) pp. 92–4.

Bamber Gascoigne

ALL THAT GLISTERS (1962)

The enraging experience of *The Alchemist*, by Sir Tyrone Guthrie, subsides slowly. . . . The great pity of it is that here were a director and a cast who could between them have achieved a marvellous production of a marvellous play. They were prevented from doing so by Guthrie's almost idiotic idea of what makes drama seem 'relevant' to a modern audience.

He argues in a programme note that 'traditionalists' like seeing old plays in period costume because it makes the plays seem quaint, delightful and totally irrelevant to the distressing realities of our everyday modern lives. He also said, in an interview in *The Times*, that modern audiences don't know enough about the Jacobean age to understand Jonson's play properly in its original form. Personally I disagree with both these assertions, though I grant that a case can be made out for altering a word here and there when the meaning is no longer generally familiar and when the poetry will not suffer from the change – Guthrie, for example, alters 'load-stone' [I iii 69] to 'magnet' in a sentence where the whole joke would be lost on anyone not knowing what a loadstone is. There is also an obvious case for anyone who wishes to rewrite such a play completely, turning it into a comedy which a twentieth-century Ben Jonson might have written. But this task does require a twentieth-century Ben Jonson.

Guthrie's alterations fall precisely between these two valid extremes. He makes no change in the core of the play, in its plot or characterisation, but he plays merry havoc with the peripheral details – chiefly in order to accommodate his beloved twentieth-century costumes. The ludicrous split in his approach is revealed, unwittingly, in his own programme note. He argues that there is nothing 'unreal' today about the idea of people believing in the Philosopher's Stone, which will turn base metal into gold; and to prove his point he quotes some relations of his who gave all their money to a charming young trickster who promised to invest it in a gold mine of fabulous prospects. Here Guthrie's argument is precisely right. He admits that we, like him, can make the imaginative jump in the theatre from an ancient to a modern type of gulling (and indeed our twentieth-century Ben Jonson might well choose a speculative stockbroker as his central character for *The Alchemist*). Yet a couple of lines later Guthrie is solemnly explaining that to give the play its full twentieth-century significance he has had to change 'coach and six' to 'limousine.' Does he seriously think, if we can see a stockbroker in an alchemist, that it will be beyond us to link a coach and six with a limousine?

What is, of course, extremely hard to see is anyone using a limousine to visit an alchemist; and because of this dichotomy almost every one of Guthrie's alterations makes for unreality where Jonson offered reality. How great is the reality of a modern lawyer's clerk who is proud of being able to 'court / His mistris out of OVID'? Where is the reality in a twentieth-century youth who wants to set up a grocery for the sale of tobacco and chemical distillations? Even Sir Epicure Mammon's boast – 'I will have all my beds, blowne up, not stuft: / Downe is too hard' – sounds a little feeble in the Dunlopillo age.

But the chief victims of Guthrie's imagination are Kastril and his sister, Dame Pliant. In Jonson, Kastril is a young provincial *nouveau riche*, with £3,000 a year, who wants to learn the proper etiquette of quarrelling so that he can become one of 'the angrie Boyes' and 'live by his wits' in gallant London society. He has brought along his sister to try and get her married to a peer. This is entirely real today, in spirit though not in detail (and the etiquette of quarrelling is still very funny – certainly Touchstone always gets plenty of laughs with it in *As You Like It*), but Guthrie doggedly turns Kastril into a creature of the purest fantasy. He now has £20,000 a year, yet he arrives in a black leather motor-cycling suit and a crash helmet. The quarrelling has had to be cut (thus also missing a lot of the humour of a later scene), and all that Kastril now wants of the learned doctor is to be provided with a flick-knife. He still brings his sister to be married to a peer, but she too is dressed in crash helmet, black trousers and baggy black sweater covered in badges. Yet in spite of her repulsive appearance the only two genuine 'gentlemen' in the play are both eager to marry her. What would seem to have happened is that Tyrone Guthrie has made the one very superficial link between 'angry boys' and 'teddy boys,' and everything else has had to tag along as best it can or else drop out altogether. Yet surely our own imaginations, while watching Jonson's play, could make better connections than this? Can there seriously be anyone who would find Guthrie's Kastril and Dame Pliant as 'real' or 'relevant' as Jonson's?

Of all Elizabethan or Jacobean dramatists Jonson is probably the one who will suffer most from the Guthrie treatment. *The Alchemist* contains many more precise references to contemporary life and manners than any of Shakespeare's plays, and also many more remarks about the precise appearance of other characters in the play. This fact forces Guthrie to cut out many of the best passages. To give only one example: when Jonson's Surly arrives in disguise as a Spanish count, he naturally wears a magnificent great ruff. Guthrie's Surly (Peruvian now, for no apparent reason) comes in a natty white suit, so a magnificent speech has to be cut where Ananias, the Puritan, sees the dago Surly and says:

> Avoid *Sathan*,
> Thou art not of the light. That ruffe of pride,
> About thy neck, betrayes thee: 'and is the same
> With that, which the uncleane birds, in *seventy-seven*,
> Were seene to pranke it with, on divers coasts.

This is splendidly funny, and provides an excellent touch of characterisation for Ananias as well as a nice satirical comment on the logical processes of the Puritan mind. The speech is sacrificed solely to make straight the way for a bunch of twentieth-century costumes. If anyone should argue that the allusion would be lost on a modern audience, unaware that the mating of birds had been observed in seventy-seven, the answer is that Jonson's original audience were equally unaware (if indeed any actual event *is* being alluded to), since the play was first performed thirty-three years after 1577.

There are many minor mysteries about Guthrie's changes. Why, for instance, does he multiply Kastril's fortune by seven, yet leave the sums paid by the Puritans at Jonson's original figure? Or why, except for a cheap laugh, is the lawyer's golden coin changed from one 'that my love gave me' to one 'which my mother kept in a tea-pot on the kitchen dresser'? The same lawyer produces from his pocket (not this time in place of anything Jonsonian, but as a free bonus), a season ticket to Grove Park.

The night I went these modernisms amused the audience more than anything else in the production. So, on this level, Guthrie's inventions do work. Yet people laugh when they see or hear anything familiar in any type of play, whether it be a mention of the football pools, Barbara Moore or the Palladium, or the sight of a teddy boy in a crash helmet. The incongruity of such things in an 'old' play adds an extra bit of merriment, and one would undoubtedly be amused by the general spirit of this production if it were a Christmas show put on by the employees of a large shop, or by a battalion in the army. But has it all anything to do with that eagerly pursued, alchemical ingredient of drama – 'relevance' to life? A play begins to be relevant when it is true in its own context. It becomes fully relevant when that truth holds good for other parallel contexts. Pompously and insistently, I repeat that Ben Jonson's play does both these things and Sir Tyrone Guthrie's neither.

Sometimes, but for me not often, the boisterousness of the production and the qualities of the cast rose above all the faults. Particularly good is Charles Gray as Sir Epicure Mammon – admittedly the richest and most indestructible character of them all, but Mr. Gray, looking like someone out of Toulouse-Lautrec, gives him the wonderfully decadent air of a gross *fin-de-siècle* hedonist, as he catalogues the sordid pleasures of his future wealth. Leo McKern as Subtle and Lee Montague as Face keep the pace brisk and are excellent foils to each other. And Priscilla Morgan's Dol Common catches to a turn the boredom of prostitution. But, in spite of all these, an evening of very high promise and hope ended, I found, in almost total disaster.[1]

SOURCE: article in the *Spectator*, 7 December 1962.

NOTE

1. [This review provoked a correspondence in the two succeeding issues of the *Spectator*. For a favourable review, see *The Times*, 29 November 1962, p. 16.]

Irving Wardle

COMIC INTRIGUE (1970)

Stuart Burge [director of the Nottingham Playhouse production at the New Theatre] has rightly seen that *The Alchemist* is a far less sententious piece than most of Jonson's comedy, and its exposure of vice is of less importance than the sheer perfection of its intrigue. Accordingly he emphasizes the pantomime element most strongly; and the character of the production is implicit in Trevor Pitt's set, a revolving house crammed with doors and spy-holes, cramped passages and stairways.

The approach is completely consistent, and sometimes most pleasingly so. For instance, when the three cheats are interrupted in the midst of gulling the blindfolded Dapper, they keep him spinning like a top as they dash about to attend to their other victims: a direct extension of the vaudeville plate-juggling routine into comic action. And there is no shortage of similar instances: such as the unwinding of Abel from an endless piece of damask, and the trick swordplay of Kastril (a good dour performance by Nicholas Clay).

All this is relevant to the play: but none of it is an acceptable substitute for Jonson's own effects, many of which are seriously underplayed. To pick one glaring example; the explosion of the 'project' following Sir Epicure's assault on Dol is a good joke but it should be thunderously crowned by Subtle's Isaiah-like curse on the wickedness of his client. Here we get multiple flashes and bangs; but the curse is merely thrown off as a subordinate line.

There is confusion in the production between speed and pace; and for all its attention to plot one misses the phrasing of events which enables you to relish the structure. Having said that, there is one glorious exception in the pause that descends on the assembled company at the voice of Dapper – the forgotten man in the privy.

Within these limits most of the performances are well conceived. The only real exception is Frank Middlemass's Sir Epicure, played for some unaccountable reason as a doddering old fool entirely remote from the lascivious grandee of the text and prevented from sheer senility from rising to those matchlessly sensual lines.

David Dodimead's interesting Subtle is an ascetic figure, suggesting a seminarist gone wrong, or Faustian parody. Peter Whitbread pulls off some bravura quick changes as Face, particularly his final transformation into the demure pink-cheeked servant who carries off the spoils. Cherith Mellor completes the trio with a rotten–ripe Hogarthian Dol.

SOURCE: article in *The Times*, 10 February 1970.

SELECT BIBLIOGRAPHY

EDITIONS

The standard edition of Jonson is C. H. Herford and P. and E. Simpson (eds), *Ben Jonson*, 11 vols (Oxford, 1925–52). The best modern-spelling editions of *Every Man in his Humour* are by J. W. Lever in the Regents Renaissance Drama Series (London, 1972), which gives parallel texts of Q and F, and Gabriele Bernhard Jackson in the Yale Ben Jonson (New Haven, Conn., and London, 1969); of *The Alchemist*, by Alvin B. Kernan in the Yale Ben Jonson (New Haven, Conn., and London, 1974) and F. H. Mares in the Revels Plays (London, 1967).

BOOKS AND ARTICLES

(a) *General*
Robert M. Adams, 'The Games of the Illusionist', *Times Literary Supplement*, 11 February 1977, pp. 142–3.
William A. Armstrong, 'Ben Jonson and Jacobean Stagecraft', *Stratford-upon-Avon Studies* 1: *Jacobean Theatre* (London, 1960) pp. 43–61.
Judd Arnold, *A Grace Peculiar: Ben Jonson's Cavalier Heroes* (Philadelphia, 1972).
Wallace A. Bacon, 'The Magnetic Field: The Structure of Jonson's Comedies', *Huntington Library Quarterly*, XIX (1955–6) 121–53.
J. B. Bamborough, 'Joyce and Jonson', *Review of English Literature*, II, no. 4 (1961) 45–50.
Jonas A. Barish (ed.), *Ben Jonson: A Collection of Critical Essays* (Englewood Cliffs, N. J., 1963).
Peter Barnes *et al.*, 'Ben Jonson and the Modern Stage', *Gambit*, VI, no. 22 (1972) 5–30.
William Blissett *et al.* (eds), *A Celebration of Ben Jonson* (Toronto and Buffalo, 1973).
J. A. Bryant, *The Compassionate Satirist: Ben Jonson and his Imperfect World* (Athens, Ga, 1972).
Alan C. Dessen, *Jonson's Moral Comedy* (Evanston, Ill., 1971).
Ian Donaldson, 'Ben Jonson', *The Sphere History of Literature in the English Language*, vol. III (London, 1971) pp. 278–305.
John J. Enck, *Jonson and the Comic Truth* (Madison, Wis., 1957).
Brian Gibbons, *Jacobean City Comedy* (London, 1968).
Thomas Greene, 'Ben Jonson and the Centred Self', *Studies in English Literature 1500–1900*, X (1970) 325–48.
Ray L. Heffner Jr, 'Unifying Symbols in the Comedy of Ben Jonson', *English Institute Essays 1954* (New York, 1955) pp. 74–97.

G. R. Hibbard (ed.), *The Elizabethan Theatre IV* (Ontario and London, 1974).
Essays commemorating Jonson's quatercentenary.

Gabriele Bernhard Jackson, *Vision and Judgment in Ben Jonson's Drama* (New
Haven, Conn., and London, 1968).

L. C. Knights, 'Ben Jonson, Dramatist', *The Pelican Guide to English Literature*,
vol. II (Harmondsworth, 1955) pp. 302–17.

Robert E. Knoll, *Ben Jonson's Plays: An Introduction* (Lincoln, Nebr., 1964).

Alexander Leggatt, *Citizen Comedy in the Age of Shakespeare* (Toronto, 1973).

Lawrence L. Levin, 'Replication in the Comedies of Ben Jonson', *Renaissance
Drama*, new ser. V (1972) 37–74.

Gail Kern Paster, 'Ben Jonson's Comedy of Limitation', *Studies in Philology*,
LXXII (1975) 51–71.

L. J. Potts, 'Ben Jonson and the Seventeenth Century', *Essays and Studies*, new
ser. II (1949) 7–24.

James D. Redwine Jr, 'Beyond Psychology: The Moral Basis of Jonson's Theory
of Humour Characterization', *Journal of English Literary History*, XXVIII
(1961) 316–34.

C. G. Thayer, *Ben Jonson: Studies in the Plays* (Norman, Okla., 1963).

Mary Olive Thomas (ed.), *Ben Jonson: Quadricentennial Essays, Studies in the
Literary Imagination*, VI, no. 1 (1973).

Edmund Wilson, 'Morose Ben Jonson', *The Triple Thinkers*, revised edition
(New York, 1948) pp. 203–20.

(b) *Every Man in his Humour*

J. D. Aylward, 'The Inimitable Bobadill', *Notes and Queries*, CXCV (1950) 2–4,
28–31.

C. R. Baskervill, *English Elements in Jonson's Early Comedy* (Austin, Tex., 1911).

J. A. Bryant, 'Jonson's Revision of *Every Man in His Humor* ', *Studies in Philology*,
LIX (1962) 641–50.

Leonard F. Dean, 'Three Notes on Comic Morality: Celia, Bobadill, and
Falstaff', *Studies in English Literature 1500–1900*, XVI (1976) 263–71.

John Hollander, '*Twelfth Night* and the Morality of Indulgence', *Sewanee
Review*, LXVII (1959) 220–38.

Lawrence L. Levin, 'Clement Justice in *Every Man in his Humour* ', *Studies in
English Literature 1500–1900*, XII (1972) 291–307.

J. C. Maxwell, 'Comic Mispunctuation in *Every Man in his Humour* ', *English
Studies*, XXXIII (1952) 218–19.

Edward B. Partridge, 'Ben Jonson: The Makings of the Dramatist (1596–
1602)', *Stratford-upon-Avon Studies* IX: *Elizabethan Theatre* (London, 1966)
pp. 221–44.

George C. Taylor, 'Did Shakespeare, Actor, Improvise in *Every Man in his
Humour?*' in J. G. McManaway *et al.* (eds), *Joseph Quincy Adams Memorial
Studies* (Washington, D.C., 1948) pp. 21–32.

(c) *The Alchemist*

Judd Arnold, 'Lovewit's Triumph and Jonsonian Morality: A Reading of *The
Alchemist*', *Criticism*, XI (1969) 151–66.

William Blissett, 'The Venter Tripartite in *The Alchemist* ', *Studies in English*

Literature 1500–1900, VIII (1968) 323–34.

Edgar H. Duncan, 'Jonson's *Alchemist* and the Literature of Alchemy', *PMLA*, LXI (1946) 699–710.

A. Richard Dutton, '*Volpone* and *The Alchemist*: A Comparison in Satiric Techniques', *Renaissance and Modern Studies*, XVIII (1974) 36–62.

James V. Holleran, 'Character Transmutation in *The Alchemist*', *College Language Association Journal*, XI (1968) 221–7.

Cyrus Hoy, 'The Pretended Piety of Jonson's *Alchemist*', *Renaissance Papers*, Southeastern Renaissance Conference (Durham, N.C., 1957) pp. 15–19.

Maurice Hussey, 'Ananias the Deacon: A Study of Religion in Jonson's *The Alchemist*', *English*, IX (1952–3) 207–12.

Harry Levin, 'Two Magian Comedies: *The Tempest* and *The Alchemist*', *Shakespeare Survey*, XXII (1969) 47–58.

Richard Levin, ' "No Laughing Matter": Some New Readings of *The Alchemist*' in M. O. Thomas (ed.), *Ben Jonson: Quadricentennial Essays* (see under (a) above) pp. 85–99.

Joseph T. McCullen, 'Conference with the Queen of Fairies: A Study of Jonson's Workmanship in *The Alchemist*', *Studia Neophilologica*, XXIII (1950–1) 87–95.

Vincent F. Petronella, 'Teaching Ben Jonson's *The Alchemist*: Alchemy and Analysis', *Humanities Association Bulletin* (Canada), XXI (1970) 19–23.

Rufus D. Putney, 'Jonson's Poetic Comedy', *Philological Quarterly*, XLI (1962) 188–204.

John Read, *The Alchemist in Life, Literature and Art* (London, 1947).

Malcolm H. South, 'The "Vncleane Birds, in *Seuenty-Seuen*": *The Alchemist*', *Studies in English Literature 1500–1900*, XIII (1973) 331–43.

NOTES ON CONTRIBUTORS

WILLIAM ARCHER (1856–1924): critic, editor, translator and journalist, he published the first English translation of Ibsen's works.

J. B. BAMBOROUGH: Principal of Linacre College, Oxford, and editor of *The Review of English Studies*. His publications include *The Little World of Man* (a study of Renaissance psychological theory), the essay on Jonson in the British Council's 'Writers and Their Work' series, and the Macmillan editions of *Volpone* and *The Alchemist*.

JONAS A. BARISH: Professor of English in the University of California at Berkeley, and editor of the Casebook on *Volpone*. His other publications include studies on Jonson and the Elizabethan drama, and the Yale edition of *Sejanus*.

HENRY HOLLAND CARTER: formerly Professor of English in the University of Indiana; author of a dictionary of Middle English musical terms. He died in 1952.

IAN DONALDSON: Professor of English in the Australian National University, and a former co-editor of *Essays in Criticism*. His publications include *The World Upside-Down: Comedy from Jonson to Fielding* and the Oxford edition of Jonson's poems.

A. RICHARD DUTTON: formerly Warden of Wroxton College, Oxfordshire (a college of Fairleigh Dickinson University, New Jersey); currently Lecturer in English in the University of Lancaster. His publications include studies of *Volpone* and *The Alchemist*.

T. S. ELIOT (1888–1965): poet, dramatist and critic. His most important works of criticism are *The Sacred Wood* (1920) and *The Use of Poetry and the Use of Criticism* (1933).

WILLIAM EMPSON: poet and critic. Professor of English Literature in the University of Sheffield, 1953–71. His publications in literary criticism include *Seven Types of Ambiguity* (1930), *Some Versions of Pastoral* (1935) and *The Structure of Complex Words* (1951).

PETER FLEMING (1907–71): author of travel-histories and belles-lettres; husband of the actress Celia Johnson.

BAMBER GASCOIGNE: writer, critic and television-programme presenter.

C. H. HERFORD (1853–1931): a co-editor of the Oxford critical edition of Jonson's works (1925–52). Author of critical studies on Wordsworth and romantic poetry, he also produced editions of Shakespeare and Spenser.

GABRIELE BERNHARD JACKSON: Professor of English in Temple University, Philadelphia. Her publications include *Vision and Judgment in Ben Jonson's Drama*.

ALVIN B. KERNAN: Dean of the Graduate school in Princeton University, his publications include *The Cankered Muse* and *The Plot of Satire*, and the Yale edition of *The Alchemist*.

L. C. KNIGHTS: formerly (1965–73) King Edward VII Professor of English Literature in the University of Cambridge, and now Emeritus Professor. His publications include *Drama and Society in the Age of Jonson*.

J. W. LEVER: formerly Professor of English in Simon Fraser University, British Columbia, his publications include *The Elizabethan Love Sonnet*, *The Tragedy of State*, the Malone Society edition of *The Wasp* and editions of *Measure for Measure* (Arden Shakespeare) and *The Rape of Lucrece* (New Penguin Shakespeare). He died in 1975.

HARRY LEVIN: Irving Babbitt Professor of Comparative Literature in Harvard University, his publications cover a wide range of subjects, including the Elizabethan and Jacobean drama.

F. H. MARES: Reader in English in the University of Adelaide; editor of *The Memoirs of Robert Carey* and of the Methuen edition of *The Alchemist*.

EDWARD B. PARTRIDGE: Professor of English in Tulane University, Louisiana, his publications include essays on Jonson, the Yale edition of *Epicoene* and the Regents Renaissance edition of *Bartholomew Fair*.

EVELYN MARY SIMPSON (1885–1963): wife of Percy Simpson and a co-editor of the Oxford critical edition of Jonson's works; her other publications include studies of Elizabethan translations of Seneca and of the prose of John Donne.

PERCY SIMPSON (1865–1962): a co-editor of the Oxford critical edition of Jonson's works, and author of important studies of early methods of proofreading and Shakespeare's punctuation.

J. B. STEANE: Senior English Master at Merchant Taylors' School, his publications include studies of Marlowe and Tennyson and the Cambridge edition of *The Alchemist*.

FREDA L. TOWNSEND: taught English in Harvard University; her publications include *Apologie for Bartholmew Fayre: The Art of Jonson's Comedies* and a study of Thomas Heywood.

KENNETH TYNAN: drama-critic, author and journalist, his publications include collections of theatre criticism.

IRVING WARDLE: drama-critic of *The Times*.

INDEX